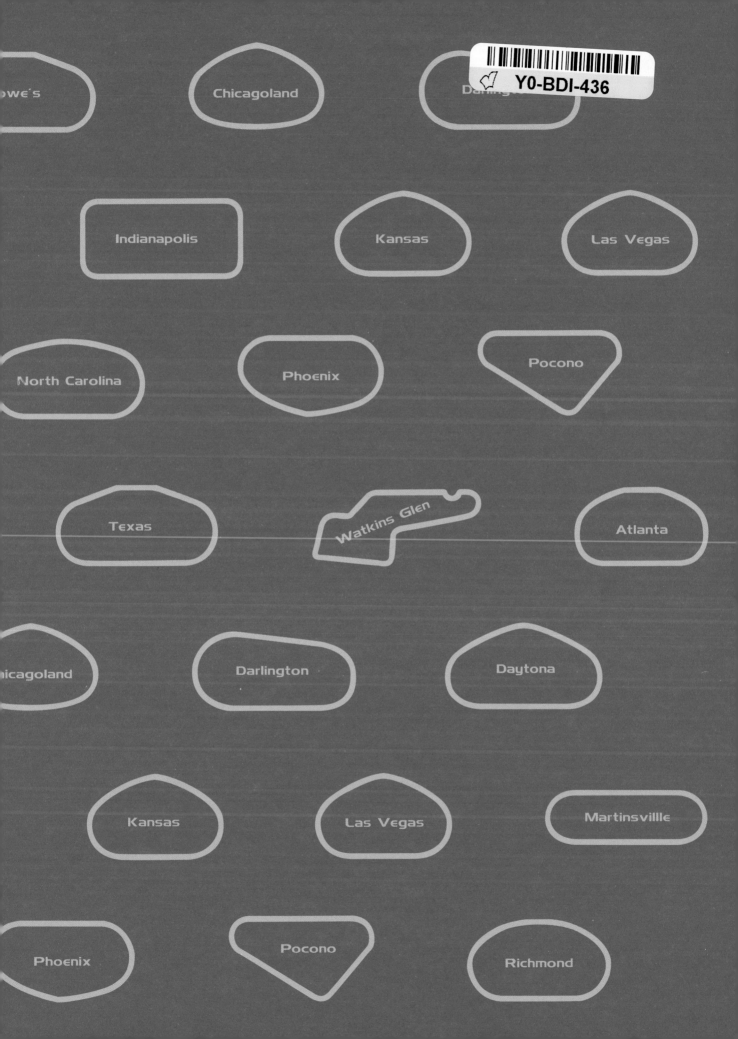

NASCAR CHRONICLE

BY GREG FIELDEN
AND THE AUTO EDITORS OF CONSUMER GUIDE®

Publications International, Ltd.

The editors gratefully acknowledge the cooperation of the following people who supplied photography to help make this book possible:

Kirk Bell, California Speedway, Jack Cansler, Chrysler Photographic, Chrysler-Plymouth Performance Publicity, Dodge Public Relations, *Chris Dolack*, Greg Fielden, Ford Motor Company and Wieck Media Services, Inc., LaDon George, David Griffin, Matt Griffith, Phil Hall, Bryan Hallman, Mike Horne, International Speedway Corporation, Dave Jensen, Brett Kelley, Don Kelly, Tom Kirkland, Mike Laczynski, Las Vegas Motor Speedway, Vince Manocchi, Larry McTighe, Motorsports Images & Archives Photography, Bill Niven, Petty Enterprises, James Price, David Schenk, Texas Motor Speedway.

A Note About Statistics: The statistics quoted in *NASCAR Chronicle* have been compiled by the author. Many of the numbers do not match official statistics recognized by NASCAR, but they do represent the best efforts of one of racing's most respected historians.

contents

4   Foreword

6   **The Birth of Stock Car Racing in America**

12   1950s: **The Manufacturers Take Notice**

24   1960s: **Superspeedways & Speedy Muscle Cars**

36   1970s: **NASCAR Enters the Modern Era**

48   1980s: **Smaller Cars, Bigger Purses, Grand Exposure**

62   1990s: **NASCAR Goes Big Time**

84   2000s: **The New Millennium**

96   Index

Foreword

Has any sport enjoyed the phenomenal, unabated growth that NASCAR has seen in its brief history? While the sport of auto racing dates to roughly 1892, NASCAR's first season didn't take the green flag until 1948.

In the latter half of the 20th century, NASCAR drove past USAC, Trans-Am, Can-Am, CART, IRL, NHRA, and Formula One to become America's most-followed motorsport. Recently, NASCAR has raced past hockey, golf, basketball, and baseball to become the country's second-most-watched professional sport on television.

This rampant growth has made billionaires of a handful and millionaires of dozens, but it has also bankrupted more than a few. And like most success stories, it began with one man and his dream.

William Henry Getty France was a smart man and a shrewd promoter whose word was his bond. He founded the National Association for Stock Car Auto Racing in 1948 to give the fledgling sport honesty and respectability. His national championship series would ensure a constant flow of membership and sanctioning fees to Daytona Beach that could be used to help the sport grow further.

France never rested on his laurels. He dreamed of a high-banked superspeedway and created his tri-oval masterpiece in Daytona Beach with borrowed money on public-owned land. Then, a decade later, France built an even-faster speedway in Alabama.

He kept his sport healthy in the late 1950s when the Detroit automakers pulled out in the wake of congressional pressure and safety concerns due to a string of fatalities throughout racing. He fought off unionization in '61, and showed his opposition to a '69 drivers' strike by climbing in a race car and driving high-speed laps. France started his own radio network in '70 to ensure weekly live coverage of the races. All along, he provided stock car rides for world-champion road racers, and helped keep struggling car owners afloat.

Without Bill France, stock car racing would just be a disconnected smorgasbord of ¼- and ½-mile ovals, racing on Saturday nights during the summer months.

There was only one world France couldn't conquer—television. The New York-based networks showed little interest in stock car racing while France was at the helm.

France's son, Bill Jr., and announcer Ken Squier brought NASCAR to network TV. CBS first televised the Daytona 500 live, flag to flag, in 1979. A close race, and a thrilling, crashing, fist-fighting finish created millions of new fans and gave the sport its biggest-ever jolt of momentum. By the mid '80s, most races were shown on network or cable TV.

Television's impact is best illustrated by the example of the ½-mile oval in Bristol, Tenn. In the sport's radio days, the track struggled to sell out its 30,000 seats. Many Sundays on the radio, Barney Hall and I often had to mention that Bristol's ticket office was open, with plenty of good seats available for the upcoming race. Once people finally saw the excitement of Bristol on ESPN, the track drew fans like an auto racing "field of dreams."

Bristol now boasts 160,000 seats and a long waiting list for tickets to its two annual NASCAR Nextel Cup races.

Where television went, Madison Avenue quickly followed. Race cars had mainly hawked automotive parts and products on their flanks. With network television came a wide range of product sponsorships, from beer to building supplies, crackers to camera film, detergents to deodorants. Financial services providers and our nation's fighting forces even got into the act.

The increased sponsor interest gave NASCAR a public reach it had never known. Every race is now televised, with FOX taking the first half of the season, and NBC and TNT splitting the second half. You can hardly walk down a supermarket aisle today without dodging a stand-up cardboard cutout of a NASCAR driver promoting his sponsor's products.

What drives the rampant fanaticism that fills the grandstands and draws stellar TV ratings every Sunday? The majority of NASCAR's heroes never received college scholarships or $1 million signing bonuses. Almost every driver started at a local short-track in a car built by his friends, hoping to develop his talent and attract backing. These are self-made men who had to prove themselves every step of the way. The American public responds to that.

Ned Jarrett, a two-time NASCAR champion, was the first expert analyst on NASCAR Cup Series broadcasts. Ned's blend of racing savvy and next-door-neighbor friendliness has helped NASCAR become welcomed into millions of American living rooms.

Thank also Richard Petty, NASCAR's all-time winner and seven-time champion, for setting the standard for driver behavior. Petty spent much of his time with the fans, signing autographs and answering questions. His grace and humility made him a perennial fan favorite.

A brash, upstart high school dropout became NASCAR's second megastar. Dale Earnhardt turned raw driving talent into seven championships, unrivaled hero worship, and a marketing empire worth untold millions. Earnhardt's self-described style of "frammin' and bammin'" redefined the limits of on-track behavior. When he stepped over the line, the line often moved with him. Earnhardt's fatal crash on the final lap of the 2001 Daytona 500 cost the sport its biggest star, but propelled NASCAR to a new proactive stance on racing safety issues.

Today, only four-time champion Jeff Gordon is within striking range of the records held by Petty and Earnhardt. While Gordon is NASCAR's poster boy, Dale Earnhardt, Jr., is the clear leader when the fans vote with their wallets. His following in the grandstands and at the numerous souvenir trailers that travel the circuit is unrivaled.

Despite the boom in popularity, NASCAR has, again, not rested on its laurels. Brian France, son of Bill France, Jr., extended NASCAR's marketing reach by opening satellite offices in New York, Charlotte, and Beverly Hills. Brian also led negotiations for the landmark network television deal with FOX, NBC, and TNT that began 2001.

In 2003, Brian France replaced his father as NASCAR's chairman and CEO. Brian's first year on the job brought continued schedule realignment, and a seamless integration of Nextel Communications as the series' title sponsor after 33 years with Winston.

The sport's management team, led by France, Mike Helton, and George Pyne, has tremendous depth, and has shouldered the burden of growing a regional sport into a national pastime. And they weren't reluctant to shake things up a bit for 2004. To bolster late-season TV ratings against the NFL, NASCAR changed the way its premier championship is decided. The ten-race, season-ending "Chase for the Nextel Cup" marked the first time ever that the series champion wasn't determined by the year's cumulative points-standing totals.

The modified playoff-style format had its critics, but the competition to make it into the "chase"—and in the season's final race—proved to be the best pure racing seen in some years. When the 2004 season's final lap began at Homestead-Miami Speedway, three drivers had a legitimate shot at the title, validating the new format.

NASCAR continues down a successful road because the compelling driving force is, and always has been, the quality of the competition. It is so much fun to follow for the same reasons it is so challenging and thrilling to broadcast:

The action can come from anywhere in the 43-car field at anytime.

The favorite rarely has an overwhelming advantage.

An underdog can often pull off a surprise.

Most of all, you never know who's going to win until the checkered flag waves.

Mike Joy
FOX Sports
December 2004

Chapter One:
The Birth of Stock Car Racing in America

As soon as the the first gasoline-powered automobile was ready to run, it was only a matter of time before someone would race the newfangled creation. As early as 1885, auto races were conducted in America. With the dawn of the twentieth century, a variety of races were run on public streets, hastily built speedways, rutted dirt tracks originally designed for other uses, and along the shoreline of Daytona Beach, Fla.

In February 1903, the first organized speed tournament was staged on the sands of Ormond Beach, Fla. Alexander Winton, sitting atop an eye-jabbing creation blistered the hard-packed sands in his Winton Bullet at a 68.19 mph clip.

Although attended by only a handful of chilly onlookers, Winton's feat would kick off an annual affair in the nearby resort town of Daytona Beach. Every winter, innovators, creators, wealthy sportsmen, and a few genuine screwballs made their way to Daytona to test the speed limits of a potpourri of vehicular oddities. Within a few years, the eyes of the world were focused on the mechanical magic taking place on Florida's beaches.

The speedy shenanigans continued on the eastern Florida coast for three decades. By 1935, speeds were approaching 300 mph, and the contemptuous sands of Daytona Beach were no longer suited for unlimited speed runs. The trials were moved to more placid conditions offered by the vast salt flats in Bonneville, Utah. Daytona Beach was in danger of losing auto racing and the travelers it attracted.

In March 1936, the town of Daytona Beach organized a race for stock cars in an effort to keep auto racing active in the coastal hamlet. The American Automobile Association, whose Contest Board had been sanctioning open-wheel racing events since 1909, came onboard to direct the scheduled 250-mile championship stock car race.

A 3.2-mile beach and road course near the center of town became the new racing "closed course." Milt Marion, driving a V-8-powered Ford, motored to victory on the choppy and rutted course. A lanky youngster named Bill France finished fifth.

The race, shortened to 240 miles due to deplorable track conditions, was an artistic and financial failure. Following the Daytona debacle, the AAA essentially bailed out of the stock car racing picture. Without a sanctioning body, Bill France tried his hand at promoting stock car racing contests on the Beach-Road course. He achieved moderate success with his low-buck, small-time operations.

In 1938, an event of major proportions was staged in Atlanta. The one-mile Lakewood Fairgrounds was selected to host a "National Championship Stock Car Race." The 150-mile marathon event was won by 18-year-old Lloyd Seay. The wild youngster outran a gathering of hard-core renegades who often deliberately crusaded on the wrong side of the law.

Other stock car racing events began popping up on rough dirt tracks across the South—as did a few north of the Mason-Dixon Line. Many of these "facilities" had been carved beneath the raw edge of a tractor blade. Few, if any, measures were taken for the safety of gladiator or spectator. The events were punctuated with little publicity, virtually no organization, crooked promoters, and nonexistent rule books. Plus, the behavior of the contestants was a crapshoot.

Stock car racing was in dire need of some organization. Bill France stepped to the forefront. A driver of considerable merit, France had joined the traveling band of rowdies in 1940 and began winning races regularly. On the strength of major victories in Ft. Wayne, Ind., and Daytona Beach, France was acknowledged as the "1940 National Stock Car Racing Champion," although there was no formal points system in place to document his title.

In his travels, France also gained a working knowledge of promoting automobile races. A man of exceptional intelligence and a keen sense of fairness, France absorbed what the drivers, teams, race officials, and the sport itself, needed to flourish. In 1941, the relentless racers crisscrossed the Eastern United States, enduring an exhaustive schedule that included four championship events at Daytona Beach promoted by France. Just as stock car racing was gaining momentum, World War II broke out. All of America's resources had to be channeled into the war effort. Every racing event in American was canceled.

The first postwar stock car race was conducted at the venerable Atlanta Lakewood Fairgrounds on Sept. 3, 1945. France ran second to madman Roy Hall, who was taking a break from his regular incarcerations in local and federal correctional facilities. Less than sixth months later, France gave up driving to devote his full attention to race promotions.

To gain immediate and widespread recognition for stock car racing, France made a pitch to the American Automobile Association to include the stocks in its repertoire of auto racing sanctions. The AAA was clearly the leader in the industry. In exchange for group insurance and sanction, France wanted to

conduct a stock car racing series under the AAA banner. Effectively, the AAA told France to get lost, and that stock car racing wasn't worth the effort.

Undaunted by the AAA's cold reception, France carried on by himself. He took a decisive step by announcing the formation of the National Championship Stock Car Circuit in 1947, a new touring series for stock car jockeys. France developed a unified set of rules, implemented a points system, and promised postseason money to the top drivers in the rankings.

France's NCSCC began in January 1947 at Daytona Beach and concluded at Jacksonville in December, having sanctioned nearly 40 events. Attendance at most of the races exceeded capacity and surpassed the visions of the ever-optimistic France. Posted awards were paid, points were accumulated, and a champion was named. Fonty Flock logged seven race wins en route to the '47 NCSCC championship and collected a postseason prize of $1000.

Near the end of the 1947 season, France advised track operators, drivers, owners, and any interested party that a big pow-wow would take place in December in Daytona Beach. Big Bill, a man of strong will and deep conviction, wanted to take the sport to a new national level, but he knew he had to have the support of the contestants. France welcomed all to the Streamline Hotel for a series of meetings.

On Dec. 14, 1947, 35 men shimmied up a creaky wooden staircase to the top floor of the Streamline Hotel. At 1:00 P.M. on that lazy Sunday afternoon, France called to order the first of four days of seminars that would outline the direction in which the sport was headed. During the meeting, France said, "Gentlemen, right here within our group rests the outcome of stock car racing in the country today. We have the opportunity to set it up on a big scale. We are all interested in one thing: improving present conditions."

At the end of the seminar, France appointed technical and competition committees, and all factions of racers—drivers, mechanics, and owners—were represented. With assistance from Daytona Beach attorney Louis Ossinski, NASCAR was formed into a private corporation with France as president.

The first official NASCAR-sanctioned stock car racing event took place on Daytona's Beach-Road course on Feb. 15, 1948, and was won by Red Byron. The 1948 NASCAR championship season consisted of 52 races, each packed with its own flair and drama. The cars, mostly five- to 10-year-old Fords, were called Modifieds, and chassis and engine work was permitted. The races were staged in seven states, with venues ranging from Birmingham, Ala., to Langhorne, Penn., and 14 drivers

earned at least one trip to victory lane. Crusty veteran Red Byron won the championship on the strength of 11 wins. In a close title chase, Byron edged Fonty Flock by only 37.75 points and earned $1250 in postseason money.

Bill France and his loyal sidekicks, pulled off the exhaustive 52-race season with few glitches. The Modifieds were successful and remained NASCAR's flagship series in 1949. However, Bill France started toying with the idea of a circuit for late-model American cars. A shortage of new, postwar automobiles delayed any serious thought to racing late models until May 1949, when France announced plans to conduct a "Strictly Stock" race in June.

News of Bill France's latest brainstorm spread quickly. With its central location, Charlotte Speedway was chosen to host the 150-mile race for stock late-model cars on June 19. The two-year-old facility was a rough ¾-mile dirt track surrounded by scraggly fences of undressed lumber. Charlotte was a regular stop on NASCAR's annual Modified tour, and its seating capacity of 10,000-plus was factor in the decision.

A total of about 13,000 spectators paid $2 to $3 to sit in the wooden grandstand for what was to become the inaugural NASCAR Late Model event. The 200-lap race was a hoot. Thirty-three new cars slapped fenders, sent up billowing clouds of red dust, and thrilled the trackside audience for a shade over two hours. At the finish, Glenn Dunnaway's '47 Ford was flagged the winner.

But Dunnaway's car, a hopped-up Ford that was used for transporting moonshine, was equipped with nonstock springs. NASCAR disqualified Dunnaway and awarded the victory to Kansas driver Jim Roper.

Seven other Strictly Stock races were staged in 1949. Attendance figures were impressive: 20,000 at Langhorne; 17,500 at Occoneechee Speedway in Hillsboro, N.C.; and 11,733 at Hamburg, N.Y. Virtually overnight, the Strictly Stocks had become a booming success.

Red Byron, twice a winner during the inaugural Strictly Stock season, captured the 1949 championship, sharing NASCAR's top honors with Fonty Flock, who was crowned champion of the Modified Circuit. Byron won $1000 in points money, while Flock earned $1250 since the Modifieds staged more shows and therefore had more money in the kitty.

As the 1940s drew to a close, Bill France was at the forefront of stock car racing. Relying on determination, a vision for the future, and polished communication skills, France had brought NASCAR's noteworthy festival of noise and color to a new level of respectability within professional motorsports.

Before NASCAR

February 1903 The first organized speed trial in the Daytona Beach, Fla., area is staged at Ormond Beach. Alexander Winton drives 68.19 mph on the hard-packed sand.

March 7, 1935 Sir Malcolm Campbell drives 276.82 mph on the sands of Daytona Beach in a record speed run. It is the final speed trial at Daytona.

March 8, 1936 Daytona Beach city officials conduct a 240-mile late-model stock car race to replace the speed trials. Milt Marion prevails.

November 12, 1938 Atlanta's Lakewood Fairgrounds stages a "National Championship Stock Car Race" on its one-mile dirt track. Lloyd Seay wins.

July 28, 1940 Bill France drives Andy Beardon's 1939 Ford to victory in a 200-mile event at Ft. Wayne, Ind.

September 1, 1941 Lloyd Seay wins the National Championship race at Atlanta's Lakewood Speedway. He is shot to death the next day by his cousin in a dispute over the family moonshine business.

November 2, 1941 Jap Brogton prevails in the Lloyd Seay Memorial race at Lakewood. It is the final stock car race before World War II.

September 3, 1945 Roy Hall outruns Bill France to win the 75-mile race at Lakewood Speedway. It is the first stock car event after World War II.

February 24, 1946 After 27 months in an Army hospital, Red Byron wins the stock car race at Orlando, Fla. Byron's plane had been shot down in the war.

Wealthy sportsman Jack Rutherford guides his #29 Auburn bobtail speedster through the rutted north turn in the inaugural 1936 Daytona Beach-Road stock car race. Rutherford was among the quickest qualifiers but he failed to finish the car-killing contest. Only 10 cars in the starting field of 27 were running at the finish.

► Cyrus Clark cuts a quick swath through the north turn in the July 27, 1941, Daytona Beach race. Newspaper reports referred to Clark as "the lunatic from Miami." Clark's wild antics behind the wheel netted him a 10th-place finish in this event.

◄ Fearless Lloyd Seay teeters on two wheels in an acrobatic jaunt through the north turn of Daytona's Beach-Road course. Seay was always spectacular. The youthful Dawsonville, Ga., driver flipped twice in one event, yet still finished fourth. On Aug. 24, 1941, Seay led the entire distance to win the 160-mile event at Daytona. Eight days later he was shot to death by his cousin.

Perhaps the most glamorous car to ever run at Daytona Beach was also the last. Malcolm Campbell's Bluebird V, a 30-foot-long bodyshell built around five tons of complicated machinery, was an outstanding example of the art of aerodynamics. With 2227 cid churning out 2700 horsepower, Campbell ran a 276.82 mph two-way average on March 7, 1935, with a one-way run of over 330 mph. On the return run, part of the cowling ripped away and Campbell spun, causing him to fall short of the 300 mph mark.

A stock car race sanctioned by the American Automobile Association replaced the land-speed vehicles on Daytona Beach in 1936. Young Bill France was one of the 27 entrants in his #10 Ford V-8 coupe. France qualified at 69.22 mph on the 3.2-mile sand and pavement course, 18th quickest. He finished fifth.

▼ The one-mile circular Langhorne Speedway near Philadelphia was one of America's most famous dirt tracks. Built in 1926, the track hosted a variety of open-wheel Champ car, sprint car, motorcycle, and stock car races. Ted Nyquist and Bill Schindler are on the front row for this '46 stock car race.

1947

January Bill France announces he will direct a series of stock car races under the National Championship Stock Car Circuit banner in 1947.

January 26 Red Byron captures the inaugural NCSCC event, billed as the "Battle of Champions," on the Beach-Road course in Daytona Beach.

May 18 Fonty Flock wins the inaugural event at North Wilkesboro (N.C.) Speedway. The race is a success, with more than 10,000 spectators.

June 15 Bob Flock wins at Greensboro, N.C. Ed Samples, the recognized 1946 stock car racing champion, rolls three times but remains in the race.

September 7 The new track in Martinsville, Va., opens to a large crowd. Red Byron wins the dusty 50-lap event.

September 14 A huge crowd of 20,000 turns out for the 160-lap race at North Wilkesboro. Marshall Teague wins.

October 17 Bob Flock, in contention for the championship, fractures his back in a spill at Spartanburg, S.C., and is forced to miss the rest of the season.

December 12 Red Byron wins the 1947 NCSCC finale at Jacksonville, Fla. Seven-race winner Fonty Flock is declared the champion.

December 14 Bill France and 35 others meet at the Streamline Hotel in Daytona Beach. A set of rules is established and Red Vogt coins the name National Association for Stock Car Auto Racing, which becomes NASCAR.

◄ This rare color photograph shows "Big Bill" France posing beside the utility vehicle he drove around during the 1947 season. Prior to the incorporation of NASCAR, France operated the National Championship Stock Car Circuit, as noted on the door of the black Ford.

▼ Bill Snowden power-slides through the corner on a dirt track in 1947. The St. Augustine, Fla., veteran was one of the most capable and well-respected drivers on the NCSCC tour.

Newcomer Lee Petty competed sparingly during the 1947 National Championship Stock Car Circuit season, driving the #87 '37 Plymouth owned by Ed Blizzard. Petty didn't begin his racing career until he was 33 years old. He would go on to form Petty Enterprises, the winningest outfit in NASCAR history.

Fisticuffs were plentiful in the early days of stock car racing. Drivers would often engage in heated battles on the racetracks, then settle personal differences in the pit area after the event was over. Drivers and crewmen weren't above occassional violent outbursts then, and some aren't above it today.

◄ Fonty Flock poses with the handsome championship trophy he received for capturing the NCSCC title. The inscription on the trophy reads: "Won by Fonty Flock —Atlanta, Ga.— Driving for Parks-Vogt Racing Team— 1765 Total Points Won—National Championship Stock Car Racing Circuit."

◄ In December 1947, the spic-and-span Streamline Hotel was the scene of a series of meetings that laid the groundwork for the NASCAR circuit. The historic hotel still stands today on Highway A-1-A in Daytona Beach.

1948

February 15 Red Byron wins the first NASCAR-sanctioned auto race in a 1939 Ford Modified. A crowd of 14,000 pays $2.50 each to watch the race on the Daytona Beach-Road course.

February 21 Louis Ossinski, an attorney for Bill France, completes the paperwork for the new stock car racing organization. NASCAR is incorporated.

May 23 NASCAR stages three championship events in different locations on the same day. Gober Sosebee wins at Macon, Ga., Bill Blair captures the feature in Danville, Va., and Johnny Rogers tops the field at Dover, N.J.

May 30 Paul Pappy outruns 19-year-old rookie Fireball Roberts to win the 40-lap Modified race at Jacksonville. It is the first time Roberts emerges as a stout contender.

June 20 NASCAR makes its first trip to Alabama. Fonty Flock wins the Modified feature at Birmingham. On the same day, Tim Flock scores his first NASCAR win at Greensboro, N.C.

July 25 Slick Davis becomes the first NASCAR driver to be fatally injured. The tragedy happens in an event at Greensboro, N.C. Curtis Turner starts on the pole and wins the race.

August 15 Al Keller spanks the 48-car field in a 200-mile NASCAR Modified race at Langhorne's circular one-mile dirt track. Runner-up Buck Barr finishes 18 laps behind Keller. Only 14 of the 48 starters manage to finish.

August 20 NASCAR is forced to cancel a number of scheduled events due to an outbreak of polio in North Carolina.

September 5 Curtis Turner bags the both ends of a doubleheader at North Wilkesboro Speedway. Turner wins the opener from the pole.

November 14 Red Byron wins the season finale at Jacksonville, Fla. Byron, winner of 11 of the 52 NASCAR-sanctioned events, edges 15-time winner Fonty Flock by 32.75 points to capture the inaugural championship. Byron collects $1250 in points fund earnings.

Red Byron is presented with a trophy for winning the Feb. 15 NASCAR race at Daytona. The postrace ceremonies were conducted as darkness descended on the Beach-Road course. Standing to the right is NASCAR Commissioner Erwin "Cannonball" Baker. The young lady is unidentified.

▼ The one-mile Occoneechee Speedway presented its inaugural race on June 27. The NASCAR Modifieds competed in a 100-mile jaunt, one of the biggest events on the '48 calendar. Jack Etheridge cocks his #6 Ford into the corner, just ahead of #7/11 Sara Christian. Others pictured are #7 Frank Mundy, #14 Bob Flock, and #44 Marshall Teague. Fonty Flock beat Teague to take the victory.

Fonty Flock waves to the sellout crowd as he takes the checkered flag to win the NASCAR race at New Atlanta Speedway on March 27. The crowd was so large that spectators stood atop the two-foot high concrete retaining wall. No protective barrier was in place at the ½-mile dirt track.

◄ Wrecks were a part of the NASCAR landscape in 1948. Most drivers were able to walk away from bone-jarring crashes such as this. One driver, W. R. "Slick" Davis, lost his life in a crash at Greensboro on July 25, becoming the first fatality in NASCAR competition.

Red Byron, a decorated war hero, prevailed in an intense battle for the 1948 NASCAR championship after a season-long struggle with '47 title-winner Fonty Flock. Byron grabbed the points lead in the 49th of 52 national championship races and edged Flock by 32.75 points.

Byron won 11 races during the 1948 campaign, including four in a row in April and May. Flock won 15 races, including six in the final two months.

Byron and Flock swapped the points lead five times during the season. Byron snared the lead for keeps after winning the Oct. 17 race at North Wilkesboro.

1948 NASCAR Modified Points Race

Rank	Driver	Points	Wins	Top 5	Top 10	Winnings
1	Red Byron	2996.5	11	25	32	$13,150
2	Fonty Flock	2963.75	15	30	34	$14,385
3	Tim Flock	1759.5	1	20	24	$5660
4	Curtis Turner	1540.5	7	20	22	$6435
5	Buddy Shuman	1350	2	15	18	$4365
6	Bill Blair	1188.5	1	11	18	$4055
7	Bob Flock	1181.5	5	12	16	$4710
8	Marshall Teague	1134.5	1	9	12	$3835
9	Bill Snowden	1092.5	0	6	14	$2665
10	Buck Baker	952.5	0	7	18	$2605

1949

January NASCAR promotes its new Roadster division. The first race scheduled at Daytona is canceled due to work on the newly designed Beach-Road course.

January 16 Marshall Teague wins the season opener at Daytona Beach.

January 23 NASCAR president Bill France promotes a 10-mile "Strictly Stock Late Model" race along with the 100-mile Modified race at the new Broward Speedway. Lloyd Christopher wins the preliminary event. Fonty Flock wins the 50-lap Modified feature.

February 27 A second Strictly Stock Late Model race is added to the card at Broward Speedway. Benny Georgeson wins the 10-mile contest.

June 19 More than 13,000 fans attend the inaugural Strictly Stock National Championship race at Charlotte Speedway. Glenn Dunnaway finishes first in a 1946 Ford, but is disqualified when NASCAR inspectors find illegal springs on the former moonshine car. Jim Roper is declared the winner.

June Hubert Westmoreland, owner of the car Dunnaway drove at Charlotte, files a lawsuit against NASCAR for disqualifying his car from the race.

August 7 A 200-mile Strictly Stock race replaces the scheduled Modified feature at Occoneechee Speedway in Hillsboro, N.C. Bob Flock wins.

October 2 Lee Petty records his first NASCAR Strictly Stock victory in the 100-mile race at Heidelberg Speedway near Pittsburgh. Sara Christian finishes fifth, the best finish ever for a female driver in NASCAR's premier division.

October 16 Bob Flock captures the eighth and final 1949 Strictly Stock race at North Wilkesboro Speedway. Red Byron is crowned the first Strictly Stock champion, while Fonty Flock is the Modified division champion.

December 16 Judge John J. Hayes dismisses the lawsuit filed by Hubert Westmoreland, and rules NASCAR is allowed to disqualify cars that don't comply with technical specifications.

Fonty Flock, behind the wheel of Joe Wolf's #47 Ford, holds a narrow advantage over a pack of cars in the March 27 NASCAR Modified race at North Wilkesboro Speedway. Chasing Flock are #16 Bill Snowden, #90 Tim Flock, #22 Red Byron, #44 Frank Mundy, and #7 Bob Apperson. Fonty Flock won 14 races during the 42-race '49 Modified season. He took the points lead following the third event of the season and remained atop the standings for the rest of the year.

◄ Female racer Louise Smith is all smiles after her spectacular tumble out of the Occoneechee Speedway during a practice run. After the car was dragged out of the woods, Smith climbed inside the crumpled machine to pose for photographers. One of the most popular competitors in NASCAR's early days, Smith always had an entourage of enthusiastic supporters in her pit area.

Circular Langhorne Speedway in Pennsylvania was the site of the fourth NASCAR Strictly Stock race of the 1949 season. The one-mile dirt track contained no straightaways. Drivers who tackled the fickle monster had to run flat out for the entire distance in a four-wheel drift. Langhorne Speedway was one of the most punishing and dangerous racing facilities ever built.

Red Byron won his second straight NASCAR title and became the first champion of the new Strictly Stock late-model tour on the strength of a pair of wins during the eight-race campaign. Byron finished 117.5 points in front of runner-up Lee Petty.

Byron took the lead in the points standings after his victory at Daytona Beach, the second Strictly Stock race of the inaugural season. His second victory at Martinsville in September locked up the championship. Byron only finished out of the top 10 in two of his six starts.

Byron drove Oldsmobiles for Raymond Parks. Chief mechanic Red Vogt kept the cars in top running order all season.

1949 NASCAR Modified Points Race

Rank	Driver	Points	Wins	Top 5	Top 10	Winnings
1	Red Byron	842.5	2	4	4	$5800
2	Lee Petty	725	1	3	5	$3855
3	Bob Flock	704	2	3	3	$4870
4	Bill Blair	567	0	3	5	$1180
5	Fonty Flock	554	0	3	3	$2015
6	Curtis Turner	430	1	1	4	$2675
7	Ray Erickson	422	0	2	3	$1460
8	Tim Flock	421	0	2	3	$1510
9	Glenn Dunnaway	384	0	1	3	$810
10	Frank Mundy	370	0	2	2	$1160

Chapter Two:
The Manufacturers Take Notice

AFTER ONLY EIGHT Strictly Stock races in 1949, NASCAR's Late Model racing division was already a hot commodity. In 1950, it became NASCAR's number-one series, replacing the Modifieds as the headlining attraction, and a new title, "NASCAR Grand National Circuit," replaced "Strictly Stock."

The development of NASCAR's Grand National Circuit and the advancement of the American passenger car were a natural mix with perfect timing. The automobile manufacturers, with accelerated research and mechanical development, were producing more powerful passenger cars to whet the appetite of a youthful car-buying public.

The NASCAR rulebook still mirrored the manufacturers' spec sheets, and the nimble and powerful Olds, with its newly developed high-compression, lightweight V-8 engine, became the car of choice for NASCAR racers. Oldsmobile won 15 of the first 24 NASCAR Grand National events. Despite this stellar performance, General Motors executives maintained only a passing interest in the sport.

Perhaps the first manufacturer to take a closer look at NASCAR's Grand National Circuit was the Nash Motor Co. The company offered cash prizes as contingency money in a few races, and delivered a new Nash to 1950 NASCAR Grand National champion Bill Rexford. Nash recruited and signed Curtis Turner at the beginning of the '51 season to drive Nash Ambassadors in NASCAR Grand National competition. Turner was NASCAR's most dynamic star, a flamboyant throttle-stomper, who won four times during the 1950 season while driving Oldsmobiles.

In the second event of the 1951 season, Turner drove his Ambassador to victory in the 150-lap NASCAR Grand National race at Charlotte Speedway. The Nash public relations office let the country know about its magnificent automobile with press releases and magazine ads. But the Charlotte win was destined to be the first and last for Nash. Turner ditched his Ambassador by late April and returned to his trusty Oldsmobile. "The Nash is an upside down bathtub that overheats all the time," Turner said.

By 1951, the best-designed automobile for NASCAR racing was actually the Hudson Hornet. Hudson developed a chassis in the late 1940s that featured wraparound perimeter-style frame rails. This design enabled the body to hang closer to the ground. The chassis also extended outside the rear wheels, giving the car a well-enclosed "low-rider" look. From ground to rooftop it was a foot lower than many of its contemporaries.

After winning the 1951 Daytona Beach race in a Hudson Hornet, Marshall Teague flew to the Hudson Motor Co. headquarters in Michigan to tell them what a nice car they had developed and how suited it was to NASCAR racing. Teague also convinced Hudson to support his racing efforts, explaining how winning on the NASCAR tracks would help sell more Hudsons to the American public. Hudson spruced up its racing package with a heavy-duty suspension kit and enhanced its engine's performance. Hudson won 61 of the 112 races from 1951 to '53 and swept the NASCAR Grand National championship all three years. Hudson's prowess on the NASCAR speedways made the other manufacturers take notice.

By the mid 1950s, General Motors, Ford, and Chrysler were developing more-powerful vehicles. Chevrolet and Ford produced V-8 engines, dual carburetors, increased horsepower, a refined chassis, and a lighter overall package. Chrysler came up with its Hemi engine, a powerful batch of bolts that produced oodles of horsepower. Meanwhile, Hudson fell behind, making only peripheral refinements. Virtually all of the Hudson drivers shifted their alliance to other makes of cars.

The 1955 season was pivotal for NASCAR. Mercury Outboard magnate Carl Kiekhaefer appeared virtually overnight with a powerful Hemi-equipped Chrysler 300. He signed Tim Flock to drive it, and the former NASCAR champion promptly won the Daytona Beach race in his first start.

An independent effort without direct backing from Chrysler, Kiekhaefer used the NASCAR playground as an advertising medium for his Mercury Outboard engines. The crusty perfectionist brought his considerable resources to NASCAR and played the game seriously. Kiekhaefer's professional discipline and deep pockets lifted him head-and-shoulders above the other "shade-tree engineering" NASCAR race teams.

Kiekhaefer's Chryslers and Dodges cleaned house in NASCAR in 1955 and '56, winning 52 of the 90 races his teams entered. Kiekhaefer drivers Tim Flock and Buck Baker took the NASCAR championship each year. In '56, his cars won 16 consecutive NASCAR Grand National races, a record that will likely live in the record books forever. After the '56 season, Kiekhaefer withdrew from NASCAR. He had accomplished all he had set out to do and his teams had performed splendidly. He got out of NASCAR as suddenly as he had arrived, having firmly left his fingerprint on stock car racing.

In a quest to get its automobiles to victory lane, Ford and Chevrolet escalated their spending on the NASCAR scene. The

two automotive giants collectively spent better than $6 million to win NASCAR stock car races and sell their product to the motoring public. The results were disappointing. Ford won 14 races while Chevrolet only won three times.

The horsepower race and the Ford-Chevrolet battle were in full gallop as the 1957 NASCAR campaign got underway. With Kiekhaefer's departure, Chrysler was no longer competitive. GM and Ford produced optimum equipment in souped-up vehicles. Fuel-injected engines and superchargers were available to the public, and, therefore, eligible for NASCAR competition.

The directors of the Automobile Manufacturers Association were becoming increasingly disturbed about the unchecked horsepower race. Congressional investigations had been going on since mid 1956. The nation's highways had become lethal with record numbers of fatalities. Fatal crashes in several racing series were also making headlines. The automakers were feeling the heat, and threats of federal regulation meant they had to do something.

On Thursday, June 6, 1957, the heads of several car companies, sitting as directors of the Automobile Manufacturers Association, recommended unanimously that the industry take no part in, or assist in any way, automobile races or other competitive events in which speed or horsepower were emphasized.

When the resolution came down, the automotive industry retreated from NASCAR stock car racing. The racing equipment remained in the hands of the NASCAR teams. Most had the resources to finish out the 1957 season. By '58, the manufacturers were itching to get back into the sport. To abide by the AMA resolution and still get the latest equipment into the hands of the competitors, the automakers had to be a little more discreet. New batches of '58 equipment found their way to select NASCAR team owners. John Holman said his newly arrived '58 Fords were the courtesy of 32 Carolina Ford dealerships, not from the Ford factory. Jim Rathmann, who owned a large Chevrolet dealership in Florida, found himself surrounded with Chevrolet's latest high-speed equipment and some of the first '58 sheetmetal. Pontiac was well-represented too, with the addition of Smokey Yunick to its team.

GM took top honors in 1958, winning 34 races, twice as many as Ford. Lee Petty won the '58 NASCAR Grand National title in an independent Oldsmobile.

By late 1958, construction had already begun on a massive new 2.5-mile speedway in Daytona Beach, and it was generating plenty of interest across the country. The huge speedway set to open in February 1959 was a temptation none of the manufacturers would be able to resist. This magnificent racing palace represented a golden opportunity for publicity and exposure for the new American cars.

The automobile manufacturers were well-represented at Daytona Beach in 1959. Pontiac supplied a new Catalina to Bill France to tool around in during the inaugural Speedweeks activities. New '59 model cars were put on display throughout the Daytona Beach area during the month and the town was decorated with hundreds of banners, all prominently displaying the GM logo. At the speedway, Chevrolet had plenty of new '59 Impalas on hand with the latest GM high-performance goodies, and Smokey Yunick fielded his '59 Pontiac with Fireball Roberts at the helm.

Ford's NASCAR teams were well-represented, too. Holman-Moody took delivery of seven new Thunderbirds, stuffed them with 430-cid Lincoln engines, and sold four of the powerful chariots to race teams for the Daytona 500. The remaining three T-Birds were entered by the Holman-Moody team.

Defending NASCAR Grand National champion Lee Petty picked up a new 1959 Oldsmobile from Newton-Chapel Motors in Reidsville, N.C., a few weeks before the Daytona 500. Petty paid $3500 for the new showroom automobile and made the car race-ready in his Randleman, N.C., garage.

The first Daytona 500 attracted the most media representatives ever to attend any auto race other than the Indianapolis 500. The show turned out to be better than a Hollywood production. For 500 miles of nonstop green-flag action, America's finest machinery battled around the new Daytona International Speedway in dizzying fashion. Speeds were much faster than any stock car had ever gone and came within a whisker of those turned at Indy.

In the late stages, the Daytona 500 boiled down to a two-car struggle between Petty's Oldsmobile and the Thunderbird driven by Johnny Beauchamp. After swapping first place a dozen times in the final 50 laps, Beauchamp and Petty crossed the finish line in a near dead heat. The finish was so close that Bill France announced the results were "unofficial" until all available film and photo evidence could be studied.

After 61 hours, Lee Petty was finally declared the official winner. A film of the finish proved he had reached the finish line first. Petty averaged 135.521 mph in his victory ride, some 33 mph faster than any other NASCAR Grand National race. The Daytona 500 was an electric success and it generated more publicity than any other stock car race in history.

The theater of NASCAR stock car racing was expanding. The sprawling facility at Daytona delivered cachet for the entire sport and momentum was building. Within weeks, several entities announced their intentions to build high-banked superspeedways, most notably in Atlanta, Charlotte, and California. NASCAR stock car racing was about to venture into a new chapter of ultrafast speedways.

1950

January NASCAR's Strictly Stock late-model division is renamed the "Grand National" division.

June 25 Jimmy Florian scores the first NASCAR Grand National win for Ford in the 100-mile race on the high banks of Dayton (Ohio) Speedway.

July 23 Curtis Turner records his fourth victory of the year in the 100-mile race at Charlotte Speedway. Lee Petty, who ranked third in the points standings, has all 809 points removed by NASCAR for competing in a stock car race not sanctioned by NASCAR.

August 13 Fireball Roberts, 21, wins the 100-mile race at Occoneechee Speedway in Hillsboro, N.C., making him NASCAR's youngest winner.

September 4 Johnny Mantz wins the first Southern Five-Hundred. Mantz collects $10,510, the largest purse so far in stock car history. The event is cosanctioned by the Central States Racing Association and NASCAR. NASCAR originally declined to sanction the race.

October 29 Lee Petty captures the season finale at Hillsboro, N.C., as Bill Rexford wraps up the NASCAR Grand National championship.

October 30 1949 NASCAR champion Red Byron, who ranked sixth in the '50 NASCAR Grand National standings, has all 1315.5 points stripped for participating in a non-NASCAR-sanctioned race at Atlanta's Lakewood Speedway.

December 18 NASCAR announces $23,024 in points fund money will be distributed to drivers based on final points standings. Champion Bill Rexford will receive $1375.

Despite mechanical problems in the season finale at Hillsboro, N.C., 23-year-old Bill Rexford held off Fireball Roberts to capture the 1950 NASCAR Grand National championship.

The 1950 title chase was quite memorable. In the 19-race campaign, the points lead changed hands nine times among seven drivers. Rexford took the points lead in the next-to-last race at Winchester, Ind., and finished 110.5 points ahead of Roberts.

Roberts, the 21-year-old from Daytona Beach, could have won the title with a fifth-place finish in the season finale. With Rexford on the sidelines, Fireball elected to charge to the front rather than employ a conservative approach. Roberts led twice for nine laps, but blew the engine in his Oldsmobile and finished 21st.

1950 NASCAR Grand National Points Race

Rank	Driver	Points	Wins	Top 5	Top 10	Winnings
1	Bill Rexford	1959.0	1	5	11	$6175
2	Fireball Roberts	1848.5	1	4	5	$6955
3	Lee Petty	1398.0	1	9	13	$5580
4	Lloyd Moore	1398.0	1	7	10	$5580
5	Curtis Turner	1375.0	4	7	7	$6935
6	Johnny Mantz	1282.0	1	1	2	$10,835
7	Chuck Mahoney	1217.5	0	3	6	$2760
8	Dick Linder	1121.0	3	5	8	$5570
9	Jimmy Florian	801.0	1	3	6	$2695
10	Bill Blair	766.0	1	5	7	$4320

Red Byron gallops out of Daytona's south turn during his runner-up effort in the opening event of the 1950 NASCAR Grand National season on Feb. 5. Byron was among the leaders in the points standings, but had all of his points stripped when he drove in independent "outlaw" races. NASCAR had a strict policy that drivers must stay within the sanctioning boundaries or accept the loss of all championship points.

◄ Jimmy Florian drove his Ford to victory in the June 25 NASCAR Grand National race at Dayton Speedway, giving Ford its first big-league NASCAR win. Temperatures soared into the 90s on that hot Ohio day. Florian removed his shirt before the race in an effort to deal with the weather. At the time, NASCAR had no rule requiring drivers to wear a shirt when driving in a race.

Seventy-five cars line up three-abreast at Darlington Raceway on Labor Day, Sept. 4. Curtis Turner, Jimmy Thompson, and Gober Sosebee qualified for the front row. Fifteen days of qualifying determined the inaugural Southern Five-Hundred field. Sosebee went down in the record books as leading the first green flag lap in Darlington history. Thompson spun out in the first turn, but, miraculously, every car avoided hitting him.

Herb Thomas and Lee Petty pose with their Plymouths following the 1950 season finale at Hillsboro's Occoneechee Speedway. Petty won the race and wound up third in the final points standings. Over the course of the season, Petty scored more points than any other driver. But, in July, he competed in a non-NASCAR-sanctioned event and lost all 809 points he had earned up until that time. The penalty cost Petty the NASCAR Grand National championship.

1951

January Bill France announces that the NASCAR Grand National division will venture into the west in 1951.

January 22 Bill Holland, winner of the 1949 Indianapolis 500, is suspended from AAA Indy Car racing for competing in a three-lap Lion's Charity race at Opa Locka, Fla., on Nov. 14, 1950.

February 11 Marshall Teague wins the season opener on Daytona's Beach-Road course. Bill France lures suspended AAA driver Bill Holland into the NASCAR fold. Holland finishes 47th.

April 8 Marshall Teague wins at Carrell Speedway in Gardena, Calif. It is the first NASCAR Grand National event on the West Coast.

May NASCAR and the Detroit Junior Chamber of Commerce plan to celebrate the 250th anniversary of the Motor City with a Grand National race at the Michigan State Fairgrounds.

June 16 Frank Mundy wins at Columbia Speedway in South Carolina. It is the first NASCAR Grand National event to be staged under the lights, Mundy's first career victory, and the first win for the Studebaker nameplate.

August 12 Newcomer Tommy Thompson outlasts Curtis Turner in a slugfest to win the Motor City 250 at Detroit.

November 12 NASCAR announces it will sanction a Speedway Division for open-wheel cars in 1952.

November 25 Frank Mundy wins the season finale at Lakeview Speedway in Mobile, Ala. Bob Flock crashes and suffers a broken neck. Herb Thomas wraps up the tightly contested NASCAR Grand National championship.

With a victory in the Southern 500 at Darlington on Labor Day, Herb Thomas leapt atop the NASCAR Grand National points standings and led the rest of the season. Thomas won seven races during the 41-race season and finished only 146.2 points ahead of runner-up Fonty Flock, who won eight races.

Thomas remained within striking distance of the points lead throughout the first half of the season, but didn't take the lead until the Darlington win netted him 1250 points. The distribution of points in 1951 was parallel to the posted awards, and the Southern 500 was the richest race on the schedule. Fonty Flock finished eighth at Darlington and earned 375 points.

The points lead changed hands nine times among four drivers during the course of the season. Tim Flock finished third in points after leading the standings for 13 races.

1951 NASCAR Grand National Points Race

Rank	Driver	Points	Wins	Top 5	Top 10	Winnings
1	Herb Thomas	4208.45	7	16	18	$21,050
2	Fonty Flock	4062.25	8	20	22	$15,535
3	Tim Flock	3722.50	7	19	21	$15,155
4	Lee Petty	2392.25	1	11	19	$7340
5	Frank Mundy	1963.50	3	8	11	$7095
6	Buddy Shuman	1368.75	0	1	6	$2755
7	Jesse James Taylor	1214.00	0	1	3	$3700
8	Dick Rathmann	1040.00	0	4	7	$3480
9	Bill Snowden	1009.25	0	3	9	$2365
10	Joe Eubanks	1005.50	0	3	3	$3350

Marshall Teague slaps his Hudson Hornet into the south turn during the Feb. 11 season opener at Daytona's Beach-Road Course. Teague took the lead from Tim Flock with 12 laps to go and sped to his first career NASCAR Grand National win. Teague had a close call in the race. A photographer ran onto the track to take a picture, and Teague commented that he "had to veer quick to miss him."

▶ An Oldsmobile convertible pace car leads the field onto the track at the start of the May 30 race at Ohio's Canfield Fairgrounds Speedway. Tim Flock flanks pole-sitter Bill Rexford on the front row. The covered grandstands were packed for the event. Staged on the same day as the Indianapolis 500, promoters named the race the "Poor Man's 500" even though it consisted of just 200 laps. Marshall Teague won, earning $1000. Lee Wallard won the Indy 500, a victory worth $63,612.

◀ With Herb Thomas in the championship chase, fellow Hudson driver Marshall Teague offered to let the title contender drive his car in a number of late-season events. Thomas' own operation was getting a little ragged around the edges during the final weeks of the exhaustive campaign. Teague's cars were well-rested, having been driven in only selected events. Thomas put Teague's #6 Hudson on the pole at Jacksonville for the Nov. 4 event, and drove to a convincing win. Frank Mundy finished fifth in the #23 Studebaker.

◀ The inaugural Motor City 250 wasn't only a much-anticipated affair, it turned out to be one of the most thrilling events in NASCAR history. Newcomer Tommy Thompson, driving a Chrysler, locked horns with the rambunctious Curtis Turner in the final laps. As both dueled for the lead, the big Chrysler and Turner's Olds collided in the third turn. As they zoomed down the front chute, Turner's busted radiator spit out a geyser of steam, leaving Thompson with a clear path to victory. Fifteen different makes of cars dotted the field, a NASCAR record.

1952

January 20 Bernard Alvarez escapes injury when his Olds flips over and the roof caves in at Palm Beach Speedway in West Palm Beach, Fla. NASCAR rules are amended to require the use of steel roll bars on all race cars.

February 9 The first two-way radio is used in NASCAR competition. Al Stevens, who operates a radio dispatch service, drives in the 100-mile Modified and Sportsman race at Daytona while talking to pit boss Cotton Bennett.

April 12 E.C. Ramsey crashes into a passenger car that attempts to cross the track during the 100-mile NASCAR Grand National race at Columbia, S.C.

April 17 Marshall Teague, who ranks sixth in the NASCAR Grand National points standings, is stripped of all points when he quits NASCAR and joins the rival AAA tour.

July 1 The first NASCAR Grand National event staged outside the U.S. is held at Stamford Park in Niagara Falls, Ontario, Canada. Buddy Shuman wins in a Hudson Hornet.

September 28 Herb Thomas wins at Wilson, N.C. Thomas averages only 35.398 mph, the slowest average speed in NASCAR Grand National history.

November 16 Donald Thomas, with relief help from older brother Herb, wins the 100-mile event at Lakewood Speedway in Atlanta. The 20-year-old Thomas becomes the youngest driver to win a NASCAR Grand National race.

November 30 Herb Thomas wins the season finale at West Palm Beach as Tim Flock finishes 12th and captures the championship.

The battle for the 1952 championship was resolved in the final event of the season at West Palm Beach, Fla. Tim Flock, who had taken the points lead from Herb Thomas at Langhorne in September, clinched the title by simply starting the finale. Flock flipped down the front chute, but he had accumulated enough points to seal the championship.

"I think I'm the only guy who ever won a championship on his head," cracked Flock afterward.

Thomas, who had taken the points lead at Darlington, only held it for two races before Flock was back in front. Flock and Thomas both won eight races during the 34-race campaign. The margin at the end of the season was 106 points.

1952 NASCAR Grand National Points Race

Rank	Driver	Points	Wins	Top 5	Top 10	Winnings
1	Tim Flock	6858.50	8	22	25	$22,890
2	Herb Thomas	6752.50	8	19	22	$18,965
3	Lee Petty	6498.50	3	21	27	$16,876
4	Fonty Flock	5183.50	2	14	17	$19,112
5	Dick Rathmann	3952.00	5	14	14	$11,248
6	Bill Blair	3449.00	1	10	13	$7899
7	Joe Eubanks	3090.50	0	4	9	$3630
8	Ray Duhigg	2986.50	0	4	10	$3811
9	Donald Thomas	2574.00	1	5	14	$4477
10	Buddy Shuman	2483.00	1	3	7	$4587

Curtis Turner hustles his #41 Oldsmobile through the south turn in the Feb. 10 race at Daytona Beach. While the wooden north-turn grandstands afforded the best view of the Beach-Road course, the south-turn grandstands attracted an equally enthusiastic throng. However, the south-turn bleachers were situated inside the track, so patrons could only see a fraction of the 4.1-mile course. The concrete blocks that held the south-turn stands are still in the ground today.

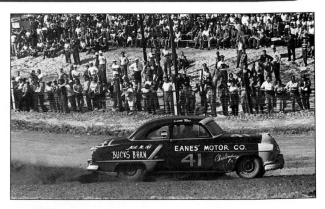

◄ The NASCAR Speedway Division ran its second race at Martinsville Speedway on May 25. Only 17 cars were ready for the 100-miler, but the new open-wheelers generated a pretty good crowd. Bill Miller is in the pole slot in his "Olds 88 Special." Flanking him on the outside is Buddy Shuman in the "GMC Special." Tex Keene, in a car powered by a stock Mercury engine, came from his 16th starting spot to win the race. Seven Speedway Division events were staged in 1952, and Buck Baker was crowned champion.

Bob Flock (shown with brother Fonty) missed the first half of the 1952 season. Flock had crashed and broken his neck in the '51 season finale at Mobile, Ala. Flock drove to Pensacola, Fla., where he visited a doctor to seek advice to deaden the pain in his neck. Doctors determined he had broken his neck. Flock made a memorable comeback by winning the Aug. 17 NASCAR Grand National race at Weaverville, N.C., in his first start since recovering.

◄ Herb Thomas went on a winning spree in the fall, winning three out of four races. Following his Oct. 26 victory at North Wilkesboro (N.C.), Thomas crept to within 146 points of NASCAR Grand National leader Tim Flock. The margin was closer than it seems. For most short-track events, the NASCAR points system awarded 200 points to the winner with a drop of eight points per position. That meant Thomas was within 20 finishing positions of Flock after 32 of the 34 races.

1953

February 11 Lee Petty is named Most Popular Driver at NASCAR's annual Victory Dinner. It is the first time the award has been presented since 1949.

February 15 Fonty Flock runs out of fuel on the final lap as Bill Blair wins at Daytona's Beach-Road course. It is the first NASCAR Grand National race to be determined by a last-lap pass.

May 16 Tim Flock, with riding companion "Jocko Flocko," prevails in the event at Hickory, N.C. Jocko, a rhesus monkey, is the first NASCAR Grand National copilot in a winning car.

May 30 The one-mile superspeedway in Raleigh, N.C., joins NASCAR and stages a 300-mile race. Fonty Flock wins. Tim Flock falls to third in the final laps when he pits to remove monkey copilot Jocko Flocko from his car.

June 21 Dick Rathmann wins the International 200 at Langhorne Speedway, the first NASCAR event open to both domestic and foreign cars. Lloyd Shaw wins the pole in a Jaguar.

November 1 Herb Thomas wraps up the NASCAR Grand National championship with a 14th-place finish in the 100-mile finale at Atlanta's Lakewood Speedway. Thomas becomes the first driver to win two titles.

November 27 NASCAR announces it will have both owner and driver points standings in 1954. Points money for the owners and drivers will be identical.

December 12 NASCAR president Bill France discloses plans for a 2.5-mile superspeedway in Daytona Beach. France estimates the cost at $1,674,000 and says it could open in 1955.

Herb Thomas took the lead in the points standings in early March and never looked back as he sailed to his second NASCAR Grand National championship. The Olivia, N.C., Hudson driver won 12 events in the 37-race season and finished comfortably ahead of runner-up Lee Petty, who won five races.

Thomas led virtually every major category during his championship run. He won the most races, led the most laps, scored the most top-five and top-10 finishes, completed the most miles and set a new record with $28,909.58 in season earnings.

1953 NASCAR Grand National Points Race

Rank	Driver	Points	Wins	Top 5	Top 10	Winnings
1	Herb Thomas	8460	12	27	31	$28,909.58
2	Lee Petty	7814	5	25	31	$18,446.50
3	Dick Rathmann	7362	5	22	25	$20,245.35
4	Buck Baker	6713	4	16	26	$18,166.20
5	Fonty Flock	6174	4	17	17	$17,755.48
6	Tim Flock	5011	1	11	18	$8281.86
7	Jim Paschal	4211	1	6	9	$5570.75
8	Joe Eubanks	3603	0	7	15	$5253.60
9	Jimmie Lewallen	3508	0	7	13	$4221.80
10	Curtis Turner	3373	1	3	5	$4371.45

Fonty Flock's #14 Olds leads the charge onto the paved section of Highway A-1-A in the Feb. 15 Daytona Beach NASCAR Grand National event. Flock started on the front row and led the entire distance until his fuel tank ran dry on the last lap. Teammate Slick Smith, playing the role of good samaritan, pushed Fonty's #14 Oldsmobile across the finish line, but NASCAR disallowed the assist and awarded Flock second place. Bill Blair was named the winner.

▲ Herb Thomas throws his Hudson Hornet into the first turn at Harnett Speedway in Spring Lake, N.C., on March 8. Thomas led all 200 laps on the ½-mile track to take his 17th career win. He became NASCAR's all-time Grand National winner in this event, and held the distinction until Lee Petty surpassed his 48 wins in 1960.

◄ Fireball Roberts steers his crippled #11 into the pits in the Sept. 7 Southern 500 at Darlington. The right front wheel collapsed on the 198th lap, forcing Roberts to retire from the event. Prior to his misfortune, Roberts led for 41 laps in the Ed Saverance-owned Oldsmobile. In the early years at Darlington Raceway, the pit area was located on the inside of the frontstretch and had no protective retaining barrier. A fatal pit accident in 1960 prompted raceway officials to build a wall to keep cars from spinning into the pits. Buck Baker went on to win the race.

▲ Drivers meetings in NASCAR's early days were held on the front straightaway just before the start of the race. Drivers, owners, pit crewmen, and race officials all gathered and stood around listening to the instructions. This photo was taken on Oct. 18 at Martinsville Speedway, an event that Jim Paschal drove to his first career NASCAR Grand National win. That's 16-year-old Richard Petty standing near the rear of the meeting in front of the door of Lee Petty's #42 Dodge.

1954

February 7 Herb Thomas wins the West Palm Beach, Fla., season opener. Thomas collects $1600 in prize money, which is sweetened by contingency money from Pure Oil Co. and Champion Spark Plugs.

February 21 Tim Flock finishes first but is disqualified at Daytona, elevating Lee Petty to the official winner. Flock quits NASCAR in disgust. Flock's car had been equipped with a two-way radio, the first such use in NASCAR Grand National competition.

May 13 NASCAR president Bill France is escorted out of the Indianapolis Motor Speedway garage. AAA chief stewart Harry McQuinn says, "We have a long-standing disagreement with NASCAR on what constitutes good racing."

June 13 The first NASCAR Grand National road-course event is held on at an airport in Linden, N.J. Al Keller wins the race in a Jaguar XK-120. A total of 20 foreign cars compete.

July Flameproof coveralls are made available to NASCAR drivers for $9.25 each by Treesdale Laboratories. It is the third NASCAR-specific product of the season. The $35 GenTex 70 helmet and special racing tires from Pure Oil Co. have already been offered.

July 24 Bill France, Jr., crashes in a NASCAR Short Track Division event. It was his second start of the season and the last of his racing career.

September 12 Hershel McGriff wins the 100-mile race at Macon, Ga. Tim Flock finishes second in his first start since rejoining the tour.

October 24 Lee Petty finishes last in the season finale at North Wilkesboro (N.C.) Speedway, but secures his first NASCAR Grand National championship.

Parlaying consistency, Lee Petty took the points lead in mid May and cruised to a 283-point victory in the 1954 NASCAR Grand National championship chase.

Two-time champion Herb Thomas gave chase, but was unable to catch Petty, who logged seven wins and 32 top-10 finishes in 34 starts. Thomas won 12 times and had 27 top-10 efforts. Buck Baker, who led the standings for six weeks in spring, posted four wins.

Petty only finished out of the top five in 10 races. The 1954 championship was sweet revenge for Petty, who lost the '50 title when NASCAR docked him 849 points for competing in a non-NASCAR-sanctioned event.

1954 NASCAR Grand National Points Race

Rank	Driver	Points	Wins	Top 5	Top 10	Winnings
1	Lee Petty	8649	7	24	32	$21,101.35
2	Herb Thomas	8366	12	19	27	$29,974.05
3	Buck Baker	6893	4	23	28	$19,367.87
4	Dick Rathmann	6760	3	23	26	$15,938.84
5	Joe Eubanks	5467	0	11	24	$8558.45
6	Hershel McGriff	5137	4	13	17	$12,999.23
7	Jim Paschal	3903	1	5	11	$5450.70
8	Jimmie Lewallen	3233	0	5	10	$4668.37
9	Curtis Turner	2994	1	7	8	$10,119.84
10	Ralph Liguori	2905	0	2	12	$3494.84

On a number of occasions in 1954, Herb Thomas picked up modest sponsorship from the Blue Crown Spark Plug Co. The Blue Crown Spark Plug Specials driven by Mauri Rose and Bill Holland won three consecutive Indianapolis 500s from 1947 to '49. Any sponsorship from a company known for its racing prowess indicated the NASCAR Grand National tour was gaining recognition.

With Ted Chester folding his racing team after the 1953 season, Tim Flock had to look for a ride. Colonel Ernest Woods was just entering NASCAR and signed Flock to drive his #88 Oldsmobile at Daytona. The car was equipped with a General Electric two-way radio, the first used in NASCAR Grand National competition. Woods could communicate with Flock during races—a major innovation for the day.

▼ Lee Petty started on the pole in the Feb. 21 Daytona Beach race and led only the first two laps. But Petty was awarded first place when Tim Flock's winning Olds was disqualified for an illegal carburetor. NASCAR disqualified winning cars that didn't comply with specs in the 1950s, a practice that has been discontinued.

▼ Al Keller poses with his Jaguar sports coupe at New Jersey's Linden Airport. NASCAR's first road-course event was staged over two miles of the airport's runways on June 13. The event was open to both American stock cars and foreign sports cars. Nearly half of the entries in the 43-car starting field were foreign cars. Keller won the race in the Jaguar, leading the final 28 laps of the 100-mile race. It remains the only win for a foreign-made automobile in the history of NASCAR's premier racing series.

1955

February 27 Tim Flock is declared the winner of the 160-mile Daytona Beach race when Fireball Roberts' Buick is disqualified on a technicality. Flock's win makes team owner Carl Kiekhaefer's maiden NASCAR voyage a success.

March 26 Fonty Flock wheels Frank Christian's Chevrolet to victory at Columbia, S.C. It is Chevrolet's first NASCAR Grand National win.

May 7 Wild youngster Junior Johnson drives an Oldsmobile to his first career NASCAR Grand National victory at Hickory Speedway in North Carolina.

July 31 Tim Flock scores his record 13th win of the season in the 250-mile NASCAR Grand National race at Bay Meadows Race Track in San Mateo, Calif. It is Flock's second win in less than 24 hours. Flock won at Syracuse, N.Y., the night before.

September 5 In his fourth start since returning from injuries suffered at Charlotte in May, Herb Thomas drives to victory in Darlington's Southern 500.

October 30 Tim Flock leads from start to finish to score his record 18th win of the season in the finale at Hillsboro, N.C. Flock's record-shattering 1955 performance includes 11 races in which he led from start to finish.

Tim Flock dominated the 1955 NASCAR Grand National season, winning 18 races in 38 starts along the way to his second championship in four years. Flock didn't take the points lead lead until the 33rd race of the season at LeHi, Ark., on Aug. 14.

Lee Petty led the points standings most of the season, but eventually succumbed to Flock and his powerful Kiekhaefer Chryslers. Petty's consistency kept him on top of the points standings, but he tapered off in the second half of the season. Petty won six races and finished third in the final standings.

Flock's record of 18 wins wasn't surpassed until 1967 when Richard Petty won 27 races.

1955 NASCAR Grand National Points Race

Rank	Driver	Points	Wins	Top 5	Top 10	Winnings
1	Tim Flock	9596	18	32	33	$37,779.60
2	Buck Baker	8088	3	24	34	$19,770.90
3	Lee Petty	7194	6	20	30	$18,919.29
4	Bob Welborn	5460	0	12	24	$10,146.76
5	Herb Thomas	5186	3	14	15	$18,023.47
6	Junior Johnson	4810	5	12	18	$13,802.78
7	Eddie Skinner	4652	0	4	15	$4736.85
8	Jim Paschal	4572	5	12	18	$10,585.88
9	Jimmie Lewallen	4526	0	4	15	$6439.51
10	Gwyn Staley	4360	3	12	20	$6546.43

Herb Thomas and Tim Flock lead the charge at the start of the May 1 NASCAR Grand National event on Charlotte Speedway's dirt track. The large letters on the side of each car were part of an experimental scoring method NASCAR used briefly in 1955. When 26 or fewer cars were in the starting grid, a typewriter was used to keep score as the cars completed each lap. An expert typist was seated in the scoring stand to assist scorers, documenting each lap while never having to take her eyes off the track. Buck Baker went on to win after starting 16th.

Lee Petty drove a Chrysler in the 1955 NASCAR Grand National season. The patriarch of the Petty kingdom won six races in 42 starts and led the points standings most of the season. He ended up third in championship points behind Tim Flock and Buck Baker.

▶ A flock of Flocks: (left to right) Fonty, Bob, and Tim pose with a pair of Kiekhaefer Chryslers. All three Flock brothers worked and drove for the Carl Kiekhaefer team in '55. Bob, who never did race a full schedule, only competed in one Grand National race, but acted as a crew member for his brothers in many races.

Junior Johnson's first full season of NASCAR Grand National racing was 1955. Having entered only five races in '53 and '54, Johnson hit the tour with a vengeance in '55, winning five races and finishing sixth in the points standings while driving an Oldsmobile. Had NASCAR named a Rookie of the Year, Johnson would have been the choice. A Rookie of the Year wasn't officially named until '57 when Ken Rush became the first recipient of the top freshman award.

1956

November 13, 1955 Tim Flock wins the 1956 season opener at Hickory Speedway as the new campaign starts early.

April 8 Tim Flock racks up his third win of the season at North Wilkesboro, N.C., then quits the championship Kiekhaefer Chrysler team. Buck Baker will replace Flock in the coveted ride.

June 3 Herb Thomas wins the 100-mile event at Merced, Calif., giving the Carl Kiekhaefer team its record 16th consecutive NASCAR Grand National victory. The record will likely live forever.

June 10 Ralph Moody wheels a DePaolo Engineering Ford to victory at West Memphis Speedway, halting the Kiekhaefer team's 16-race win streak.

August 4 Lee Petty dismounts his car in disgust on the 32nd lap, climbs the flagstand, grabs the red flag from the official starter, and waves the scheduled 100-mile NASCAR Grand National race at Tulsa, Okla., to a halt. Dusty conditions blinded the drivers and Petty acted to prevent a catastrophe.

August 12 Tim Flock wins the only NASCAR Grand National event ever held at Elkhart Lake, Wisconsin's Road America. The race is run despite rain.

October 23 Buck Baker tiptoes around a nasty crash involving former Kiekhaefer teammate Herb Thomas and wins the 100-mile race at Shelby, N.C. The crash is triggered by Speedy Thompson, also member of the Kiekhaefer team, and leaves Thomas gravely injured.

November 11 Speedy Thompson wins the 100-mile race at Hickory and Marvin Panch wins the same-day event at Lancaster, Calif. Thompson's win counts as a 1956 race, while Panch's triumph is the opener of the '57 NASCAR Grand National season.

November 18 Buck Baker is declared the winner of the 1956 season finale at Wilson, N.C. Joe Weatherly reaches the checkered flag first, but Baker is the first to pass the scoring stand. Baker also wraps up the '56 NASCAR Grand National championship.

Junior Johnson climbed out of the rear window of his overturned Pontiac after a crash in the late stages of the Feb. 26 Daytona Beach race. Johnson had spun out twice earlier in the race, but continued to charge into the north and south turns with reckless abandon. His courage finally caught up to him with a series of tumbles as he entered the north turn.

NASCAR's third road-course event was staged on the four-mile track in Elkhart Lake, Wis., on Aug. 12. Carl Kiekhaefer entered three cars in the 258.3-mile event. Frank Mundy qualified Buck Baker's Dodge on the pole in a three-lap qualifying session. After relinquishing the pole car to Baker, Mundy started 23rd and finished 14th in the #300 Chrysler. Baker finished 8th. Tim Flock won in a Mercury, beating the Kiekhaefer cars in his former boss's backyard. NASCAR Grand Nationals never returned to Road America.

▲ Russ Truelove's tumble midway through the Daytona Beach NASCAR Grand National was quite spectacular. Truelove's Mercury was one of the quickest cars, qualifying fifth. The beach conditions were awful. Truelove hit a soft patch in the sand and flipped almost a dozen times near the north end of the beach. Afterward, Truelove stepped out of the smoldering machine through the passenger door.

A horrendous crash took Herb Thomas out of the championship hunt late in the season, allowing Buck Baker to cruise to the 1956 NASCAR Grand National title. Thomas led the points race until the October event at Shelby, N.C., where he suffered critical injuries in a multicar crash.

Speedy Thompson, Baker's teammate on the Carl Kiekhaefer team, hooked Thomas' bumper, triggering the crash. Controversy flared. Kiekhaefer had leased the track and quickly scheduled a race to give Baker another opportunity to catch up in the points race. Thomas, who quit the Kiekhaefer team at midseason, had taken over the points lead a month earlier.

Baker won 14 races en route to his first NASCAR Grand National championship.

1956 NASCAR Grand National Points Race

Rank	Driver	Points	Wins	Top 5	Top 10	Winnings
1	Buck Baker	9272	14	31	39	$34,076.35
2	Speedy Thompson	8788	8	24	29	$27,168.62
3	Herb Thomas	8710	5	22	36	$19,351.19
4	Lee Petty	8324	2	17	28	$15,337.08
5	Jim Paschal	7878	1	16	27	$17,203.08
6	Billy Myers	6796	2	13	21	$15,829.08
7	Fireball Roberts	5794	5	17	22	$14,741.27
8	Ralph Moody	5528	4	13	21	$15,492.27
9	Tim Flock	5062	4	11	13	$15,768.19
10	Marvin Panch	4680	1	12	13	$11,519.40

1957

December 30, 1956 Fireball Roberts leads a 1-2-3-4 sweep for Peter DePaolo Fords in the 90-mile NASCAR Grand National race on the Titusville-Cocoa Airport runways in Florida.

February 17 Cotton Owens drives the Ray Nichels Pontiac to victory in the Daytona Beach event, recording the first NASCAR win for Pontiac.

June 6 The Automobile Manufacturers Association recommends unanimously that the auto industry divorce itself entirely from all forms of racing, including the NASCAR Grand National series. The factory-supported teams will be disbanded and all machinery will be given to the drivers.

July 4 Paul Goldsmith wins the 250-mile NASCAR Grand National race at Raleigh Speedway. Herb Thomas makes his first start of the season after injuries suffered in October 1956.

September 2 Speedy Thompson wins the Southern 500, averaging 100.094 mph. It is the first Southern 500 to average better than 100 mph.

October 6 Bob Welborn, with relief help from Possum Jones, wins the Sweepstakes 500 at Martinsville Speedway. Welborn's Chevy convertible outruns the 40-car field of sedans and convertibles. It is Welborn's first NASCAR Grand National win.

October 12 Only 900 spectators watch Fireball Roberts win the 100-mile race at Newberry Speedway in South Carolina. To this day, it remains the smallest trackside attendance in NASCAR history.

October 27 Buck Baker wraps up his second straight NASCAR Grand National championship campaign by winning the 250-lap season finale at Central Carolina Fairground in Greensboro, N.C.

November 27 The first spade of dirt is turned on the tract of land that will become the Daytona International Speedway. After nearly five years, the red tape has been cleared to proceed with the construction of the world's most modern racing facility.

Paul Goldsmith fishtails in his Smokey Yunick Chevrolet during the Feb. 17 Daytona Beach race. Goldsmith assumed command late in the race, but a blown engine with eight laps to go foiled his victory bid. Five of Goldsmith's nine career NASCAR Grand National wins came in cars groomed by the capable hands of Yunick. Cotton Owens won the race, giving Pontiac its first NASCAR Grand National victory.

Buck Baker, who drove for the #87 Chevrolet factory team when Carl Kiekhaefer disbanded his operation after the 1956 season, enjoyed a successful '57 campaign. Baker won 10 races, claimed the championship, and only finished out of the top 10 twice in 40 starts. Here, Baker leads #46 Speedy Thompson en route to a win in the March 24 race at Hillsboro's Orange Speedway.

Fireball Roberts salutes to the crowd as he receives the checkered flag in the inaugural Rebel 300 at Darlington Raceway on May 12. Roberts breezed to a two-lap victory over runner-up Tim Flock. The Convertible division was born in 1956 and Bob Welborn was the first champion, even though he posted three wins to Curtis Turner's 22. Welborn won the title again in '57.

Herb Thomas' twisted and deformed Pontiac lays still after a savage crash in the early laps of the Sept. 2 Southern 500 at Darlington. Fonty Flock, who drove the car, spun along the backstretch and stopped broadside at the entrance to the third turn. Paul Goldsmith and Bobby Myers plowed full bore into the idle car. Goldsmith and Flock suffered serious injuries. Myers was killed. Flock announced his retirement from a hospital bed soon thereafter.

Buck Baker assumed command of the 1957 points race in mid May and easily won his second straight NASCAR Grand National championship. Baker finished 760 points ahead of Marvin Panch, who led the points standings for the first 16 races.

Baker was consistently excellent throughout the season. He began the year with 26 consecutive top-10 finishes and finished the campaign with 38 top-10 efforts in 40 starts. The veteran from Charlotte, N.C., won 10 races.

Panch won six races in 42 starts in his first full season. He led the points standings until the May 19 race at Martinsville, when Baker took the points lead with a victory.

1957 NASCAR Grand National Points Race

Rank	Driver	Points	Wins	Top 5	Top 10	Winnings
1	Buck Baker	10,716	10	30	38	$30,763.40
2	Marvin Panch	9956	6	22	27	$24,306.60
3	Speedy Thompson	8560	2	16	22	$26,840.58
4	Lee Petty	8528	4	20	33	$18,325.28
5	Jack Smith	8464	4	17	25	$14,561.10
6	Fireball Roberts	8268	8	21	27	$19,828.04
7	Johnny Allen	7068	0	4	17	$9814.01
8	L.D. Austin	6532	0	1	13	$6484.68
9	Brownie King	5740	0	1	16	$5588.68
10	Jim Paschal	5124	0	9	17	$7078.68

1958

February 23 Paul Goldsmith drives Smokey Yunick's Pontiac to victory in the NASCAR Grand National race on Daytona's Beach-Road course. It is the final NASCAR race staged on the picturesque 4.1-mile course on the shore.

March 2 Four days after the race, Lee Petty is declared the winner of the 100-mile event at Concord Speedway. Scorecard data indicates that Petty finishes the 200 laps first, even though Curtis Turner starts on the pole and leads the entire distance.

May 30 Fireball Roberts wins the race at Trenton, N.J. It is the first 500-miler staged north of Darlington.

June 1 Riverside International Raceway in Southern California opens with three 500-mile races in one weekend. Eddie Gray captures the Crown America 500 for NASCAR Grand National cars.

July 18 Richard Petty makes his first career NASCAR Grand National start in the 100-lap race at Toronto's Canadian National Exposition Speedway. The 21-year-old finishes 17th out of 19 cars.

September 1 Fireball Roberts wins Darlington's Southern 500. Roberts has won four of his first seven starts.

October 26 Junior Johnson edges Fireball Roberts to win the NASCAR Grand National season finale at Atlanta's Lakewood Speedway. Lee Petty captures the championship.

▼ Eddie Pagan's Ford blasts through the steel guardrail after blowing a tire on the 137th lap of the Sept. 1 Southern 500. The car tumbled down the embankment outside the track, but Pagan miraculously escaped injury. NASCAR completed the race devoid of proper retaining barriers. Drivers were warned not to drive too close to the gaping hole in the wall. Fireball Roberts went on to win the race by five laps over Buck Baker.

Old pro Lee Petty was a dominant force in 1958 NASCAR Grand National competition, leading the points standings after all but the first race of the season.

The Oldsmobile-driving Petty won seven of his 50 starts and finished 644 points ahead of runner-up Buck Baker. Petty finished out of the top 10 in only six races and held a comfortable margin in the points race nearly the entire season.

Rex White won the season opener at Fayetteville, N.C., to claim the early points lead. Petty took the lead for keeps with a sixth-place finish at Daytona. White didn't make a concerted run at the title, though, competing in only 22 of the season's 51 races.

1958 NASCAR Grand National Points Race

Rank	Driver	Points	Wins	Top 5	Top 10	Winnings
1	Lee Petty	12,232	7	28	44	$26,565.00
2	Buck Baker	11,588	3	23	35	$25,840.20
3	Speedy Thompson	8792	4	18	23	$15,214.56
4	Shorty Rollins	8124	1	12	22	$13,398.08
5	Jack Smith	7666	2	15	21	$12,633.28
6	L.D. Austin	6972	0	0	10	$6245.96
7	Rex White	6552	2	13	17	$12,232.40
8	Junior Johnson	6380	6	12	16	$13,808.40
9	Eddie Pagan	4910	0	11	18	$7471.52
10	Jim Reed	4762	4	10	12	$9643.60

The Holman-Moody Ford team bolted a top on Curtis Turner's Ford convertible late Saturday Feb. 22 following that day's Daytona Beach Convertible race. Turner won the ragtop event, then drove the same car in Sunday's NASCAR Grand National race. NASCAR rules permitted the use of "zipper tops" for teams that wanted to use the same car in different divisions. Turner ran a close second to Paul Goldsmith in Sunday's premier division race.

◄ Johnny Bruner, Jr., waves the checkered flag for Paul Goldsmith at the finish of the Feb. 23 Daytona Beach NASCAR Grand National race. Driving a Smokey Yunick Pontiac, Goldsmith won the final event on the storied beach course. A week later, Goldsmith quit NASCAR and joined the rival USAC tour so he could compete in the Indianapolis 500. Goldsmith ran in five Indy 500s from '58 to '63, twice finishing in the top five. He later returned to NASCAR.

▼ Fireball Roberts and pole-sitter Glen Wood sit on the front row at the start of the Oct. 12 Martinsville Speedway Sweepstakes race. Both NASCAR Grand Nationals and Convertibles were eligible; 21 hardtops and 19 Convertibles participated. Roberts won the race, which was curtailed to 350 of the scheduled 500 laps due to darkness.

1959

February 22 Johnny Beauchamp is flagged the winner of the first Daytona 500 in a photo finish with Lee Petty. Bill France announces the results are unofficial and solicits photos so a decisive winner can be determined.

February 25 Lee Petty is officially declared the winner of the Daytona 500-mile race 61 hours after the checkered flag fell.

May 2 Junior Johnson rolls his Ford in practice, but drives the hastily repaired car to victory in the NASCAR Grand National race at Hickory Speedway.

June 14 Richard Petty finishes first at Atlanta's Lakewood Speedway, but the win is protested by second-place finisher Lee Petty. After NASCAR officials study the scorecards, Lee is declared the winner with Richard second.

July 29 Groundbreaking ceremonies for the new Charlotte Motor Speedway are held. The new speedway will be built by Curtis Turner and Bruton Smith, and the first race is scheduled for May 1960.

August 1 Ned Jarrett records his first NASCAR Grand National win at Myrtle Beach, S.C. Jarrett had purchased the car only a couple days earlier with a postdated check that wouldn't clear the bank until the Monday after the race.

September 7 Jim Reed wins the 10th annual Southern 500 at Darlington, giving Goodyear Tire & Rubber Co. its first NASCAR win on a superspeedway.

October 25 Jack Smith wins the season finale at Concord, N.C. Rather than the winner's check for $1500, Smith elects to take home a new '60 Ford offered by promoter Bruton Smith. Lee Petty wraps up his third championship.

Lee Petty became the first three-time winner of the NASCAR Grand National championship by dominating the 1959 season. Petty's victory in the inaugural Daytona 500 pushed him atop the standings, a perch he never relinquished.

The 45-year-old Petty won 11 of his 42 starts to finish 1830 points ahead of runner-up Cotton Owens. Bob Welborn won the season's first two races and led the early standings, but the veteran from Greensboro, N.C., concentrated his efforts more heavily on NASCAR's Convertible circuit.

Petty established an all-time NASCAR record by leading the points standings after 92 of the 95 races in 1958 and '59.

1959 NASCAR Grand National Points Race

Rank	Driver	Points	Wins	Top 5	Top 10	Winnings
1	Lee Petty	11,792	11	27	35	$49,219.15
2	Cotton Owens	9962	1	13	22	$14,639.35
3	Speedy Thompson	7684	0	5	9	$6815.63
4	Herman Beam	7396	0	1	12	$6379.48
5	Buck Baker	7170	1	14	19	$11,060.04
6	Tom Pistone	7050	2	12	18	$12,724.43
7	L.D. Austin	6519	0	0	13	$4670.35
8	Jack Smith	6150	4	9	12	$13,289.38
9	Jim Reed	5744	3	7	9	$23,533.58
10	Rex White	5526	5	11	13	$12,359.85

In perhaps the bravest display of the 1959 Speedweeks festivities, Johnny Bruner, Sr., threw the flag for the start of the inaugural Daytona 500 from the apron of the track. Bob Welborn and Shorty Rollins were on the front row. Thirty-nine NASCAR Grand Nationals and 20 Convertibles started the inaugural 500-mile grind on Feb. 22. A packed house of 41,921 spectators jammed the grandstands and infield to watch the historic event.

◄ The cars of #48 Joe Weatherly, #42 Lee Petty, and #73 Tom Beauchamp approach the finish line at Daytona in a three-abreast cluster. Weatherly was two laps behind and would finish fifth. Petty took the lead with four laps to go, but Beauchamp caught a good draft in the final turn and pulled alongside Petty at the stripe.

◄ Richard Petty, shown here in a sleeveless driver's "uniform" that was routine apparel in the late 1950s, was the third recipient of the Rookie of the Year award in 1959. Petty started 21 races and recorded nine top-10 finishes while driving Oldsmobiles and Plymouths from the Petty Enterprises shops. In addition to NASCAR Grand National races, Petty competed in a dozen NASCAR Convertible events, winning once and finishing fourth in the points standings.

► A tired Bill France, along with Ed Otto and Dick Dolan, study miles of film footage of the Daytona 500 finish. As more photos and film came into NASCAR headquarters, more and more evidence built up to support Lee Petty as the winner. On Wednesday, Feb. 25, film arrived from the *Hearst Metrotone News of the Week*. The footage removed all doubt and Petty was declared the winner, 61 hours after the inaugural Daytona 500 had ended.

Chapter Three:
Superspeedways & Speedy Muscle Cars

In June 1957, factory representation in NASCAR stock car racing came to an abrupt halt with the resolution adopted by the American Manufacturers Association. Under intense congressional pressure, the automotive industry unanimously adopted a "hands off" policy when it came to stock car racing. The gravy train from Detroit to the NASCAR teams was officially derailed, though backroom deals were still conducted.

When the Daytona International Speedway opened in 1959, the NASCAR stock car races became major sporting events that drew the attention of the national media. The sport was in a measurable transition as more and more superspeedways were in the planning stages and trackside attendance was increasing.

The automobile industry began to realize that the 1957 AMA resolution was hindering its efforts in promotions, sales, and performance. By 1961, ABC's *Wide World of Sports* began to televise a number of the major NASCAR superspeedway races using a tape-delayed format. New Pontiacs, Chevrolets, Fords, and Plymouths were performing on a speedy stage in the living rooms of a car-buying public.

In June 1962, Ford Motor Co. president Henry Ford II announced that Ford was stepping out of the 1957 AMA agreement and would actively—and publicly—become involved in NASCAR racing. "We feel that the resolution has come to have neither purpose nor effect," said Ford. "Accordingly, we have notified the AMA that we feel we can better establish our own standards of conduct with respect to the manner in which the performance of our vehicles is to be promoted and advertised."

Under its "Total Performance" moniker, Ford began racking up major wins on NASCAR's Grand National tour. Their winning ways included a 1-2-3-4-5 sweep in the celebrated 1963 Daytona 500. As Fords took top honors on the speedways, its showroom sales flourished.

As the curtain lifted on the 1964 season, Chrysler was ready to give Ford a run for the money. The Plymouth and Dodge cars were more streamlined aerodynamically and they were packed with a bundle of horsepower. Chrysler bolted hemispherical heads to its 426-cid engine to come up with the 426 Hemi. The Chrysler contingent swept all the '64 Daytona Speedweeks events and young star Richard Petty bagged the championship in a Hemi-powered Plymouth Belvedere.

But with the increased speeds came danger. The unlimited horsepower race exacted a heavy toll. Three drivers, including two-time NASCAR champion Joe Weatherly and popular icon

Fireball Roberts, lost their lives in racing accidents. To address the situation, NASCAR developed a new set of rules for the 1965 season. The limited-edition engines and some of the smaller cars were banned.

Reigning NASCAR champion Richard Petty said the effect of the 1965 rules "amounts to us going back to 1963 running against 1965 equipment." Dodge team owner Cotton Owens declared the '65 rules "have put the Chrysler teams out of business." Having only big luxury cars like the Plymouth Fury to race, with old outdated engines to power them, Chrysler packed up and pulled out of NASCAR. Richard Petty would not defend his championship, and other top-ranking Chrysler drivers were on the sidelines.

The 1965 NASCAR Grand National season turned out to be a high-speed Ford parade. Fords scooped up all the marbles, winning a record 32 straight NASCAR Grand National races, a mark that still stands today. Ticket sales were lagging with the Ford domination and promoters were taking it on the chin. The dissent within the NASCAR ranks was greater than at any time in history. No one was happy, not even the Ford drivers, who felt their lofty records were tainted by the lack of competition.

After the 1965 season, NASCAR was licking its wounds. The Chrysler boycott had produced a box-office disaster. When the new '66 guidelines were announced, NASCAR approved the Chrysler Hemi engine since it had become a high-volume production item.

Back in the fold for 1966, Chrysler reeled off victories at Daytona, Rockingham, and Atlanta to begin the season. Ford began a boycott of its own in '66 after NASCAR failed to approve a limited-production overhead-cam engine. While not as devastating as the Chrysler boycott of '64, the Ford walk-out also created sluggish ticket sales.

By 1967, the Ford and Chrysler factories were back in NASCAR in full force as GM remained on the sidelines. Ford had refined its tunnelport 427-cid engine and had bolted it into a fleet of smaller Ford Fairlanes, but it was Richard Petty who rewrote the record books in his Hemi-powered Plymouth. During the second half of the '67 campaign, Petty strung together a 10-race winning streak. From Aug. 12 through Oct. 1, Petty was undefeated. He won 27 races out of 46 starts, grabbed his second NASCAR Grand National championship and earned the nickname "The King." Meanwhile, Chrysler won 36 races, while Ford managed only 10 victories.

Having taken its lumps in 1967, Ford went to work to come up with an answer to the Petty/Plymouth stampede. The answer was a sleek, slope-backed body for the '68 Ford Torino and Mercury Cyclone models. Chrysler, on the other hand, had only done peripheral aerodynamic refinements. The '68 season would pit the sleek Fords against the brute horsepower of Chrysler's Hemi.

The Ford teams and Cale Yarborough's lone Mercury were the top dogs on the superspeedways in 1968, winning nine of the 12 major races on big tracks. David Pearson captured the championship on the strength of 16 victories driving Fords.

With full factory representation in place for two years, NASCAR Grand National racing was enjoying an explosion of popularity. And a gaggle of new superspeedways were being built in areas outside NASCAR's traditional domain. A two-mile oval had opened in Michigan, and construction had already begun on new tracks in Dover, Del.; College Station, Texas; and Talladega, Ala. All would host NASCAR events in 1969.

Ford enhanced its aerodynamic package with a new 1969 Torino Talladega, which featured a sloped and narrowed nose. Mercury had the Cyclone Spoiler in its arsenal. And with a new 429-cid "Blue Crescent" engine with semihemispherical combustion, the future looked rosy for the Blue Oval. Richard Petty, winner of 92 races in Plymouths since 1960, parked his Plymouth and agreed to drive Fords in '69. "Ford has a vast storehouse of racing knowledge, much more than Chrysler has," said Petty.

Petty scored a victory in his first start for Ford in the 1969 Riverside 500 road-course event, and LeeRoy Yarbrough followed up with a big win for Ford in the Daytona 500. On the superspeedways, Ford and Mercury were virtually unbeatable. On the big tracks hosting races of 300 miles or more, Ford tied together a 13-race winning streak, and ran first and second in eight of the 13 events.

NASCAR refrained from changing the rules to maintain a level playing field in the 1960s. The rules were established before the season and, with rare exceptions, remained unchanged no matter what car make was winning. Chrysler went back to the drawing board in hopes of competing with Ford.

The creation was a needle-nose, high-winged Dodge Charger Daytona, an aerodynamic wonder. The Dodge Daytona made its first NASCAR appearance at the inaugural Talladega 500 on Sept. 14, 1969. Bill France was the mastermind behind the Talladega project, an ultrafast speedway that would be the fastest closed course on the planet. Early tests indicated the 200-mph barrier was within reach.

As the new Alabama International Motor Speedway was nearing completion, a disturbing undercurrent of dissent grew within the driver ranks. NASCAR Grand National racing was in the midst of a popularity explosion with grand new facilities popping up all over the country. The well-financed teams and the independent privateers found expenses rising sharply, yet the posted awards at most tracks showed only a minor increase.

In August 1969, the drivers held a secret meeting in Ann Arbor, Mich., to discuss a number of concerns. The topics of the discussion included facilities for drivers at the speedways, the perceived lack of prize money, and the alarming speeds at the new Talladega track. The 11 drivers who were present at the Ann Arbor meeting formed the Professional Drivers Association. Richard Petty was elected president of the new union.

When teams arrived at Talladega and began their initial practice runs, drivers quickly discovered that tires were shredding at speeds over 190 mph. Members of the PDA approached Bill France and asked him to postpone the 500-miler until suitable tires could be produced. France refused, telling the drivers to slow down and run at a more comfortable pace. He even hopped into a 1969 Ford and ran about 175 mph to prove the cars were safe. New tire compounds were tested daily, but concerns escalated. With no solution in sight, most of the drivers loaded up their cars and went home the day before the race. It was the first official driver boycott in NASCAR history.

Sophomore driver Richard Brickhouse was offered a ride in one of the winged Dodge Daytonas owned by Ray Nichels. Brickhouse and a dozen other Grand National drivers competed against 23 drivers from the NASCAR Grand Touring ponycar division. Several mandated caution flags kept the remaining drivers in check. The sandy-haired Brickhouse scampered into the lead 11 laps from the finish and won the controversial Talladega 500, an event that was run without a crash or a spin out. Dodge's first superspeedway win of the season was cloaked in controversy.

In the final months of the 1969 campaign, the PDA drivers returned to the speedway, albeit with considerable tension. Ford drivers Donnie Allison and LeeRoy Yarbrough won at Charlotte and Rockingham as Bobby Isaac won the season finale at the new Texas track in his winged Dodge Daytona.

The decade of the 1960s was the most progressive in NASCAR history. The automobiles had advanced from stock productions to specialized mechanical creations capable of running 200 mph. Crowds had increased and new speedways were built. The entire sport was on a roll, but there were rumblings beneath the surface. Tension was high and despite an encouraging outlook in general, NASCAR stock car racing was at a crossroads.

1960

January 31 CBS television sends a production crew to Daytona International Speedway to televise the pole position and compact car races during the opening of Speedweeks. Bud Palmer is the anchorman for the first live telecast of NASCAR competition.

February 12 Herman Beam becomes the first driver to be black-flagged in a NASCAR event at Daytona. Race officials notice that Beam forgot to put on his helmet before the Twin 100-mile qualifying race. NASCAR officials park Beam for the remainder of the race.

February 28 Richard Petty scores the first win of his career in the 100-mile NASCAR Grand National event at the Charlotte Fairgrounds Speedway.

March 27 Lee Petty wins the 100-mile race at North Wilkesboro Speedway. It is Petty's 49th career NASCAR Grand National win, making him the top race winner in NASCAR history. Petty surpasses 48-time-winner Herb Thomas.

June 19 Unheralded Joe Lee Johnson gallops to a four-lap victory in the inaugural World 600 at the new Charlotte Motor Speedway.

July 4 Jack Smith wins the second annual Firecracker 250 at Daytona. Smith becomes the first driver to win on a superspeedway using radio communication with his pit crew.

October 30 Bobby Johns drives Cotton Owens' Pontiac to his first career NASCAR Grand National victory in the inaugural Atlanta 500 at Atlanta International Raceway. Rex White finishes fifth and is officially declared the 1960 NASCAR Grand National champion.

Don O'Dell's Pontiac skids after hitting Lenny Page's Thunderbird in the Oct. 16 National 400 at Charlotte Motor Speedway. Page was badly injured in the crash. Chris Economaki, a journalist covering the race for *National Speed Sport News*, saved Page's life. Economaki administered emergency aid to Page until the ambulance arrived.

Rex White took the points lead in June and sped to his first NASCAR Grand National championship.

White grabbed first place in the standings following a sixth-place finish in the inaugural World 600 at the new Charlotte Motor Speedway on June 19. He won six races in 40 starts.

Runner-up Richard Petty suffered a major setback in the points race when he was disqualified at Charlotte for making an improper entrance to pit road. Petty had finished fourth in the 600-miler, worth 3520 points, but when NASCAR disqualified him, he lost all of the points he earned that day. Petty won three times during the season, including his first career win.

The points lead changed hands seven times among five drivers during the season. Junior Johnson, Jack Smith, and Bobby Johns also led the standings.

1960 NASCAR Grand National Points Race

Rank	Driver	Points	Wins	Top 5	Top 10	Winnings
1	Rex White	21,164	6	25	35	$57,524.85
2	Richard Petty	17,228	3	16	30	$41,872.95
3	Bobby Johns	14,964	1	8	9	$46,114.92
4	Buck Baker	14,674	2	15	24	$38,398.31
5	Ned Jarrett	14,660	5	20	26	$25,437.38
6	Lee Petty	14,510	5	21	30	$31,282.19
7	Junior Johnson	9932	3	14	18	$38,989.16
8	Emanuel Zervakis	9720	0	2	10	$12,123.97
9	Jim Paschal	8968	0	3	7	$15,095.94
10	Banjo Matthews	8458	0	0	4	$15,616.99

A crowd of 7489 witnesses history from the covered grandstands at Charlotte's Fairgrounds Speedway on Feb. 28. Lined up on the inside of the fourth row is young Richard Petty in the white #43 Plymouth. In his 35th start, Petty, with an assist from his father Lee, scored his first of 200 NASCAR Grand National wins. The elder Petty popped Rex White out of the way in the closing stages, allowing Richard to make the decisive pass.

◄ Lee Petty and Bobby Johns, wheeling a pair of Petty Plymouths, cut through the fourth turn during the inaugural World 600 at Charlotte Motor Speedway. The June 19 race was a survival of the fittest, as the new track, paving for which had been completed during qualifying, broke up badly. The Petty Plymouths finished third, fourth, and fifth, but third- and fourth-place finishers Richard and Lee Petty were disqualified for improper pit entrances. They were sent to the rear of the field, losing all money and championship points earned that day.

► Number 12 Joe Weatherly leads #4 Rex White into Martinsville Speedway's first turn during the Sept. 25 Old Dominion 500. Weatherly led most of the way, but White took the lead with nine laps to go. White went on to claim the NASCAR Grand National championship. His ascent to NASCAR's pinnacle was meteoric, rising from a lightly regarded independent to a top-ranked pilot in less than two years.

1961

February 24 Fireball Roberts and Joe Weatherly share victory lane in Daytona's crash-marred Twin 100-mile qualifying races. Lee Petty is badly injured when he sails over the guardrail in the second event.

April 9 Former USAC champion Fred Lorenzen racks up his first NASCAR win in the rain-shortened Virginia 500 at Martinsville Speedway.

May 28 Sophomore David Pearson scores his first career win in the second annual World 600 at Charlotte Motor Speedway.

July 4 David Pearson wins Daytona's Firecracker 250. The event is taped by ABC's *Wide World of Sports* and televised a few days later.

August 8 Curtis Turner announces that "most of the NASCAR drivers" have joined the Teamsters Union and the Federation of Professional Athletes. NASCAR president Bill France says, "No known union member can compete in a NASCAR race, and I'll use a pistol to enforce it."

August 11 Fireball Roberts withdraws from the Teamsters Union. NASCAR reinstates Roberts upon his resignation. Rex White and Ned Jarrett also submit resignations and are permitted to resume racing.

August 13 Junior Johnson wins the shortened Western North Carolina 500 at Asheville-Weaverville Speedway. The race is halted after 258 laps due to a deteriorating track. About 4000 angry spectators hold the drivers and team owners hostage in the infield for nearly four hours.

August 15 NASCAR president Bill France bans Curtis Turner and Tim Flock "for life" from all NASCAR racing. Turner and Flock are the only two drivers who refuse to abandon the Teamsters Union project.

October 29 Joe Weatherly dominates the season finale at Orange Speedway in Hillsboro, N.C., for his ninth win of the season. Ned Jarrett, winner of only one race during the season, is declared the NASCAR Grand National champion.

◀ Lee Petty and Johnny Beauchamp, principles in the photo finish ending of the inaugural Daytona 500 in 1959, were involved in a horrible last-lap crash in the second Twin 100-miler on Feb. 24, 1961. Beauchamp's #73 Chevy snagged the rear bumper of Petty's #42 Plymouth and both cars soared out of the speedway. Petty suffered multiple life-threatening injuries, while Beauchamp sustained less-serious head injuries.

NASCAR vs. The Teamsters Union

The most critical battle ever to confront NASCAR occurred in 1961. A snowballing episode with the mighty Teamsters Union threatened to shake the foundation of how NASCAR did business.

Top-ranked driver Curtis Turner and track promoter Bruton Smith built the Charlotte Motor Speedway, which opened in June 1960. Building costs exceeded estimates, and the speedway was gripped in financial hardship from the moment it opened. In a last-ditch effort to save the track, Turner approached the Teamsters Union in the summer of 1961 for a loan of more than $800,000. In return for the loan, Turner was asked to organize NASCAR-licensed drivers into a Teamsters-affiliated union called the Federation of Professional Athletes.

On Aug. 8, Turner announced that a majority of Grand National drivers had joined the FPA. NASCAR president Bill France responded with an ultimatum: "No known Teamster member can compete in a NASCAR race. And I'll use a pistol to enforce it."

The first domino tumbled in France's favor on Aug. 11 when popular driver Fireball Roberts resigned from the FPA. Soon, virtually every other driver followed suit. Only Turner and Tim Flock sided with the Teamsters, and France promptly banned both drivers from NASCAR "for life." Turner was eventually reinstated in 1965, having lost four years of racing privileges in NASCAR.

The Teamsters' efforts to gain inroads into NASCAR never materialized, and Bill France prevailed in the greatest battle that NASCAR has ever faced.

Ned Jarrett races with teammate Johnny Allen in the Daytona 500. Jarrett and Allen, along with "Tiger" Tom Pistone, were all members of the Chevrolet factory team under the guise of Bee Gee Holloway's "independent" operation. Holloway had catchy nicknames for his three race teams. Jarrett was in the Dash-Dash-Dash Corp. Chevrolet, Allen drove the Win-Win-Win Corp. Chevy, and Pistone piloted the Go-Go-Go Corp. car. Jarrett finished seventh in the Daytona 500 and Allen finished eighth. Pistone placed 10th.

About 4000 fans gather at Asheville-Weaverville Speedway after the Aug. 13 Western North Carolina 500. The scheduled 500-lapper was halted after 258 laps due to a disintegrating track surface. Junior Johnson was declared the winner. Nearly half the fans refused to leave, and a handful began rioting. All teams were held hostage in the infield. Pop Eargle, a giant of a man and Bud Moore crew member, hit one of the mob leaders over the head with a 2×4. A few minutes later, the teams were permitted to leave and a full-scale riot was averted.

Ned Jarrett won only one race during the 1961 season, a 100-miler at Birmingham in June, but it was good enough to walk away with the NASCAR Grand National championship.

Jarrett and 1960 champion Rex White engaged in a tight duel throughout the summer for top honors. Jarrett took the points lead after the 34th race of the 52-race season at Columbia, S.C., and led the rest of the way.

White won seven races and logged 38 top-10 finishes in 47 starts, while Jarrett had 34 top-10 finishes in 46 starts. The points lead changed hands seven times among five drivers during the season.

1961 NASCAR Grand National Points Race

Rank	Driver	Points	Wins	Top 5	Top 10	Winnings
1	Ned Jarrett	27,272	1	23	34	$41,055.90
2	Rex White	26,442	7	29	38	$56,394.60
3	Emanuel Zervakis	22,312	2	19	28	$27,280.65
4	Joe Weatherly	17,894	9	14	18	$47,078.36
5	Fireball Roberts	17,600	2	13	14	$50,266.09
6	Junior Johnson	17,178	7	16	22	$28,540.44
7	Jack Smith	15,186	2	10	14	$21,409.81
8	Richard Petty	14,984	2	18	23	$25,238.52
9	Jim Paschal	13,922	2	12	16	$18,099.91
10	Buck Baker	13,746	1	11	15	$13,696.91

1962

February 18 Fireball Roberts caps off a perfect Speedweeks in which he won the American Challenge invitational event, the pole position for the Daytona 500, the Twin 100-mile qualifier, and the Daytona 500.

June 11 Ford Motor Co. announces that it will actively support selected NASCAR Grand National racing teams, breaking from the 1957 resolution established by the American Manufacturers Association.

July 4 Fireball Roberts continues his mastery of Daytona International Speedway by winning the Firecracker 250. Track officials announce the July 1963 race will be lengthened to 400 miles.

July 20 Joe Weatherly captures the 100-mile Grand National at Savannah Speedway. African American driver Wendell Scott earns his first career pole position and finishes eighth.

August 21 Richard Petty wins the 100-mile race at Hub City Speedway in Spartanburg, S.C. It is the sixth consecutive victory for the Petty Enterprises team. Teammate Jim Paschal won two of the races, while Richard Petty bagged the other four.

September 16 Fred Lorenzen drives a Ford owned by 19-year-old Mamie Reynolds to victory in the 100-mile race at Augusta Speedway in Georgia. Reynolds is the daughter of U.S. Senator Robert R. Reynolds, and is the first female car owner to win a race.

October 28 Rex White posts his first superspeedway win in Atlanta's Dixie 400. Joe Weatherly wraps up his first NASCAR Grand National championship.

Joe Weatherly, in his second year driving Bud Moore's Pontiacs, won the 1962 NASCAR Grand National championship. Weatherly won nine races and posted 31 top-three finishes in 52 starts in his impressive drive to the title.

Weatherly took the points lead following a runner-up finish in Charlotte's World 600 on May 27. The Norfolk, Va., veteran only finished out of the top 10 in seven of his 52 starts.

The points lead swapped hands five times among three different drivers. Weatherly held the lead most of the way, relinquishing it briefly to Jack Smith for two races in May.

Richard Petty won eight races, including three in a row, to claim second in the points race.

1962 NASCAR Grand National Points Race

Rank	Driver	Points	Wins	Top 5	Top 10	Winnings
1	Joe Weatherly	30,836	9	39	45	$70,742.10
2	Richard Petty	28,440	8	31	38	$60,763.30
3	Ned Jarrett	25,336	6	19	35	$43,443.12
4	Jack Smith	22,870	5	28	36	$34,747.74
5	Rex White	19,424	8	18	23	$36,245.36
6	Jim Paschal	18,128	4	17	24	$27,347.88
7	Fred Lorenzen	17,554	2	11	23	$46,100.00
8	Fireball Roberts	16,380	3	9	23	$66,151.22
9	Marvin Panch	15,138	0	5	8	$26,745.84
10	David Pearson	14,404	0	1	7	$19,031.44

The father and son team of Lee and Richard Petty pose beside their 1962 Plymouths during Daytona's Speedweeks. Lee had recovered from his nasty spill a year earlier, but decided against competing in the '62 Daytona events. Bunkie Blackburn drove the #42 Plymouth in the Twin 100-miler and the Daytona 500. Richard finished a surprising second in the 500, while Blackburn brought Lee's car home 13th.

Glen "Fireball" Roberts swept all of Daytona's Speedweeks offerings in 1962, winning the Race of Champions, the Pole Position race, the 100-mile qualifier, and the Daytona 500. Roberts had led in '59, '60, and '61, but never finished due to mechanical problems. Team owner Smokey Yunick parked the winning Pontiac after the 500, and Roberts joined the Banjo Matthews Pontiac team for the rest of the season.

◄ Joe Weatherly and Ned Jarrett contended for the title in 1962. Both were on the factory payroll, though GM denied any support of NASCAR. Weatherly's car had Gillman Pontiac on the quarter panels, a Pontiac dealership in Houston. Jarrett's car was "sponsored" by Jim Rathmann Chevrolet in Melbourne, Fla., which was one of the hot spots for the delivery of newly designed racing parts from Chevrolet.

► Ralph Moody (left) and Fred Lorenzen were at center stage when Ford Motor Co. announced it would actively support Moody's NASCAR Grand National racing team. The automotive manufac-

turers officially had been out of racing since the summer of 1957, but NASCAR stock car racing was just too fertile a ground to resist. Ford's announcement of public support kicked off the most progressive period of race car development in NASCAR Grand National history.

1963

February 22 Johnny Rutherford wins the second Twin 100-mile qualifying race at Daytona, becoming only the sixth driver to win in his first career NASCAR Grand National start.

February 24 Tiny Lund, filling in for the injured Marvin Panch, drives the Wood Brothers Ford to victory in the Daytona 500. Fords take the top five spots.

May 11 Joe Weatherly prevails in a two-part running of the Rebel 300 at Darlington. Weatherly wins the opening 150-miler and Richard Petty takes the second half. A complicated points system determines the winner.

July 13 Glen Wood wins the 200-lap race at Bowman Gray Stadium in Winston-Salem, N.C. Lee Petty finishes fourth in his first start start since a bad accident at Daytona in 1961.

July 21 Richard Petty posts his first career road-course victory in the 100-mile race at Bridgehampton Race Circuit on Long Island.

August 16 Junior Johnson wins the International 200 at Bowman Gray Stadium. The race is open to foreign cars, but only one makes the field—an MG that Smokey Cook drives to a 17th-place finish.

September 2 Fireball Roberts wins the only caution-free Southern 500 in history. Fred Lorenzen tops the $100,000 mark for season earnings, making him the first driver to reach six digits.

November 3 Darel Dieringer posts his first career victory in the season finale at Riverside, Calif. Joe Weatherly wraps up the NASCAR Grand National championship.

Joe Weatherly authored the most unlikely championship run in NASCAR history in 1963, driving for nine different team owners. Weatherly's primary team, owned by Bud Moore, only entered selected major events, leaving Weatherly without a ride for most of the short-track races. Weatherly showed up at each track and borrowed a car in an effort to accumulate points.

Weatherly won three races. Richard Petty took second in the points race with 14 wins. Weatherly claimed the lead for keeps after a fourth-place finish in the June 2 World 600 at Charlotte.

Under NASCAR's points system, more points were available in high-dollar events. Weatherly averaged an eighth-place finish in the 10 races on large tracks while Petty averaged 17th place.

Fred Lorenzen, the first driver to win over $100,000 in a single season, finished third despite missing 26 of the 55 races.

1963 NASCAR Grand National Points Race

Rank	Driver	Points	Wins	Top 5	Top 10	Winnings
1	Joe Weatherly	33,398	3	20	35	$74,623.76
2	Richard Petty	31,170	14	30	34	$55,964.00
3	Fred Lorenzen	29,684	6	21	23	$122,587.28
4	Ned Jarrett	27,214	8	32	39	$45,843.29
5	Fireball Roberts	22,642	4	11	14	$73,059.30
6	Jimmy Pardue	22,228	1	7	20	$20,358.34
7	Darel Dieringer	21,418	1	7	15	$29,724.50
8	David Pearson	21,156	0	13	19	$24,985.66
9	Rex White	20,976	0	5	14	$27,240.76
10	Tiny Lund	19,624	1	5	12	$49,396.36

Although Marvin Panch suggested Tiny Lund take his place in the Feb. 24 Daytona 500, team owner Glen Wood also considered Johnny Allen. Lund had never won in NASCAR competition, while Allen was a highly capable driver with one victory to his credit. Wood decided to go with Lund after discussing it with his brothers. They figured Lund would be the driver others would fear most. Wood's hunch paid off, as Lund won in an upset. Lund ran the whole race on one set of tires and made one less pit stop than his rivals. It was his first win in nine years on the circuit.

◄ Hollywood starlet Jayne Mansfield attended the Hillsboro NASCAR Grand National race on March 10 and presented the winner's trophy to Junior Johnson after the race. Johnson was almost speechless in the victory lane ceremonies, though he did flash a big smile.

▼ Johnny Allen survived this spectacular tumble outside Atlanta International Raceway in the June 30 Dixie 400. A tire blew on Allen's Ford, sending him over the guardrail. The engine was ripped from the chassis and landed more than 100 feet from the car. Miraculously, Allen suffered only a cut on his nose.

Number 8 Joe Weatherly leads Paul Goldsmith in the March 17 Atlanta 500. Weatherly began the year with the General Motors team, but car owner Bud Moore switched to Mercury midseason when the factory-blessed bag of GM goodies stopped coming from the Detroit headquarters. Weatherly drove for Moore in the major races, and hitchhiked his way in pick-up rides at the short tracks. Weatherly's title run in 1963 remains the most unlikely in NASCAR history.

1964

January 19 Dan Gurney wins the Riverside (Calif.) 500. Joe Weatherly loses his life when he crashes into a concrete wall in the late stages.

February 23 Driving a potent Plymouth with the new Hemi engine, Richard Petty wins the Daytona 500. Plymouths run 1-2-3 at the finish. The triumph is Petty's first on a superspeedway.

May 9 Fred Lorenzen wins his fifth consecutive NASCAR Grand National start in Darlington Raceway's Rebel 300. Fords finish 1-2-3-4.

May 24 Jim Paschal wins Charlotte's World 600. NASCAR great Fireball Roberts is near death after a fiery pileup on the eighth lap.

July 2 Fireball Roberts succumbs to burns suffered at Charlotte.

July 19 Billy Wade wins the 150-miler at Watkins Glen. The victory makes Wade the first driver to win four consecutive NASCAR Grand National races.

July 26 Fred Lorenzen takes advantage of Richard Petty's engine failure to win the Volunteer 500 at Bristol International Speedway. Petty's car creeps to a halt on the final lap.

September 20 Jimmy Pardue, fourth in the points race, dies in a tire-test crash at Charlotte Motor Speedway.

November 8 Ned Jarrett wins his 15th race of the year in the season finale at Jacksonville, N.C. Richard Petty wraps up his first NASCAR Grand National championship. The Jacksonville event ends the 62-race campaign, the most races ever staged in a NASCAR season.

Richard Petty posted nine wins, including his first superspeedway victory in the Daytona 500, and ran away with the 1964 NASCAR Grand National championship. Petty finished 5302 points ahead of runner-up Ned Jarrett, who won 15 races.

Petty took the points lead after the 25th race of the season with a runner-up finish in the World 600 at Charlotte. He continued to pad his lead during the balance of the 62-race season.

The points lead changed hands six times among four drivers in '64. Marvin Panch led from late February through late May, but fell to 10th in the final tally.

David Pearson made his first concentrated effort for the championship and finished third with eight wins.

1964 NASCAR Grand National Points Race

Rank	Driver	Points	Wins	Top 5	Top 10	Winnings
1	Richard Petty	40,252	9	37	43	$114,771.45
2	Ned Jarrett	34,950	15	40	45	$71,924.05
3	David Pearson	32,146	8	29	42	$45,541.65
4	Billy Wade	28,474	4	12	25	$36,094.58
5	Jimmy Pardue	26,570	0	14	24	$41,597.18
6	Curtis Crider	25,606	0	7	30	$22,170.46
7	Jim Paschal	25,450	1	10	15	$60,115.68
8	Larry Thomas	22,950	0	9	27	$21,225.64
9	Buck Baker	22,366	2	15	18	$43,780.88
10	Marvin Panch	21,480	3	18	21	$34,835.88

Fireball Roberts drives his Ford on the Augusta International Speedway road course during the Nov. 17, 1963, NASCAR Grand National event. The scheduled 500-miler was shortened to 417 miles because speeds on the three-mile track were far below expected. Still, the race took nearly five hours to complete. Roberts scored his 33rd and final NASCAR Grand National victory. He lost his life in a crash at Charlotte six months later. In an eerie twist of fate, six of the top seven finishers in the Augusta event would die within 14 months, including reigning champion Joe Weatherly, who died two months later in a crash at Riverside.

Number 25 Paul Goldsmith, #43 Richard Petty, and #26 Bobby Isaac battle for the lead in the early laps of the Feb. 23 Daytona 500. Goldsmith won the pole with a record speed of 174.910 mph. Petty qualified nearly 20 mph faster than he did in 1963 when his Plymouth was equipped with a conventional Chrysler engine. Petty drove his Hemi-powered Plymouth to a lopsided victory in the 500, leading 184 of the 200 laps. Goldsmith finished third, while Isaac fell out late and was credited with a 15th-place finish.

A.J. Foyt sprints toward the finish line just ahead of Bobby Isaac at the end of the July 4 Firecracker 400 at Daytona International Speedway. Foyt was the nation's most successful auto racer of 1964, winning the Indianapolis 500 and scoring victories in 10 of the 13 USAC Indy Car races he entered. He became the first man to win at Indy and Daytona in the same year.

Two movie cameras were mounted on Larry Frank's Ford in the Oct. 18 National 400 at Charlotte Motor Speedway. Frank was assigned to gather close-action racing shots for the upcoming film *Red Line 7000*. Frank had to make repeated pit stops so Paramount Pictures producer Howard Hawkes and his crew could load film into the cameras. Frank finished 122 laps behind winner Fred Lorenzen and earned only $400 for his race effort. However, Paramount paid him well for carrying the camera.

1965

January 1 New NASCAR rules go into effect that eliminate the Chrysler Hemi engine and the Plymouth and Dodge models that were raced in 1964. Chrysler balks at the new rules and announces it will boycott all NASCAR races in 1965.

January 5 Billy Wade is killed during a tire test at Daytona. Wade had replaced the late Joe Weatherly on the Bud Moore Mercury team.

February 14 Fred Lorenzen wins the rain-shortened Daytona 500. Fords and Mercurys take the top 13 positions as Chrysler continues its boycott.

February 27 Ned Jarrett wins the 100-mile race at Spartanburg by an incredible 22 laps. Only 16 cars start the race.

June 27 Cale Yarborough drives Kenny Myler's Ford to his first career NASCAR Grand National win at Valdosta, Ga.

July 25 Ned Jarrett wins the Volunteer 500 at Bristol. It is Ford's 32nd consecutive win, an all-time NASCAR record. Richard Petty returns to NASCAR after NASCAR relaxes the rules against the Hemi engine on short tracks.

July 31 Bill France lifts the lifetime ban on Curtis Turner. Turner plans to enter selected NASCAR Grand National events for the first time since 1961.

September 6 Ned Jarrett wins the Southern 500 at Darlington, 14 laps (19.25 miles) ahead of runner-up Buck Baker. It is the largest margin of victory in NASCAR Grand National history.

October 24 Rookie Dick Hutcherson claims his ninth win of the season at Hillsboro. Hutcherson's feat is the all-time record for race wins during a freshman campaign.

October 31 Curtis Turner returns from exile by winning the American 500 at the new North Carolina Motor Speedway.

November 7 Ned Jarrett wins the 100-mile race at Dog Track Speedway in Moyock, N.C. Jarrett's 13th win of the season helps him wrap up his second championship.

Number 28 Fred Lorenzen and #27 Junior Johnson battle side-by-side in the Feb. 12 Twin 100-mile qualifier at Daytona. Lorenzen took the white flag a car length ahead of Johnson, but thought he had seen the checkered flag. He backed off and Johnson sprinted to victory.

▼ When Chrysler pulled out of NASCAR Grand National racing in a dispute over new rules, 1964 champion Richard Petty drove the #43 Jr. Plymouth Barracuda in drag racing events.

Cale Yarborough's Ford sails over the guardrail after tangling with Sam McQuagg's #24 Ford during the Sept. 6 Southern 500. Yarborough tried to make a daring pass on leader McQuagg, but their fenders touched and Yarborough's Ford went airborne. Yarborough, who was uninjured, said, "I knew I was in trouble when I saw grass, because I know there ain't no grass on a racetrack."

▶ One of the best duels in NASCAR history came in the Oct. 17 National 400 at Charlotte Motor Speedway. Number 29 Dick Hutcherson, #28 Fred Lorenzen, and #41 Curtis Turner battled three-abreast for the lead, with A.J. Foyt also in the mix. With six laps to go, Foyt spun as he attempted to pass Lorenzen for the lead. Hutcherson had to take evasive action and Turner was forced to spin to avoid hitting Foyt. Lorenzen won with Hutcherson close behind. Turner recovered and finished third.

Veteran Ned Jarrett prevailed in a season-long struggle with rookie Dick Hutcherson to capture his second NASCAR Grand National championship. Jarrett and Hutcherson traded the points lead five times during the season.

Jarrett's quest for a second NASCAR title was in jeopardy when he injured his back in a race at Greenville, S.C., in June. With the aid of a back brace, Jarrett continued and managed to overtake Hutcherson after the 34th race of the season at Bristol. Jarrett won 13 races during the season, while Hutcherson set an all-time record for a rookie winning nine events. Hutcherson led the standings after 13 races, another rookie record.

1965 NASCAR Grand National Points Race

Rank	Driver	Points	Wins	Top 5	Top 10	Winnings
1	Ned Jarrett	38,824	13	42	45	$93,624.40
2	Dick Hutcherson	35,790	9	32	37	$57,850.50
3	Darel Dieringer	24,696	1	10	15	$52,213.63
4	G. C. Spencer	24,314	0	14	25	$29,774.72
5	Marvin Panch	22,798	4	12	14	$64,026.29
6	Bob Derrington	21,394	0	3	19	$20,119.90
7	J. T. Putney	20,928	0	10	24	$22,328.75
8	Neil Castles	20,848	0	6	28	$22,328.75
9	Buddy Baker	20,672	0	12	17	$26,836.21
10	Cale Yarborough	20,192	1	13	21	$26,586.21

1966

April 7 David Pearson wins the 100-mile race at Columbia, S.C., as Ford announces its factory teams will boycott the 1966 NASCAR Grand National season in a dispute over engine rules.

April 30 Richard Petty dominates the Rebel 400 at Darlington. The Ford boycott has a telling effect on the attendance as only 7000 paying spectators attend.

May 13 Darel Dieringer wins an all-independent 125-mile NASCAR Grand National race at Starlite Speedway in Monroe, N.C. Promoters at the track refuse to allow any Chrysler factory entries in wake of the Ford boycott.

July 4 Sophomore Sam McQuagg wins Daytona's Firecracker 400. McQuagg's Dodge has a strip of aluminum on the rear deck to make the car more stable. It is the first NASCAR Grand National race to permit "spoilers."

July 12 Bobby Allison wins the 100-mile race at Oxford, Maine. It is the first win for the Chevrolet nameplate since Junior Johnson won at Charlotte Motor Speedway on Oct. 13, 1963.

August 7 The Dixie 400 at Atlanta International Raceway is marked with controversy. David Pearson's Dodge is ruled illegal, while the Junior Johnson Ford driven by Fred Lorenzen is permitted to compete despite unapproved aerodynamic enhancements. Bill France admits that "rules were bent at Atlanta" but adds he was hoping to lure Fords back into NASCAR racing.

October 30 Fred Lorenzen wins the American 500 at Rockingham as David Pearson is crowned champion. Ned Jarrett and Junior Johnson, who have both won 50 NASCAR Grand National races, compete in their final race.

David Pearson took the lead in the 1966 NASCAR Grand National points standings in the second event of the season and sprinted to an easy win over rookie James Hylton. Pearson finished 1950 points ahead of Hylton in the final tally.

Hylton's runner-up effort marked the second straight season a rookie driver finished second in the points race.

Pearson, driving Cotton Owens' Dodge, scored 15 victories during the season. Hylton failed to post any wins, but finished in the top 10 in 32 of his 41 starts. Pearson's car was ruled ineligible for the 400-miler at Atlanta in August when NASCAR officials determined it didn't conform to specifications. Despite sitting out, Pearson maintained his points lead.

1966 NASCAR Grand National Points Race

Rank	Driver	Points	Wins	Top 5	Top 10	Winnings
1	David Pearson	35,638	15	26	33	$78,193.60
2	James Hylton	33,688	0	20	32	$38,722.10
3	Richard Petty	22,952	8	20	22	$85,465.11
4	Henley Gray	22,468	0	4	18	$21,900.96
5	Paul Goldsmith	22,078	3	11	11	$54,608.53
6	Wendell Scott	21,702	0	3	17	$23,051.62
7	John Sears	21,432	0	11	30	$25,191.35
8	J. T. Putney	21,208	0	4	9	$18,652.72
9	Neil Castles	20,446	0	7	17	$19,034.09
10	Bobby Allison	19,910	3	10	15	$23,419.09

David Pearson developed into one of NASCAR's best road racers. Driving Cotton Owens' #6 Dodge, Pearson won the pole for the Jan. 23 Motor Trend 500 at Riverside International Raceway. Pearson led the race on two occasions and finished second to road-racing expert Dan Gurney.

Number 42 Marvin Panch prepares to lap #34 Wendell Scott in the May 22 World 600 at Charlotte Motor Speedway. Panch, who ignored the Ford boycott and accepted a ride in a Petty Enterprises Plymouth, led 115 of the final 121 laps and scored a two-lap victory. Scott came from the 40th starting spot to finish seventh.

◄ Bobby Allison became an immediate crowd favorite in the summer of 1966 when his little 327-cid Chevrolet gave General Motors fans something to cheer about. Allison drove the car to victories at Oxford, Maine; Islip, N.Y.; and Beltsville, Md. Under NASCAR's 1966 power-to-weight ratio rules, Allison's Chevy had to weigh only 3060 pounds. Cars equipped with the 426-cid Hemi engine had to tip the scales at 3997 pounds. On the short tracks, Allison's nimble Chevy was able to run circles around most of the heavier cars.

▲ The Junior Johnson-built #26 Ford, driven by Fred Lorenzen in Atlanta's Dixie 400, was one of the most radical cars to ever compete in NASCAR. The front end of the car sloped downward, the roofline was lowered, the side windows were narrowed, the front windshield was sloped in an aerodynamic position, the tail was kicked up, and the body sat low over the wheels. Several rival drivers called the car "The Yellow Banana," "Junior's Joke," and "The Magnafluxed Monster." Despite the rules violations, NASCAR allowed the car to race. Lorenzen crashed while leading on the 139th lap. "No wonder," one wag in the pit area quipped. "I ain't never seen anybody who could drive a banana at 150 mile 'n hour."

1967

February 26 USAC star Mario Andretti leads the final 33 laps and wins the Daytona 500. It is Andretti's first NASCAR Grand National win.

April 2 Cale Yarborough posts his first career victory on a superspeedway by winning the Atlanta 500.

May 13 Richard Petty wins Darlington's Rebel 400. It is Petty's 55th career NASCAR Grand National win, putting him first on the all-time victory list. Fred Lorenzen retires before the race.

June 18 Richard Petty wins the Carolina 500 at Rockingham. The win, Petty's 11th of the season, pushes him atop the points standings for the first time.

August 12 Richard Petty wins his 19th race of the season in the 250-lapper at Bowman Gray Stadium. With the victory, Petty surpasses Tim Flock's record of 18 wins set in 1955.

October 1 Richard Petty continues his winning streak by taking the Wilkes 400 at North Wilkesboro Speedway. It is Petty's record-setting 10th straight win.

October 15 In his 215th start, Buddy Baker grabs his first career NASCAR Grand National win in the Charlotte National 500. Baker halts Richard Petty's 10-race winning streak.

October 29 Bobby Allison gives Ford its first NASCAR Grand National win in nearly three months by winning the American 500 at Rockingham.

November 5 Bobby Allison wins the season finale at Asheville-Weaverville Speedway. Richard Petty wraps his dominating championship season with a second-place finish.

Richard Petty rewrote the record book in 1967, winning 27 races in 46 starts. The newly crowned "king" of stock car racing also won 10 races in a row. The 27 wins and 10-race streak set records that may never be matched.

Despite his domination, Petty didn't grab the points lead until his 11th win of the season at Rockingham in late June. Winless James Hylton held the lead for six months based on consistency. Petty hit his stride in the second half of the season, and sprinted to a 6028-point cushion over Hylton by the time the 49-race season ended in November.

Petty became the all-time NASCAR victory leader, passing his father Lee by posting his 55th triumph in the May 13 400-miler at Darlington.

1967 NASCAR Grand National Points Race

Rank	Driver	Points	Wins	Top 5	Top 10	Winnings
1	Richard Petty	42,472	27	38	40	$150,196.10
2	James Hylton	36,444	0	26	39	$49,731.50
3	Dick Hutcherson	33,658	2	22	25	$85,159.28
4	Bobby Allison	30,812	6	21	27	$58,249.64
5	John Sears	29,078	0	9	25	$28,936.74
6	Jim Paschal	27,624	4	20	25	$60,122.28
7	David Pearson	26,302	2	11	13	$72,650.00
8	Neil Castles	23,218	0	4	16	$20,682.32
9	Elmo Langley	22,286	0	10	24	$23,897.52
10	Wendell Scott	20,700	0	0	11	$19,509.76

◄ Curtis Turner became the first driver to surpass 180 mph on a Daytona 500 qualifying run. Turner's #13 Smokey Yunick Chevelle was clocked at 180.831 mph. It was a controversial achievement for two reasons. First, it meant an unsponsored GM car had beaten the Ford and Chrysler factory cars. Second, the car was roughly ⅞ scale, making it illegal. A late-race engine failure put Turner out of the Feb. 25 Daytona 500, which was won by Mario Andretti.

► NASCAR began using templates at the midpoint of the 1967 season. Some innovative mechanics were getting downsized versions of full-size automobiles through the inspection procedure. Templates measured the body and contour of each car to make sure they conformed to stock guidelines. Here, Armond Holley's Chevrolet goes through the ritual prior to the July 4 Firecracker 400. Of the 50 entries for the event, 49 initially failed inspection. Bud Moore's Mercury was the only car to pass the first time.

◄ Fred Lorenzen posted his 26th and final NASCAR Grand National win in the second Twin 100-miler at Daytona on Feb. 24. Lorenzen went the distance without a pit stop. NASCAR tacked on an additional 25 miles thereafter so teams would have to pit at least once. Lorenzen retired before the May 13 race at Darlington. He returned in 1970 but never won again.

Richard Petty's Plymouth rolls into victory lane following his triumph in the May 13 Rebel 400 at Darlington. It was Petty's 55th career NASCAR Grand National win, moving him into first place on NASCAR's all-time win list. He surpassed his father Lee, who had won 54 races from 1949 to 1964.

1968

November 12, 1967 Bobby Allison wins the season opener at Middle Georgia Raceway in Macon. An elaborate moonshine operation is discovered beneath the track.

February 25 Cale Yarborough wins the Daytona 500 by less than a second over LeeRoy Yarbrough. Gordon Johncock's Smokey Yunick-prepared Chevrolet is not permitted to compete when NASCAR officials find a number of rules violations during inspection.

May 11 David Pearson scores his first superspeedway victory since 1961 in the Rebel 400 at Darlington Raceway. Pearson's Holman-Moody Ford is powered by a small 396-cid engine, which allows him to run 293 pounds lighter than most of his rivals under the new power-to-weight ratio rules.

June 16 Donnie Allison scores his first career NASCAR Grand National victory in Rockingham's Carolina 500.

September 2 Cale Yarborough nips David Pearson by four car lengths and wins the Southern 500 at Darlington. It is Yarborough's record fourth superspeedway win of the season.

November 3 Cale Yarborough wins the season finale at Jefferson, Ga., as David Pearson is declared the NASCAR Grand National champion.

November 25 Richard Petty announces he will leave Plymouth to drive Fords in the 1969 season. All of Petty's 92 wins have come in Plymouths.

David Pearson and Bobby Isaac engaged in a ferocious duel for superiority in the 1968 NASCAR Grand National championship race before Pearson pulled away in the closing months. It was Pearson's second title.

Pearson won 16 races en route to the championship, while Isaac won three times. Pearson took the lead from Isaac in the points race after a victory in the Aug. 8 event at Columbia, S.C. The driver of the Holman-Moody Ford survived two disqualifications, but still won the title by 126 points.

NASCAR instituted a new points system for 1968, with 150 points to the winner in races of 400 miles or more, 100 points for major short-track events, and 50 points for small short-track races.

1968 NASCAR Grand National Points Race

Rank	Driver	Points	Wins	Top 5	Top 10	Winnings
1	David Pearson	3499	16	36	38	$133,064.75
2	Bobby Isaac	3373	3	27	35	$60,341.50
3	Richard Petty	3123	16	32	35	$99,534.60
4	Clyde Lynn	3041	0	2	35	$29,225.55
5	John Sears	3017	0	5	24	$29,178.75
6	Elmo Langley	2823	0	6	28	$25,831.85
7	James Hylton	2719	0	16	27	$32,607.50
8	Jabe Thomas	2687	0	1	15	$21,165.70
9	Wendell Scott	2685	0	0	10	$20,497.20
10	Roy Tyner	2504	0	4	14	$20,246.95

Number 16 Cale Yarborough, #27 Bosco Lowe, Charlie Glotzbach, and #43 Richard Petty gun their cars through the turn at Middle Georgia Raceway in the 1968 season opener on Nov. 12, 1967. Petty finished second to Bobby Allison. The other three drivers failed to finish. The 500-lap race on the short track in Macon, Ga., almost didn't run on schedule. Federal authorities discovered a moonshine still beneath the track. Track promoter Lamar H. Brown, Jr., was charged with possession of an apparatus for the distillery of illegal whiskey. He was found not guilty 13 months later.

Bobby Isaac sits on Daytona's pit road, awaiting a signal from the NASCAR official to return to the track under caution. Isaac and his K&K Insurance Dodge team made their first attempt at the NASCAR Grand National championship in 1968. Isaac won three short-track races and led the points race from April through July, but finished second to David Pearson.

David Pearson's #17 Holman-Moody Ford Torino flashes past the finish line to win the May 5 Fireball 300 at Asheville-Weaverville Speedway. Pearson started on the pole and led 299 of the 300 laps around the ½-mile high-banked paved oval. It was Pearson's fourth win of the season.

Richard Petty sidestepped his familiar electric-blue paint scheme for both Daytona races in 1968. In the Daytona 500, the Petty Enterprises crew attached a black vinyl top to his Plymouth. In July, Petty showed up with a blue-and-white Plymouth. The roof and hood were painted white to deflect the hot summer sun and keep the driver's compartment and the engine a little cooler.

1969

February 1 In his first start in a Ford, Richard Petty wins the Motor Trend 500 on the Riverside road course.

March 30 Cale Yarborough wins the Atlanta 500 in a Mercury at Atlanta International Raceway. Yarborough's win marks a successful debut for the Blue Crescent Boss 429-cid engine.

July 20 David Pearson wins the Volunteer 500 at Bristol International Speedway. It is the first race on the ½-mile oval since the turns were banked to a staggering 36 degrees.

August 22 Richard Petty wins the 250-lap race at Winston-Salem's Bowman Gray Stadium. It is Petty's 100th NASCAR Grand National victory.

September 14 Richard Brickhouse drives a winged Dodge Daytona to victory in the inaugural Talladega 500 at the new Alabama International Motor Speedway. The event is boycotted by virtually all the top NASCAR drivers.

October 26 LeeRoy Yarbrough scores his seventh superspeedway win of the season in Rockingham's American 500.

December 7 Bobby Isaac claims his first career superspeedway victory in the inaugural Texas 500 at the new Texas International Speedway. Cale Yarborough is seriously injured when his Mercury clobbers the wall.

December 17 NASCAR signs a contract with ABC Television, which will televise nine NASCAR Grand National races, including five live broadcasts during the 1970 season.

▶ With threats of a drivers' boycott at Talladega, NASCAR president Bill France took a 1969 Ford out for a practice run. He then filed an entry for the race, hoping to gain admission to the new Professional Drivers Association's meetings. The PDA prevented France from joining the discussions, which centered on the possible boycott due to track conditions and tire problems related to the track's high speeds. Less than 24 hours before the inaugural Talladega 500, 32 drivers pulled out of the race. Richard Brickhouse (#99) and Bobby Isaac (#71) drove the only two Dodge Daytonas on race day. Brickhouse won the race, which featured several mandatory pit stops to keep tire temperatures in check.

David Pearson racked up his third NASCAR Grand National championship in 1969. With his win in the 250-miler at Richmond on April 13, Pearson took the points lead from Richard Petty, never to relinquish it. Petty, who had switched from Plymouth to Ford products, had his bid for a third title derailed in May when he missed two races due to broken ribs suffered in a crash.

Pearson's third NASCAR championship came in only his fourth concerted attempt at NASCAR's highest honor. He finished third in 1964, and won in '66, '68, and '69.

Bobby Isaac was the most prolific winner in 1969, winning 17 NASCAR Grand National races. He finished 6th overall.

1969 NASCAR Grand National Points Race

Rank	Driver	Points	Wins	Top 5	Top 10	Winnings
1	David Pearson	4170	11	42	44	$229,760
2	Richard Petty	3813	10	31	38	$129,906
3	James Hylton	3750	0	27	39	$114,416
4	Neil Castles	3530	0	14	30	$54,367
5	Elmo Langley	3383	0	13	28	$73,092
6	Bobby Isaac	3301	17	29	33	$92,074
7	John Sears	3166	0	17	27	$52,281
8	Jabe Thomas	3103	0	0	12	$44,989
9	Wendell Scott	3015	0	0	11	$47,451
10	Cecil Gordon	3002	0	1	8	$39,679

After his Plymouth Roadrunner produced only one superspeedway win in 1968, Richard Petty asked that Chrysler shift him to the more aerodynamic Dodge for '69. When Chrysler balked, Petty bailed out of the Chrysler camp and joined forces with Ford. Petty won his first start in a Ford at Riverside and went on to score eight other wins in the Torino Talladega.

LeeRoy Yarbrough erased an 11-second deficit in the final 10 laps and stormed past Charlie Glotzbach on the final lap to win the the Feb. 22 Daytona 500. Having crashed his primary car in practice, Yarbrough was driving a backup #98 Ford out of the Junior Johnson shops. It was the first Daytona 500 determined by a last-lap pass.

◀ David Pearson won his second straight and third overall NASCAR Grand National championship in 1969. He compiled an envious record, winning 11 races and 14 poles and finishing among the top three 38 times in 51 starts. Counting post-season awards, Pearson also became the first driver to surpass $200,000 in single-season winnings. After the exhausting season, Pearson reduced his schedule and vowed never to take another stab at the championship. During his career, Pearson made four concentrated efforts at the NASCAR title and won three of them.

Chapter Four:
NASCAR Enters the Modern Era

Auto racing in the United States was billed as "The Sport of the '70s" as the new decade approached. With ultramodern facilities popping up all over the country and millions of dollars being poured into NASCAR stock car racing by the automakers, the sport seemed to be on a roll.

Despite the rosy appearance, the earth was rumbling under the NASCAR domain. The automakers were considering significant cutbacks. Ford and Chrysler had spent untold millions developing cars for NASCAR, but most of the cars bought by the public were more conservative. Speeds in NASCAR's Grand National series were also a concern yet to be addressed.

During Daytona's 1970 Speedweeks, Ford announced it was drastically cutting back its financial backing, leaving the Wood Brothers, Junior Johnson, Banjo Matthews, and Holman-Moody teams with fewer operating funds.

On the heels of the Ford cutback, the winged Dodges and Plymouths swept 10 of the top 13 spots in the Daytona 500 as Pete Hamilton drove a Petty Superbird to a narrow victory. Hamilton hit stride quickly and also won convincingly in the 1970 Alabama 500 at Talladega. While only 36,000 spectators dotted the grandstands for the first spring race at the new track, the overall audience was well over five million, thanks to NASCAR's new contract with ABC television.

In December 1969, Roone Arledge, president of ABC Sports, announced that the network would begin live coverage of NASCAR Grand National events, citing good ratings and viewer interest for expanded auto racing coverage.

The 1970 spring race at Talladega was ABC Sports' first live telecast, though only the second half was aired. The exciting early laps were never shown and Hamilton won by nearly a full lap. By Talladega standards, the race was a dud.

Other ABC telecasts of races at North Wilkesboro, Darlington, Charlotte, and Nashville also proved unspectacular. Every car running at the finish at Nashville was in a lap by itself—not exactly high-pitched drama. After the Nashville event, ABC abandoned plans to televise any more races live. The remainder of the TV schedule returned to the *Wide World of Sports* with races taped, edited, and aired up to six weeks later.

By midsummer, NASCAR introduced the restrictor plate to curb speeds. The restrictive device limited fuel flow to the carburetor. The Aug. 16 event at Michigan International Speedway became the first NASCAR Grand National event to be run with restrictor plates. Charlie Glotzbach won, and restrictor plates were used in all the remaining 1970 NASCAR Grand National races, including short-track events.

By 1971, Ford had pulled up stakes and withdrawn entirely from NASCAR Grand National racing. Chrysler cut back its factory effort too, trimming their potent six-car effort to a pair of cars fielded by Petty Enterprises.

The loss of factory support was a big blow to NASCAR. With the unlimited conveyor belt of parts and technical support being reduced to a trickle, the hand-me-down pieces the independent campaigners received were no longer available.

Racing teams were forced to seek outside sponsorship to continue operation. Junior Johnson approached the R.J. Reynolds Tobacco Co. about possible sponsorship. At the same time, NASCAR was courting the tobacco giant about sponsoring the entire Grand National series. Due to a new congressional mandate, the tobacco companies were no longer able to advertise on television. They had huge advertising budgets and a lot of that went into auto racing starting in 1971.

R.J. Reynolds agreed with NASCAR's proposal, and became title sponsor. The new name of NASCAR's premier stock car racing tour became the "Winston Cup Grand National Series." The biggest news was the addition of a $100,000 points fund.

Winston's plunge into NASCAR was one of the few highlights in an otherwise troubled 1971 season. Many of the top teams folded due to a lack of funds. With a scarcity of first-class rides, the sport lost several of its top stars. Things looked bleak.

Car counts were dwindling, ticket sales were off, and the sport was clearly in a deep-rooted recession. Richard Howard, general manager at Charlotte Motor Speedway, became the savior of the 1971 season. Howard talked Junior Johnson into building a Chevrolet for the upcoming World 600 at Charlotte. With the restrictor plates choking off the beefy Chrysler and Ford engines, the time was ripe for a competitive Chevrolet to return to NASCAR. Charlie Glotzbach was hired to drive.

Glotzbach put the Chevy on the pole for the World 600, and a record crowd of 78,000 was on hand. Glotzbach crashed in the race, but the huge throng had seen the first competitive Chevy in six years. The Howard-Johnson-Glotzbach team entered selected races for the balance of the 1971 season and came away with a win in Bristol's Volunteer 500.

With the dwindling car count, NASCAR permitted the lower tier Grand American Ford Mustangs and Chevy Camaros to compete on the short tracks in the late summer of 1971. Bobby Allison, driving a Mustang, won the first of the "mixed" races on August 6 at Winston-Salem's Bowman Gray Stadium. The lightweight Mustang was much more nimble on the flat ¼-mile track. Tiny Lund won twice in his Grand American Camaro.

By the end of the 1971 season, Chrysler announced it would get out of NASCAR stock car racing entirely. It would be 30 years before Mopar would reappear in NASCAR racing.

In 1972, NASCAR announced that the Winston Cup Grand National season would consist of only 31 races, each consisting of 250 miles or more. However, the biggest news came on Jan. 11, when Big Bill France stepped aside and gave the NASCAR reins to his son, William Clifton France—Bill France, Jr.

Locating sponsorship was again a struggle for the racing teams. The STP Corp., Coca-Cola, and Purolator Filters were the only major corporate sponsors to line up with NASCAR teams. More drivers found themselves on the sidelines without cars to drive, and a few more team owners were forced to quit.

The early part of the 1972 campaign was rather lethargic. Only five cars had a shot at winning the Daytona 500, which A.J. Foyt won by nearly five miles. Richard Petty lost a cylinder midway through the 250-miler at Martinsville in April, but still won by *seven laps*. With the lack of competition, trackside attendance began tapering off. Only 12,000 showed up at Richmond, and only 16,000 came out at North Wilkesboro.

Richard Petty and Bobby Allison, who collectively won 18 of the 31 races, livened up the 1972 campaign by rekindling a feud that dated back to '66. The pair engaged in on-track scuffles at Richmond, Martinsville, and North Wilkesboro. The media played it up. NASCAR was back in the headlines in the South's newspapers. Petty edged Allison for the championship.

In 1973, Allison left the Richard Howard-owned, Junior Johnson-managed Chevrolet team to form his own operation. Petty's two-car team had filtered down to a one-car effort and David Pearson was content to drive a limited schedule with the Wood Brothers. Cale Yarborough was back in NASCAR's fold after a disappointing two-year stint in USAC.

Bud Moore, one of the top team owners of the 1960s, had departed in '69 to campaign Mustangs on the SCCA Trans-Am tour. He, too, was back in NASCAR with a small 351-cid Ford. Restrictor plates were still part of the equation, but teams campaigning the small engines were able to run without the plates.

David Pearson enjoyed a record-wrecking year in 1973. Pearson won 10 of 15 starts on superspeedways and 11 of 18 for the season. The unsponsored team of L.G. DeWitt and Benny Parsons won a single race and took the championship in an upset. The only race won by a car with a small engine was Mark Donohue's upset win at Riverside in an AMC Matador.

NASCAR was confronted with an issue in early 1974 that threatened to shut down the entire sport of auto racing. In late '73, the Organization of the Petroleum Exporting Countries (OPEC) announced a general boycott on oil exports to Europe, Japan, and the United States. The Federal Energy Office was established to monitor fuel usage nationwide, and NASCAR was facing the possibility of a congress-mandated shutdown.

Retired NASCAR president Bill France took the bull by the horns. Groomed in politics, Big Bill represented the entire auto racing fraternity in a meeting with FEO authorities. Under France's guidance, NASCAR took immediate steps to conserve fuel. The length of all races was reduced by 10 percent, and a 30-gallon fuel limit for practice sessions was introduced. Practice days were shortened, and the starting fields at most races were reduced. Following the '74 Daytona Speedweeks, NASCAR reported that it used 30 percent less fuel than it had in '73. NASCAR conducted the full slate of 30 Winston Cup Grand National events. Petty and Cale Yarborough each won 10 races in '74, with Petty taking his fifth title.

By 1975, the transition from the big to small engines was complete. All teams ran the same size engines and the restrictor plates were gone. NASCAR also initiated the Awards and Achievement Plan, which was basically appearance money. To offset the costs of the switch to small engines, NASCAR mandated that promoters pay up to $3000 each for top-ranked teams and $500 for independents who competed in all races.

With a standard set of rules, NASCAR had achieved some stability. However, many of the smaller teams still couldn't afford to continue. Filling out the fields was tough. Only 22 cars showed up at Richmond and only 23 were on hand at Bristol. Junior Johnson's potent team only ran selected events.

Despite the small fields and continued turbulence in 1975, NASCAR Winston Cup Grand National racing was getting more television time. ABC Sports was in its second year of presenting the second half of the Daytona 500 live. CBS also signed on to show tape-delayed coverage of some races.

By the late 1970s, NASCAR was pulling itself out of the shackles of the postfactory days. Corporate sponsors were jumping on the bandwagon, new teams found NASCAR appealing, and a few of the surviving independent teams had beefed up their operations. The starting fields were full again, the grandstands were close to capacity, competition was closer, and television ratings were climbing steadily. The NASCAR drivers were even invited to the White House by Jimmy and Rosalyn Carter. NASCAR was coming of age.

By February 1979, CBS Sports had wrangled the Daytona 500 contract away from ABC. CBS announced it would televise the entire Daytona 500 live, a first for a 500-mile race.

A snowstorm that blanketed the East Coast gave CBS a captive audience. The 21st annual running of the Daytona 500 was spectacular from start to finish. In the frantic finish, Richard Petty came from a half lap behind to win as leaders Cale Yarborough and Donnie Allison crashed on the final mile.

As Petty cruised around on his victory lap, Yarborough and Donnie and Bobby Allison were throwing punches and kicking each other. Bobby Allison had stopped on the track to check on the condition of his brother and soon got into the fracas. The CBS cameras captured the fisticuffs, and about 16 million were tuned into the telecast. The Daytona 500 was the top-rated show during each half hour.

The 1979 NASCAR Winston Cup Grand National season was memorable for other reasons. Freshman Dale Earnhardt drove like a savvy veteran, winning in his 13th career start. Petty and Waltrip battled down to the wire for the championship, with Petty winning the title in the final race. Petty became the NASCAR champion for a record seventh time.

By the end of the 1970s, NASCAR had regained and surpassed the popularity it enjoyed at the start of the decade. It had overcome a numerous setbacks, including retreating factory support, thinning fields, competitor unrest, the energy crisis, and weak team sponsorships. It had encountered many bumps along the way, but by the decade's end, NASCAR had emerged as one of the sporting industry's strongest entities.

1970

February 22 Pete Hamilton posts an upset victory in the Daytona 500.

March 24 During a Goodyear tire test at Talladega, Buddy Baker runs a lap at 200.447 mph to become the first man to break 200 mph on a closed course.

April 12 Pete Hamilton wins the Alabama 500 at Talladega. It is the first NASCAR race televised live by ABC Sports, but only the second half of the event is shown.

April 18 Richard Petty wins the Gwyn Staley Memorial 400 at North Wilkesboro, the second event televised live by ABC Sports. Petty leads every lap shown during ABC's telecast.

May 24 Donnie Allison wins the Charlotte World 600. Fred Lorenzen ends a three-year retirement, but exits with a blown engine.

August 16 Restrictor plates make their first NASCAR appearance at Michigan International Speedway. Charlie Glotzbach wins in a winged Dodge Daytona.

September 30 Richard Petty wins the final dirt-track race in NASCAR Grand National history, which is run at State Fairgrounds Speedway in Raleigh, N.C.

October 4 Legendary NASCAR driver Curtis Turner perishes in a private plane crash in Pennsylvania.

November 15 Cale Yarborough wins the American 500 at Rockingham, and announces from victory lane that he will move to USAC Indy Cars in 1971.

November 19 Ford announces that it will cut back its factory effort in 1971. Jacques Passino, director of Ford's racing program, quits the company.

November 22 Bobby Allison captures the season finale at Hampton, Va., as Bobby Isaac is declared the 1970 NASCAR Grand National champion.

December R.J. Reynolds announces its Winston brand of cigarettes will become the title sponsor of NASCAR's premier stock car racing series. The official title will be NASCAR Winston Cup Grand National Series.

Following a one-year stint with Ford, Richard Petty was lured back into the Plymouth fold in 1970 with the development of the new winged Superbird. Chrysler had to produce more than 1500 of the new models (1920 were built) to enter NASCAR Grand National competition. Prior to '70, only 500 factory examples were required to make a car eligible. Chrysler officials determined it was necessary to build the increased number of units to reacquire the services of NASCAR's leading driver.

Pete Hamilton, a youngster from Dedham, Mass., was hired by Petty Enterprises to drive the #40 Superbird in major NASCAR events. Hamilton was a hit, winning the Daytona 500 after a tremendous late-race battle with three-time champion David Pearson. Hamilton was the 1968 NASCAR Grand National Rookie of the Year, but he missed most of the '69 season when he couldn't find a full-time ride.

On March 24, Buddy Baker took Chrysler's company car, a royal blue Dodge Daytona, to Talladega for a special closed-circuit world-record attempt. In an officially timed run, Baker became the first driver to surpass the magic 200-mph barrier on a closed oval. His best lap was 200.447 mph.

Bobby Isaac drove the K&K Insurance Dodge to the 1970 NASCAR Grand National championship. Team owner Nord Krauskopf started his operation in '66 with a five-year plan to win the NASCAR title. With Isaac driving and Harry Hyde filling the role of crew chief, Krauskopf realized his dream in the allotted time frame. Isaac won 11 races and finished second nine times in 47 starts.

Bobby Isaac overtook James Hylton in late August and went on to win the 1970 NASCAR Grand National championship. It was the most competitive title chase in NASCAR history. Seven drivers swapped the points lead 12 times during the 48-race campaign, a record that still stands.

Isaac moved to the front with a runner-up finish in the Talladega 500 and stayed atop the standings for the final 14 events. Hylton lost his fading hopes for the championship when he crashed in Charlotte's National 500 in October. Bobby Allison surged past Hylton to capture second place in the final standings.

For the second straight year, Richard Petty's hopes for a third title were dashed by injury; he missed five races due to a broken shoulder suffered at Darlington. The King managed to climb to fourth place in the standings at the end of the season.

1970 NASCAR Grand National Points Race

Rank	Driver	Points	Wins	Top 5	Top 10	Winnings
1	Bobby Isaac	3911	11	32	38	$199,600
2	Bobby Allison	3860	3	30	35	$149,745
3	James Hylton	3788	1	22	39	$78,201
4	Richard Petty	3447	18	27	31	$151,124
5	Neil Castles	3158	0	12	24	$49,746
6	Elmo Langley	3154	0	1	19	$45,193
7	Jabe Thomas	3120	0	0	23	$42,958
8	Benny Parsons	2993	0	12	23	$59,402
9	Dave Marcis	2820	0	7	15	$41,111
10	Frank Warren	2697	0	0	2	$35,161

1971

February 14 Richard Petty bags his third Daytona 500 win. Dick Brooks finishes seventh in the final appearance for a winged Dodge Daytona in a NASCAR event.

February 28 A.J. Foyt drives the Wood Brothers Mercury to victory in the 500-miler at Ontario Motor Speedway. It is the 1000th NASCAR Winston Cup Grand National race.

April 10 Bobby Isaac wins the 100-mile race at Greenville-Pickens Speedway. The short-track event is televised live flag to flag by ABC Sports.

May 9 Sophomore Benny Parsons scores his first career NASCAR win in the 100-mile event at South Boston Speedway in Virginia.

May 21 Seven independent drivers stage a boycott of the 100-mile event at Asheville, N.C. Protesting the payoff structure and a lack of appearance money, the drivers pull out of the race early, leaving only five cars running at the finish. Richard Petty wins.

May 30 Driving a Junior Johnson-built Chevrolet, Charlie Glotzbach wins the pole for Charlotte's World 600. He is poised to make a competitive run, but crashes on the 234th lap.

July 11 Charlie Glotzbach, with relief help from Friday Hassler, wins Bristol's Volunteer 500. It is Chevrolet's first NASCAR win since 1967.

August 6 Bobby Allison drives a Ford Mustang to victory in the race at Winston-Salem. The event is the first race to mix NASCAR Winston Cup Grand National cars and the ponycars of NASCAR's Grand American division.

November 21 Tiny Lund drives a Chevy Camaro to victory in the Wilkes 400 at North Wilkesboro Speedway. It is the third win for the smaller Grand American cars since NASCAR permitted them to compete in short-track events.

December 12 Richard Petty roars to his 21st win of the season in the finale at Texas World Speedway. Petty also wraps up his third NASCAR Winston Cup Grand National championship.

► A.J. Foyt pitches his Wood Brothers Mercury into the first turn in the inaugural race at Ontario Motor Speedway in Ontario, Cal. Foyt manhandled the 51-car field on the 2.5-mile rectangular course and scored an easy victory. The 500-mile Feb. 28 event marked the 1000th NASCAR Winston Cup Grand National race, a noteworthy milestone that wasn't reported.

Number 71 Bobby Isaac and #22 Dick Brooks battle through the fourth turn in the Feb. 14 Daytona 500. Brooks was driving a Dodge Daytona powered by a small 305-cid engine. The aerodynamic wonder had been all but legislated out of NASCAR with the new 1971 rules. Team owner Mario Rossi, with the blessing of Chrysler, defied the odds and entered the underpowered car in Daytona's Speedweeks events. Brooks finished third in the Twin 125 and seventh in the Daytona 500. Brooks' run marked the Dodge Daytona's final appearance in NASCAR competition.

▲ Charlie Glotzbach and relief driver Friday Hassler piloted the Richard Howard-owned #3 Chevrolet to victory in the July 11 Volunteer 500 at Bristol International Speedway. Glotzbach and Hassler scored a three-lap victory in a caution-free event. To this day, it remains the only NASCAR Winston Cup race in Bristol history without a caution flag.

▼ A shortage of teams in the Winston Cup Grand National and lower-ranked Grand American divisions prompted NASCAR to permit cars from both series to compete in short-track races in 1971. Bobby Allison won the opening event with the mixed field, driving Melvin Joseph's #49 Mustang in the Aug. 6 race at Winston-Salem's Bowman Gray Stadium.

Richard Petty won 21 races in 46 starts and breezed to his third NASCAR Winston Cup Grand National championship. Petty took command of the points chase after the eighth race of the season at Hickory, N.C., in March and never trailed in the points battle again.

James Hylton, Bobby Allison, Benny Parsons, and Bobby Isaac jockeyed for the points lead in the early part of the season before Petty set sail. King Richard posted 38 top-five finishes in 46 starts to post a thoroughly dominating performance.

Allison, who joined the Holman-Moody team in May, won 11 races and finished fourth overall. Among the top-ten finishers, only Allison and Petty won races during the 1971 campaign.

1971 NASCAR Winston Cup GN Points Race

Rank	Driver	Points	Wins	Top 5	Top 10	Winnings
1	Richard Petty	4435	21	38	41	$351,071
2	James Hylton	4071	0	14	37	$90,282
3	Cecil Gordon	3677	0	6	21	$69,080
4	Bobby Allison	3636	11	27	31	$254,316
5	Elmo Langley	3356	0	11	23	$57,037
6	Jabe Thomas	3200	0	2	15	$48,241
7	Bill Champion	3058	0	3	14	$43,769
8	Frank Warren	2886	0	1	10	$40,072
9	J.D. McDuffie	2862	0	2	8	$35,578
10	Walter Ballard	2633	0	3	11	$30,974

1972

January NASCAR announces the 1972 NASCAR Winston Cup Grand National season will be reduced to 30 events. Only races of 250 miles or more will be part of the schedule.

January 11 NASCAR founder Bill France steps down as president and turns the reins over to his son, Bill France, Jr.

February 20 A.J. Foyt blisters the field to win the Daytona 500 by nearly five miles. Foyt leads the final 300 miles.

March 5 A.J. Foyt wins the second annual 500-miler at Ontario Motor Speedway. ABC Sports, which televises the second half of the race live across the nation, reports that the final half hour draws a 12.3 Nielsen rating.

March 26 Bobby Allison drives a Chevrolet to victory in the Atlanta 500. Allison records the first superspeedway win for Chevrolet since 1963.

August 6 Independent driver James Hylton wins the Talladega 500. New tires introduced by Goodyear fail to withstand the high-speed punishment and eliminate most of the favorites.

September 10 Richard Petty prevails in a wild duel with Bobby Allison in the Capital City 500 at Richmond Fairgrounds Speedway. At one point, Petty's Dodge climbs on top of the guardrail, but he returns to the track, retains the lead, and motors to victory.

October 1 Richard Petty outruns Bobby Allison in the final laps of an epic slugfest to win the Wilkes 400 at North Wilkesboro Speedway. Petty and Allison tangle repeatedly in the final laps and both cars are badly crumpled when the checkered flag falls.

October 8 Bobby Allison posts his 10th victory of the season at Rockingham's American 500. Allison leads in his 39th consecutive race, an all-time mark that is acknowledged as stock car racing's "Joe DiMaggio Record."

November 12 Buddy Baker wins the season finale at Texas World Speedway. Richard Petty takes third and clinches his fourth NASCAR Winston Cup Grand National championship.

◀ A.J. Foyt relaxes in victory lane following his dominating performance in the Daytona 500. Foyt was unchallenged for the final 300 miles, and he became the second USAC Indy Car driver to pluck NASCAR's sweetest plum in the last six years. No visiting driver from another sanctioning body has won the Daytona 500 since Foyt's victory.

▼ Bobby Allison joined the Richard Howard and Junior Johnson Chevrolet team in 1972. Team owner Howard needed a sponsor to compete on the full schedule and Allison's close ties with Coca-Cola provided the operating funds. The Coca-Cola sponsorship was roughly $80,000 for the full season, but team manager Johnson said he needed a minimum of $100,000. Allison had to pay the additional $20,000 to secure the ride.

▼ David Pearson took over the #21 Wood Brothers/Purolator Mercury after A.J. Foyt left the team to return to the USAC Indy Car tour. In his first race, Pearson won the April 16 Rebel 400 at Darlington. Many observers felt Pearson was washed up after a lackluster 1971 campaign. "Nothing bothers me as long as I know the truth," said Pearson, who went on to win six of 12 starts with the Wood Brothers in '72.

▼ One of the most thrilling moments in NASCAR history came during the final laps of the Oct. 1 race at North Wilkesboro Speedway. Richard Petty and Bobby Allison rekindled their feud, which dated back to 1967. Allison led Petty under the white flag, but Petty passed Allison after both cars hit the wall on the final lap and Petty won the final sprint to the finish line. Petty was attacked by a drunk fan in victory lane after the race, but order was restored when Richard's brother Maurice smacked the fan on the head with Richard's helmet.

Richard Petty claimed a record fourth NASCAR Winston Cup Grand National championship in 1972, leading the points standings most of the season.

A new points system was introduced, which awarded points per lap completed. This system prevented Petty from taking the points lead until the 11th race of the season at Talladega. Petty had finished higher than James Hylton in nine of the first 10 races, including victories in four events, but Hylton maintained the points lead due to more laps completed. When Hylton was involved in a crash at Talladega, Petty claimed the lead, which he held for the balance of the season.

Petty won eight races and finished 127.9 points in front of runner-up Bobby Allison, who won 10 events. Hylton finished third. Petty, Hylton, and Allison swapped the points lead six times during the season.

1972 NASCAR Winston Cup GN Points Race

Rank	Driver	Points	Wins	Top 5	Top 10	Winnings
1	Richard Petty	8701.40	8	25	28	$339,405
2	Bobby Allison	8573.50	10	25	27	$348,939
3	James Hylton	8158.70	1	9	23	$126,705
4	Cecil Gordon	7326.05	0	4	16	$73,126
5	Benny Parsons	6844.15	0	10	19	$102,043
6	Walter Ballard	6781.45	0	0	7	$59,745
7	Elmo Langley	6656.25	0	1	9	$59,644
8	John Sears	6298.50	0	2	7	$51,314
9	Dean Dalton	6295.05	0	0	4	$42,299
10	Ben Arnold	6179	0	0	7	$44,547

1973

January 21 Mark Donohue drives his Roger Penske Matador to victory in the season-opening Winston Western 500 at Riverside. Donohue's first win comes in his fifth NASCAR Winston Cup Grand National start.

March 25 Cale Yarborough, back in NASCAR after a two-year stint in USAC Indy Cars, drives Junior Johnson's Chevrolet to an overwhelming victory in the Southeastern 500 at Bristol.

May 6 David Pearson steers clear of a 21-car crash and wins the Winston 500 at Talladega. Only 17 cars in the 60-car starting field finish.

August 12 Dick Brooks posts perhaps the biggest upset win in NASCAR history in the Talladega 500. Brooks is driving a Plymouth owned by the Crawford Brothers, a team that has never finished above 16th in a NASCAR Winston Cup Grand National event since forming in 1966.

October 7 Cale Yarborough and Richard Petty finish 1-2 in the National 500 at Charlotte Motor Speedway. Controversy flares as NASCAR inspectors find the engines in Yarborough's Chevrolet and Petty's Dodge measure larger than the cubic inch limit. The finish stands with no penalties.

October 9 Bobby Allison, who finished third in the controversial Charlotte race, announces he is quitting NASCAR. "On account of NASCAR's arbitrary and capricious conduct, I find it necessary to withdraw from the remaining races this season," Allison remarks.

October 15 Bobby Allison settles his differences with NASCAR in a tense meeting with Bill France, Jr., in Atlanta. NASCAR promises to increase scrutiny in the prerace inspections.

October 21 David Pearson captures his 11th win in 18 starts with a season-ending victory in the American 500 at Rockingham. Benny Parsons pits for repairs after an early crash. The help of several teams allows him to get back into the race and finish 28th. Parsons holds on to win the NASCAR Winston Cup Grand National championship by 67.15 points over Cale Yarborough.

► The backstretch of Talladega's Alabama International Motor Speedway is littered with wrecked cars and debris following a 21-car crash in the May 6 Winston 500. The accident, which occurred on the 11th lap, took out 19 cars. The caution flag was out for more than 25 laps while safety crews cleaned up the mess. Many of the drivers blamed the huge crash on the 60-car starting field, the most cars to start a NASCAR Winston Cup Grand National race in 13 years. "They wanted to fill up the track with those extra cars," said Bobby Allison. "They filled it up alright—all over the backstretch."

◄ David Pearson scored his eighth win of the season in Daytona's Firecracker 400. During a 10-race stretch from March through August, Pearson won nine races and finished second in the other event. Pearson won 14 of his first 22 starts with the Wood Brothers including 13 on superspeedways. It was one of the most dominating performances in NASCAR history.

◄ The Feb. 18 Daytona 500 came down to a battle between the Dodges of Buddy Baker and Richard Petty. Baker won the pole and led most of the way, but Petty scrambled into contention late. Petty assumed command with a lightning-fast 8.6-second pit stop with a dozen laps remaining. Baker shortened Petty's lead each lap, but his engine let go with six laps remaining. Petty went on to win his fourth Daytona 500.

▲ Cale Yarborough and Richard Petty battle in the final laps of the Oct. 7 National 500 at Charlotte. Yarborough made the decisive pass 22 laps from the finish. In a postrace inspection, NASCAR discovered disturbing engine readings in Yarborough's Chevy and Petty's Dodge. Both cars had oversized engines, but both drivers kept their 1-2 finishes without penalty.

Benny Parsons, driving the unsponsored #72 L.G. DeWitt Chevrolet, pulled off a major upset by winning the 1973 NASCAR Winston Cup Grand National championship despite posting only one win.

Parsons took the points lead with a third-place finish at Talladega in early May and never gave it up. He held off a late rally by Cale Yarborough to win by only 67.15 points.

Under NASCAR's points system, in which points per lap completed were factored in, Parsons was unaware of what position he would have to finish in at the finale at Rockingham to seal the championship. Five drivers had a mathematical chance to win the championship entering the final event of the 28-race season. Parsons crashed early, but, with the help of other crews, his team made miraculous repairs to get him back into the race and he completed enough laps to wrap up the title.

1973 NASCAR Winston Cup GN Points Race

Rank	Driver	Points	Wins	Top 5	Top 10	Winnings
1	Benny Parsons	7173	1	15	21	$182,321
2	Cale Yarborough	7106	4	16	19	$267,513
3	Cecil Gordon	7046	0	8	18	$102,120
4	James Hylton	6972	0	1	11	$82,512
5	Richard Petty	6877	6	15	17	$234,389
6	Bobby Baker	6327	2	16	20	$190,531
7	Bobby Allison	6272	2	15	16	$161,818
8	Walter Ballard	5955	0	0	4	$53,875
9	Elmo Langley	5826	0	0	4	$49,542
10	J. D. McDuffie	5743	0	3	10	$56,140

1974

January 3 In the wake of the energy shortage, NASCAR announces all races will be reduced 10 percent in length to conserve fuel. In addition, NASCAR plans for smaller starting fields and limited practice sessions.

February 17 Richard Petty rallies from a flat tire and drives to victory in the 450-mile Daytona 500.

April 21 Richard Petty wins the Gwyn Staley Memorial 400 at North Wilkesboro Speedway using a small engine in his Dodge. Under NASCAR rules, the small engines can compete without carburetor restrictor plates, while the large 426–429-cid engines must run with the restrictive devices.

May 26 David Pearson racks up his 80th career NASCAR Winston Cup Grand National victory in the World 600 at Charlotte Motor Speedway.

August 11 Richard Petty edges David Pearson to win the Talladega 500, an event marred by a mass sabotage in the garage the night before the race. More than two dozen of the top-contending cars are tampered with by an unknown assailant during the night.

September 29 Rookie Earl Ross wins the Old Dominion 500 at Martinsville, becoming the first Canadian driver to win a NASCAR Winston Cup Grand National race.

November 24 Bobby Allison drives an AMC Matador to victory at Ontario Motor Speedway. During the postrace inspection, NASCAR officials discover the Roger Penske-owned Matador is equipped with illegal roller tappets. The team keeps the win but is fined a record $9100. Richard Petty wins his fifth championship.

NASCAR changed its points system for the 1974 season, and it proved to be the most confusing method ever used. Fractions of points were multiplied and remultiplied after each race. The idea was to award points in direct relation to money won.

Under the peculiar system, the 1-2 finishers in the rich Daytona 500 were virtually assured of a 1-2 finish in the final standings. Richard Petty and Cale Yarborough finished first and second at Daytona and, not surprisingly, ranked 1-2 in the final standings. All drama for the points chase ended in February. Petty and Yarborough had their Daytona points added to their point total after each event, making it virtually impossible for anyone to overtake them.

In the Darlington Southern 500, Petty crashed early and placed 35th, yet still had more points added to his total than Darrell Waltrip, who finished second. Petty accumulated 5037.75 points, compared to Waltrip's runner-up total of 4470.30. Thankfully, the system was changed after only one year.

1974 NASCAR Winston Cup GN Points Race

Rank	Driver	Points	Wins	Top 5	Top 10	Winnings
1	Richard Petty	5037	10	22	23	$432,019.00
2	Cale Yarborough	4470	10	21	22	$363,781.10
3	David Pearson	2389	7	15	15	$252,818.92
4	Bobby Allison	2019	2	17	17	$178,436.90
5	Benny Parsons	1591	0	11	14	$185,079.72
6	Dave Marcis	1378	0	6	9	$83,376.01
7	Buddy Baker	1016	0	11	12	$151,024.62
8	Earl Ross	1009	1	4	9	$81,198.50
9	Cecil Gordon	1000	0	1	10	$66,165.32
10	David Sisco	956	0	2	9	$58,312.32

In his second season on the NASCAR Winston Cup Grand National circuit, Darrell Waltrip posted seven top-five and 10 top-10 finishes, proving he would become one of the elite. His best effort was a second-place finish at Darlington's Southern 500. Waltrip earned $67,774.30 for his 1974 efforts and finished 19th in the points race.

Donnie Allison's DiGard Chevrolet leads Richard Petty's Dodge in the closing stages of the Feb. 17 Daytona 500. Petty suffered a flat tire with 19 laps to go and was forced to make an unscheduled pit stop. Seemingly out of the hunt with 10 laps remaining, Petty was nearly a lap behind when Allison cut a tire. Allison spun out, allowing Petty to breeze to victory. By the time Allison righted his path, he had fallen to sixth place.

◀ Nord Krauskopf's K&K Insurance Dodge team ended its boycott of NASCAR races in late 1974. In Charlotte's National 500, Dave Marcis and Bobby Isaac both drove the familiar poppy-red machines. Here, Isaac's #17 Dodge leads #5 Harry Gant, who was competing in one of his early NASCAR Winston Cup Grand National events. Mechanical problems forced Isaac and Gant to the sidelines before 100 laps had been completed.

Bobby Allison drove the Roger Penske AMC Matador to a surprising victory in the Nov. 24 season finale at Ontario Motor Speedway. It was only the third race all season won by a driver other than Richard Petty, David Pearson, or Cale Yarborough. After the race, NASCAR technical inspectors discovered illegal roller tappets on the Matador. The victory was upheld, but the Penske team was fined $9100—at the time the largest fine in NASCAR history.

1975

January NASCAR announces a new points system, the fourth different system in the last five years. For the first time, each race will carry an equal points value throughout the season.

February 16 Benny Parsons takes the lead with three laps to go and wins the Daytona 500 when leader David Pearson spins on the backstretch.

May 10 Darrell Waltrip posts his first career NASCAR Winston Cup Grand National victory in the Music City USA 420 at Nashville Speedway.

May 25 Dale Earnhardt, making his first NASCAR Winston Cup Grand National start, finishes 22nd in a Dodge owned by Ed Negre.

August 16 Buddy Baker noses out Richard Petty in a photo finish to win the Talladega 500, an event marred by the death of DeWayne "Tiny" Lund.

September 28 Journeyman Dave Marcis drives a Dodge to his first career NASCAR Winston Cup Grand National victory in the Old Dominion 500 at Martinsville Speedway.

November 23 Buddy Baker bags his fourth win of the season in the Los Angeles Times 500 at Ontario Motor Speedway. Richard Petty claims his sixth NASCAR championship.

NASCAR instituted another new points system in 1975. It was the first time that every race on the NASCAR Winston Cup Grand National schedule carried an equal point value.

Richard Petty, who won 13 of the 30 races, won his sixth championship by a whopping 722-point margin over Dave Marcis. Petty snatched the points lead from Bobby Allison in the third race of the season and never trailed.

The new points system drew mixed reviews. While it was designed to encourage more teams to commit to running the full schedule, many observers felt a greater amount of points should be awarded at the major superspeedway races than the short tracks. Petty received more points for winning Richmond and leading the most laps than Benny Parsons did for winning the Daytona 500.

NASCAR officials said they approved of the way the points system worked and indicated it would likely remain unchanged for several years to come. It remains in place today.

1975 NASCAR Winston Cup GN Points Race

Rank	Driver	Points	Wins	Top 5	Top 10	Winnings
1	Richard Petty	4783	13	21	24	$481,750.80
2	Dave Marcis	4061	1	16	18	$240,645.40
3	James Hylton	3914	0	2	16	$113,641.86
4	Benny Parsons	3820	1	11	17	$214,353.32
5	Richard Childress	3818	0	2	15	$96,779.78
6	Cecil Gordon	3702	0	7	16	$101,466.24
7	Darrell Waltrip	3462	2	11	14	$160,191.35
8	Elmo Langley	3399	0	2	7	$67,599.16
9	Cale Yarborough	3295	3	13	13	$214,690.62
10	Dick Brooks	3182	0	6	15	$93,000.62

Richard Petty whips his #43 Dodge around Lennie Pond on his way to victory in Martinsville Speedway's April 27 Virginia 500. Petty out-ran Darrell Waltrip in the last 20 laps to secure his 14th career win on the flat ½-mile track. Petty went unchallenged in the NASCAR Winston Cup Grand National title chase in 1975, leading the standings after all but the first two races.

▲ Dale Earnhardt made his NASCAR Winston Cup Grand National debut in the May 25 World 600 at Charlotte Motor Speedway. Driving the #8 Dodge Charger owned and maintained by independent driver Ed Negre, Earnhardt qualified third on the grid. Earnhardt completed 355 of the 400 laps and finished 22nd.

▶ A wobbly but unhurt Dick Brooks is helped from his car following a tumble down the backstretch in the Aug. 17 Talladega 500. Brooks was running in the top five when he touched fenders with Donnie Allison. Brooks' Ford darted off the track, dug into the infield, and flipped numerous times. Unfortunately, a crash on the sixth lap claimed the life of veteran Tiny Lund.

▲ Number 88 Donnie Allison, #15 Buddy Baker, and #17 Darrell Waltrip occupied the front positions at the start of Daytona's July 4 Firecracker 400. These front-running cars were devoid of major sponsorships in 1975 as corporate America's recession took its toll on NASCAR. Baker's Ford was sponsored by Coppertone suntan lotion, but it was only a one-shot deal. Despite the lack of solid backing, all three drivers finished strong. Baker was second, Waltrip fourth, and Allison fifth.

▲ Buddy Baker enjoyed one of his finest years in 1975, despite not having a full-time sponsor. While picking up local sponsorships, Baker drove the Bud Moore Ford to four wins, including two in the season's last two events.

1976

February 8 NASCAR disallows the speeds of the three fastest qualifiers for the Daytona 500, leaving unheralded Ramo Stott on the pole. A.J. Foyt, Darrell Waltrip, and Dave Marcis have to requalify.

February 15 David Pearson beats Richard Petty in a stunning finish to the Daytona 500. Pearson and Petty swap the lead four times on the final lap and tangle off the fourth turn. Pearson gets his Mercury straightened out and crosses the finish line first.

May 2 Buddy Baker wins Talladega's Winston 500, averaging a record speed of 169.887 mph.

May 30 David Pearson wins the Charlotte World 600. Janet Guthrie makes her NASCAR Winston Cup Grand National debut, finishing 15th.

September 6 David Pearson wins the Southern 500 at Darlington, giving him a victory in all three crown-jewel races on the NASCAR calendar: the Daytona 500, World 600, and Southern 500.

October 10 Donnie Allison posts his first NASCAR Winston Cup Grand National victory since 1971 in Charlotte's National 500.

November 21 David Pearson wins his 10th race of the year at Ontario Motor Speedway. Cale Yarborough claims his first NASCAR Winston Cup Grand National championship.

Janet Guthrie entered, but never competed in, the 1976 Indianapolis 500. After her Indy efforts fell through, Charlotte Motor Speedway promoter Humpy Wheeler hatched a plan to get Guthrie a ride in the World 600. Lynda Ferreri, vice president of First Union Bank in Charlotte, paid $21,000 to become a NASCAR Winston Cup Grand National team owner. Ralph Moody organized the team. Guthrie, pictured here with Ferreri and Moody, qualified 27th and finished 15th in the May 30 600-miler.

Cale Yarborough broke out of a close points race with Benny Parsons at midseason to score his first NASCAR Winston Cup Grand National championship. Yarborough won nine races and beat runner-up Richard Petty by 195 points.

Yarborough took the points lead for keeps with a 26th-place finish at Talladega in August. Parsons finished 39th after his engine let go in the early laps. Petty passed Parsons in the points race in September and held on for the runner-up spot.

The points lead changed hands eight times among four drivers. Yarborough, Petty, Parsons, and David Pearson traded first place in an early season flurry. Pearson won 10 races in 22 starts, but finished ninth in the final standings because he ran a limited schedule.

1976 NASCAR Winston Cup GN Points Race

Rank	Driver	Points	Wins	Top 5	Top 10	Winnings
1	Cale Yarborough	4644	9	22	23	$453,404.40
2	Richard Petty	4449	3	19	22	$374,805.62
3	Benny Parsons	4304	2	18	23	$270,042.98
4	Bobby Allison	4097	0	15	19	$230,169.72
5	Lennie Pond	3930	0	10	19	$159,700.54
6	Dave Marcis	3875	3	9	16	$218,249.32
7	Buddy Baker	3745	1	16	16	$239,921.10
8	Darrell Waltrip	3505	1	10	12	$204,192.88
9	David Pearson	3483	10	16	18	$346,889.66
10	Dick Brooks	3447	0	3	18	$111,879.66

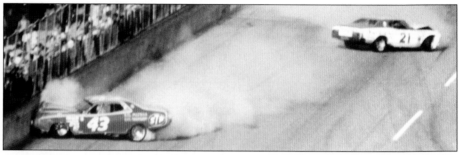

Richard Petty's Dodge hits the wall as David Pearson's Mercury slides backward in the Feb. 15 Daytona 500's heart-stopping last-lap crash. Pearson passed Petty on the backstretch, but when Petty attempted to reclaim the lead in the third turn, the cars slapped together. Both cars spun and Petty's Dodge came to a stop on the infield about 100 feet from the finish line. Pearson managed to keep his car running and rolled across the finish line at about 20 mph. It was perhaps the most thrilling finish in NASCAR history.

Buddy Baker pushes his #15 Ford under Richard Petty at Talladega during the May 2 Winston 500. Baker held command most of the way, leading for 135 of the 188 laps. Baker ran away from the field, finishing 35 seconds ahead of runner-up Cale Yarborough. He averaged 169.887 mph, which at that time was a 500-mile record.

Cale Yarborough drove his #11 Junior Johnson/Holly Farms Chevrolet to the 1976 NASCAR Winston Cup Grand National championship. Yarborough won nine races along the way to the first of three consecutive titles. He finished last in the Daytona 500, but grabbed the points lead in August. Yarborough beat Richard Petty by 195 points. Petty had pulled within 97 points with two races to go, but a 28th-place finish in the next race dashed his title hopes.

1977

February 20 Cale Yarborough pulls away from Benny Parsons in the final laps to win in his second Daytona 500.

July 4 Richard Petty wins the Firecracker 400 at Daytona. For the first time since 1949, three women are in the starting field. Janet Guthrie, Christine Beckers, and Lella Lombardi all start the race.

August 28 Cale Yarborough racks up his eighth win of the year at Bristol's Volunteer 400. Yarborough's Junior Johnson Chevrolet fails the postrace inspection for the second time in a row. Team owner Johnson is fined $500. Janet Guthrie finishes sixth, her best NASCAR Winston Cup Grand National effort.

September 11 Neil Bonnett scores his first career NASCAR Winston Cup Grand National win in the Capital City 400 at Richmond.

November 6 Darrell Waltrip denies David Pearson his 100th victory at Atlanta International Raceway. Waltrip makes a final-lap pass as darkness descends on the track. Unable to see through his tinted windshield, Pearson backs off and accepts second place.

November 20 Neil Bonnett outruns Richard Petty to win at Ontario Motor Speedway. Third-place finisher Cale Yarborough takes his second straight NASCAR Winston Cup championship.

▲ In the summer of 1977, George Elliott purchased the Mercury equipment that Roger Penske had campaigned. Penske was making a switch to Chevrolet, and the Mercury cars were an upgrade for the independent Elliott team. George's son Bill, in his sophomore season, drove the car in the Oct. 9 NAPA National 500 at Charlotte Motor Speedway, finishing a strong 10th.

▶ Number 11 Cale Yarborough, leads #1 Donnie Allison, and #88 Darrell Waltrip in the Oct. 23 American 500 at North Carolina Motor Speedway. Yarborough clinched his second straight NASCAR Winston Cup Grand National championship with his fourth-place finish. Allison went on to win and Waltrip came home third.

Cale Yarborough was running at the finish in all 30 NASCAR Winston Cup Grand National races as he dominated the 1977 season to wrap up his second consecutive title. Yarborough won nine races in 30 starts and finished 386 points ahead of runner-up Richard Petty.

Petty captured the points lead briefly at midseason, taking first place after the July 31 race at Pocono. But a runner-up finish the following week at Talladega lifted Yarborough atop the standings again, a lead that he never relinquished.

Benny Parsons finished third in the final standings, posting four race wins.

1977 NASCAR Winston Cup GN Points Race

Rank	Driver	Points	Wins	Top 5	Top 10	Winnings
1	Cale Yarborough	5000	9	25	27	$561,641.16
2	Richard Petty	4614	5	20	23	$406,607.80
3	Benny Parsons	4570	4	20	22	$359,340.52
4	Darrell Waltrip	4498	6	16	24	$324,813.24
5	Buddy Baker	3961	0	9	20	$224,846.96
6	Dick Brooks	3742	0	7	20	$151,373.68
7	James Hylton	3476	0	0	11	$108,391.40
8	Bobby Allison	3467	0	5	15	$94,574.12
9	Richard Childress	3463	0	0	11	$97,011.84
10	Cecil Gordon	3294	0	0	2	$86,311.84

◀ Cale Yarborough and wife Betty Jo celebrate in victory lane on Feb. 20 after the Timmonsville, S.C., driver won his second of four Daytona 500s. Driving Junior Johnson's #11 Chevrolet, Yarborough shook the draft of Benny Parsons and motored across the finish line 1.39 seconds ahead of the runner-up. Yarborough collected $63,700 for his three hour, 15 minute drive.

▼ Skip Manning's #92 Chevrolet runs ahead of #1 Donnie Allison late in the Aug. 7 Talladega 500 at Alabama International Motor Speedway. Manning, the 1976 Rookie of the Year, made a surprise run and was poised to win until smoke billowed from his car in the final laps. Allison's Hawaiian Tropic Chevy, with Darrell Waltrip driving in relief, took the lead from Manning with six laps remaining. Allison got credit for the victory, the eighth of his career.

1978

January 22 Cale Yarborough wins the Winston Western 500 at Riverside International Raceway. It is the first win for Oldsmobile since 1959.

March 5 David Pearson rallies from a late spin to post his 100th career win in the Carolina 500 at Rockingham's North Carolina Motor Speedway.

May 14 Cale Yarborough wins the Winston 500 at Talladega. Car owner Harold Miller and driver Keith Davis are suspended for 12 weeks when NASCAR discovers a nitrous-oxide bottle in their #91 Chevy in prerace inspections.

May 15 African American Willy T. Ribbs fails to appear for two special practice sessions in preparation for the upcoming World 600 at Charlotte. Team owner Will Cronkrite, irked with Ribbs' absence, replaces him with little-known Dale Earnhardt.

August 6 Lennie Pond posts his first career NASCAR Winston Cup Grand National victory in the Talladega 500. Pond averages a record 174.700 mph.

August 20 David Pearson wins the Champion Spark Plug 400 at Michigan International Speedway. Richard Petty makes his first start in a Chevrolet, having parked his uncompetitive Dodge Magnum, and finishes 14th.

September 4 Cale Yarborough wins the Southern 500. D.K. Ulrich is suspended for the remainder of the season after a wreck reveals he has a nitrous-oxide bottle in his Chevrolet.

November 5 Donnie Allison is declared the winner of the Dixie 500 at Atlanta International Raceway after the crowd of 40,000 thought Richard Petty had nipped Dave Marcis in a race to the finish. NASCAR scorers failed to notice that Allison had passed both Petty and Marcis with three laps to go. Rookie Dale Earnhardt finishes fourth in his first start with the Rod Osterlund team.

November 19 Bobby Allison scores his fifth win of the year in the finale at Ontario Motor Speedway. Runner-up Cale Yarborough wins his third consecutive NASCAR Winston Cup Grand National championship.

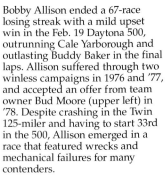

Bobby Allison ended a 67-race losing streak with a mild upset win in the Feb. 19 Daytona 500, outrunning Cale Yarborough and outlasting Buddy Baker in the final laps. Allison suffered through two winless campaigns in 1976 and '77, and accepted an offer from team owner Bud Moore (upper left) in '78. Despite crashing in the Twin 125-miler and having to start 33rd in the 500, Allison emerged in a race that featured wrecks and mechanical failures for many contenders.

David Pearson's #21 Wood Brothers Mercury battles with Richard Petty's STP Dodge Magnum in the early stages of the March 5 Carolina 500 at Rockingham. Temperatures were in the mid 20s at race time, but Pearson blistered the one-mile track to record his 100th career victory. Petty finished fourth in his Magnum, a bulky beast that The King struggled with for most of the 1978 season.

Dale Earnhardt drove Will Cronkrite's #96 Cardinal Tractor Ford to a seventh-place finish in the July 4 Firecracker 400 at Daytona. The car was meant for African American Willy T. Ribbs, but when he failed to appear for two practice sessions in May and was arrested in Charlotte for reckless driving, Cronkrite dumped Ribbs and signed Earnhardt.

Lennie Pond whips his #54 Harry Rainier Oldsmobile under #27 Buddy Baker and #11 Cale Yarborough in the Aug. 6 Talladega 500. Pond grabbed the lead five laps from the finish and held off a quartet of challengers in a near photo finish to snare his first and only NASCAR victory. He averaged a then record 174.700 mph in the event, which featured 67 official lead changes.

Cale Yarborough motored to his record-setting third consecutive NASCAR Winston Cup Grand National championship in 1978. Yarborough's Junior Johnson team won 10 races and finished 474 points ahead of runner-up Bobby Allison. Yarborough clinched the 1978 title at Rockingham in October.

Benny Parsons led the points standings from March through June, but Yarborough grabbed the lead with a victory at Nashville on July 15 and never gave it up. Yarborough scored 23 top-five finishes in 30 starts in a near-perfect campaign. Allison won five races, including the Daytona 500.

Darrell Waltrip, a six-time winner, finished third in the standings, while Parsons fell to fourth by the end of the season.

1978 NASCAR Winston Cup GN Points Race

Rank	Driver	Points	Wins	Top 5	Top 10	Winnings
1	Cale Yarborough	4841	10	23	24	$623,505.80
2	Bobby Allison	4367	5	24	22	$411,516.40
3	Darrell Waltrip	4362	6	19	20	$413,907.26
4	Benny Parsons	4350	3	15	21	$329,992.12
5	Dave Marcis	4335	0	14	24	$205,870.98
6	Richard Petty	3949	0	11	17	$242,272.84
7	Lennie Pond	3794	1	11	19	$181,095.70
8	Dick Brooks	3769	0	5	17	$137,589.99
9	Buddy Arrington	3626	0	1	7	$112,959.84
10	Richard Childress	3566	0	1	12	$108,701.42

1979

January CBS Sports prepares for its live, flag-to-flag telecast of the Daytona 500. It marks the first time in history that a 500-mile NASCAR Winston Cup Grand National event will be televised by a major network in its entirety.

February 18 Richard Petty hustles past the crashed cars of Cale Yarborough and Donnie Allison to win the Daytona 500. Yarborough and Allison fight in the infield following their last-lap crash. The Nielsen ratings for the CBS live telecast are a remarkable 10.5, with the final half hour drawing an amazing 13.5 rating.

April 1 Outstanding rookie driver Dale Earnhardt scoots around Darrell Waltrip with 27 laps to go and grabs his first career NASCAR Winston Cup Grand National victory in Bristol's Southeastern 500.

April 8 Darrell Waltrip prevails in a last-lap battle with Richard Petty to win the Rebel 500 at Darlington. The two drivers swap the lead four times on the final lap. After the race, David Pearson is released as driver of the Wood Brothers Mercury. A pit mishap is cited as the reason for Pearson's release.

May 20 Neil Bonnett, making his third start for the Wood Brothers, wins the Mason-Dixon 500 at Dover Downs International Speedway.

July 30 Cale Yarborough wins the Coca-Cola 500 at Pocono International Raceway. Rookie Dale Earnhardt fractures both collar bones in a crash.

August 5 Darrell Waltrip wins the Talladega 500. Young Kyle Petty makes his NASCAR Winston Cup Grand National debut, finishing ninth.

November 4 Neil Bonnett edges Dale Earnhardt to win the Dixie 500 at Atlanta. Darrell Waltrip carries a narrow two-point lead over Richard Petty into the season finale at Ontario.

November 18 Benny Parsons wins the Los Angeles Times 500 at Ontario Motor Speedway. Richard Petty claims his seventh NASCAR Winston Cup Grand National championship.

▲ Richard Petty leads Darrell Waltrip down the backstretch during the hectic final lap of the Feb. 18 Daytona 500. Leaders Donnie Allison and Cale Yarborough crashed on the final lap, opening the door for Petty, who was more than a mile behind, to end a 45-race winless skid.

◄ After the final-lap crash in the Daytona 500, Cale Yarborough, Donnie Allison, and Bobby Allison engaged in fisticuffs. Bobby stopped on the track to check on his brother's condition. Cale approached Bobby and punched him as he sat in the car. Bobby dismounted and wrestled with Cale as Donnie came over to join the free-for-all. Later, Bobby described the incident with Cale: "For some reason, Cale kept hitting my fist repeatedly with his nose." The finish and the fight made great television, and helped increase the general public's interest in NASCAR.

▼ Richard Petty and Darrell Waltrip engaged in one of the most heated and exciting duels in the history of the legendary Darlington Raceway on April 8. Petty's #43 STP Chevrolet and Waltrip's #88 Gatorade Chevy swapped the lead four times in the four laps before the final lap of the Rebel 500, plus an additional three times on the final lap alone. On that last lap, Waltrip passed Petty in turn one, only to lose the lead in turn three. Waltrip fought back and passed Petty off turn four and won by a car length.

▲ Dale Earnhardt was tabbed to drive the Osterlund Racing Chevrolets and Oldsmobiles in 1979, and the rookie responded brilliantly. In the April 1 Southeastern 500 at Bristol, Earnhardt edged Bobby Allison and Darrell Waltrip to post his first NASCAR Winston Cup Grand National win in only his 16th start.

Richard Petty won an unprecedented seventh NASCAR Winston Cup Grand National championship after making a furious rally late in the 1979 season. Petty trailed Darrell Waltrip by 187 points with just seven races to go. From that point on, Petty never finished lower than sixth.

Waltrip led the points chase most of the season. He assumed command in May and built a healthy lead until his advantage began to slip away. The lead changed hands in each of the last four races. Waltrip led after the 28th race at North Wilkesboro in October. Petty won at Rockingham the following week and took an eight-point lead. Waltrip finished one spot ahead of Petty at Atlanta and carried a two-point lead into the season finale at Ontario Motor Speedway in California.

In the finale, Waltrip spun out trying to avoid a spinning car and lost a lap. Unable to make up the lap, Waltrip finished eighth, while Petty came home fifth and won the title by 11 points.

1979 NASCAR Winston Cup GN Points Race

Rank	Driver	Points	Wins	Top 5	Top 10	Winnings
1	Richard Petty	4830	5	23	27	$561,933.20
2	Darrell Waltrip	4819	7	19	22	$557,011.60
3	Bobby Allison	4633	5	18	22	$428,800.44
4	Cale Yarborough	4604	4	19	22	$440,128.28
5	Benny Parsons	4256	2	16	21	$264,929.12
6	Joe Millikan	4014	1	5	20	$229,712.88
7	Dale Earnhardt	3749	1	11	17	$274,809.96
8	Richard Childress	3735	0	1	11	$132,921.64
9	Ricky Rudd	3642	0	4	17	$150,897.48
10	Terry Labonte	3615	0	2	13	$134,652.48

Chapter Five:
Smaller Cars, Bigger Purses, Grand Exposure

THE 1980S BEGAN with a refreshing outlook for a sport that had endured a tumultuous trek through the preceding decade. NASCAR overcame innumerable obstacles in the '70s, from the loss of factory support to the crippling energy crisis and a gripping recession.

Unpolished sophomore driver Dale Earnhardt, a rugged short-track warrior, had driven his way into the starry world of NASCAR Winston Cup Grand National racing with relative ease. He emerged from obscurity to instant fame, fortune, and headlines. Following in the footsteps of his famous father Ralph, the second-generation Earnhardt possessed the fortitude and supreme self-confidence to make the grade at NASCAR's highest level.

With a full season under his belt, Earnhardt blazed his way out of the starting blocks in 1980. Back-to-back victories at Atlanta and Bristol in March put Earnhardt atop the points standings. Showing maturity far beyond his 29 years, Earnhardt never broke stride, winning at Nashville, Martinsville, and Charlotte. He held off Cale Yarborough in a spirited title battle, and prevailed by a scant 19-point margin.

At the start of the 1981 campaign, the team owners worked feverishly to deal with the new NASCAR guidelines and the smaller, downsized race cars. The maximum wheelbase was reduced to 115 inches, down from 120. The '81 models built by Detroit were boxy and devoid of aerodynamic enhancements. Everyone was back to square one.

Richard Petty scored his seventh Daytona 500 win in 1981. It was an entertaining race that featured 49 lead changes, a sign of what was to come during the rest of the season. The two Michigan races produced 65 and 47 lead changes, respectively. The total of 112 lead changes for two races at one track hasn't been approached since. Talladega had a combined 82 lead changes for its two races, and Daytona had 84. Over the course of the 31-race season, there were a total of 772 lead changes, a mark that still stands. A record five races were also determined by a last-lap pass, another standard that hasn't been surpassed.

Two rookies and three teams logged their first career wins during an energized season. In the end, Darrell Waltrip nosed out Bobby Allison for the NASCAR Winston Cup Grand National title in a spirited points chase.

Much of the 1981 season was aired on television. CBS and ABC produced their usual telecasts, but a new entity was forging its way into the NASCAR empire. The Entertainment Sports Programming Network televised the Nov. 8 Atlanta Journal 500 live flag to flag. After that initial production, ESPN

knew it had fertile grounds in NASCAR. ESPN picked up a number of races that didn't already have a TV contract in place. The stock car racing fraternity welcomed the addition of the cable sports network.

Acquiring team sponsorship was becoming even more paramount. Costs were rising, and teams had to perform well to secure and keep sponsorship. Winning races was a prerequisite, and crews often challenged the savvy of the NASCAR technical inspectors in their efforts to gain a "competitive edge."

In October 1983, the NASCAR Winston Cup Grand National Series was at Charlotte Motor Speedway and several teams were scrambling to line up sponsorship for '84. Richard Petty had won twice in '83, but both victories had come in the early weeks. On more than one occasion, Petty told his brother Maurice, the engine builder for Petty Enterprises, that he needed more horsepower to keep up with the front-runners.

Petty qualified 20th and spent most of the day lagging behind the leaders. During a late caution flag, Petty made a pit stop for new rubber, and his crew bolted four left-side tires on the STP Pontiac, a violation of NASCAR's rules. On the restart, Petty blasted past the competition and drove to a convincing victory, the 198th of his career. As Petty went through the routine victory lane proceedings and postrace interviews, NASCAR inspectors noticed the numbers "D2881" on all four of Petty's tires. Those were the left-side serial numbers Goodyear used.

NASCAR technical director Dick Beaty and Maurice Petty were huddled in a conference in the inspection area. Maurice braced Beaty for another shock. The engine was too big, he confessed. The engine in Petty's car measured 381.983 cid, well above the maximum of 358 cid.

NASCAR allowed Petty to keep his 198th win, but stripped him of 104 NASCAR Winston Cup Grand National points and fined the team a then-record $35,000. Petty admitted he had grown "out of touch" with his crew. "I didn't know what was going on. As I get further and further away from the business aspect, I become only the driver. I've been telling the crew I needed more horsepower. I guess they took me at my word."

Bobby Allison went on to record his first NASCAR Winston Cup Grand National championship in 1983 after six runner-up finishes. After two painful losses to Darrell Waltrip in '81 and '82, Allison had finally achieved NASCAR's top honor.

Richard Petty, on the other hand, was deeply hurt by the Charlotte fiasco. At the end of the season, he departed Petty Enterprises and hooked up with California music producer Mike Curb, who was forming a team for the 1984 season. Petty

took the STP sponsorship with him, leaving Petty Enterprises with third-generation driver Kyle Petty to carry on the flame.

The 1984 season got off to a shaky start for Richard and Kyle. Both were felled by repeated engine failures. The elder Petty was able to shake off the mechanical gremlins to win race number 199 at Dover in May. In the July 4 Firecracker 400 at Daytona, he took win number 200, beating Cale Yarborough in a photo finish as both cars crossed the finish line grinding against each other. President Ronald Reagan arrived trackside midway through the race and witnessed one of the most memorable races in NASCAR history.

Petty was escorted to the VIP suites for a meeting with the President and radio interviews. "We all shook hands and then the President and I talked," said Petty. "I think it blowed his mind that Cale and I were really running into each other at 200 miles per hour." Petty had finally posted his magical 200th NASCAR Winston Cup Grand National victory. It turned out to be the final win of his illustrious career.

Bill Elliott emerged as a bona fide superspeedway hero in 1985, clicking off a string of victories on NASCAR's speediest tracks. Elliott led 136 of the 200 laps to win the Daytona 500. He followed that with victories at Atlanta and Darlington, then made a miraculous comeback to take Talladega's Winston 500, overcoming a two-lap deficit to win going away.

The Talladega victory gave Elliott a win in the first two crown-jewel races of 1985, Daytona and Talladega. At the beginning of the season, title sponsor R.J. Reynolds inaugurated "The Winston Million," a million-dollar prize that would go to any driver winning three of the four major races (Daytona, Talladega, Charlotte, and Darlington) during the campaign. Another big-buck plum tossed into the fray was The Winston, NASCAR's version of an all-star race, a special event that would offer $200,000 to the winner.

The all-star race was a big bonus for the drivers and fans. The inaugural running of the event was staged at Charlotte Motor Speedway on May 25, the day before the World 600. The media attention during the Charlotte race week was incredible. After his win at Dover the week before, Elliott commented that he "dreaded" going to Charlotte. The quiet and unassuming boy from the Georgia hills was thrust into the limelight. The distractions were too much for Elliott and his team. Elliott finished a distant seventh in the 12-car field in The Winston, and wound up 18th in the World 600.

Elliott got back on track after Charlotte. He won twice at Pocono, bagged both Michigan races, and regained a narrow lead in the points race. Darlington's Southern 500 in September represented his last shot at winning The Winston Million. This time Elliott was braced for the onslaught of media attention. He had armed deputies in his garage, shielding him from the herd of media. Interviews were scheduled in advance so Elliott and his team could concentrate on the job at hand.

The Southern 500 was a memorable event. Elliott led early, then dropped off the pace due to handling problems. In the middle stages, Elliott was nearly lapped, but timely caution flags enabled his pit crew to make pivotal chassis adjustments. Elliott scrambled back into serious contention and passed Cale Yarborough in the closing laps to score a million-dollar victory.

Elliott went on to win 11 superspeedway races in 1985, still a single-season record. He gobbled up every postseason award, yet didn't win the NASCAR Winston Cup Grand National title. That honor went to Darrell Waltrip, who won three races.

Late in 1985, NASCAR announced it would change the names of its two top divisions. For '86, "Grand National" would be shifted to the old Late Model Sportsman division. "We feel our friends at Winston deserve a name of their own," said NASCAR president Bill France, Jr. The new official titles would be NASCAR Winston Cup and NASCAR Busch Grand National.

Dale Earnhardt, NASCAR's darling youngster in the early 1980s, rebounded from a few sluggish seasons after his electrifying championship in '80. Between '81 and '83, Earnhardt drove for four teams before settling down with the Richard Childress operation in '84.

It took a couple of years for the chemistry to mesh, but once they hit stride, Earnhardt's Wrangler Jeans machine ran up front every week. Along the way, Earnhardt ruffled a few feathers, crumpled some sheetmetal, shoved rivals out of the way, and acquired the nickname "The Intimidator." In 1986, Earnhardt won five races and ran away from the field in the NASCAR Winston Cup title race. The following year, the formidable team went for the jugular early, winning six of the first eight races of the season. The outcome of the '87 title race was never in doubt after April.

The 1988 campaign was sweet redemption for Bill Elliott. Elliott won six races and claimed the NASCAR Winston Cup title by 24 points over Rusty Wallace, who would claim the championship in '89.

As the 1980s drew to a close, the popularity of NASCAR stock car racing was spiraling dramatically upward. Sponsorship from corporate America was strong, the dynamic heroes behind the wheel were becoming household names, and all of the NASCAR Winston Cup events were being televised live. Trackside attendance was running at record levels and promoters were adding new grandstands to accommodate the demand for tickets. The problems of the chaotic 1970s were a distant memory. With adequate financing, superlative public relations, and intelligent leadership, NASCAR Winston Cup racing had rapidly developed into one of the most efficient endeavors in big league sports.

1980

February 17 In his 18th Daytona 500 start, Buddy Baker shakes the monkey off his back with a resounding victory. Baker averages a record 177.602 mph.

March 16 Sophomore Dale Earnhardt fends off a pesky Rusty Wallace to score his first superspeedway victory in the Atlanta 500. Earnhardt comes from the 31st starting position to win.

April 13 David Pearson wins the rain-shortened Rebel 500 at Darlington. It is Pearson's 105th and final NASCAR Winston Cup Grand National victory.

April 27 Darrell Waltrip wins the Virginia 500 at Martinsville Speedway. Waltrip violates a new rule stating teams aren't permitted to change tires during caution periods.

July 27 Neil Bonnett wins the Coca-Cola 500 at Pocono. Title contender Richard Petty crashes hard on the 57th lap and suffers a broken neck.

September 1 Sophomore driver Terry Labonte scores his first NASCAR Winston Cup Grand National victory in the Southern 500 at Darlington.

November 2 Cale Yarborough wins the Atlanta Journal 500 at Atlanta International Raceway to move to within 29 points of Dale Earnhardt. Earnhardt, who has led the standings since the second race of the year, finishes third.

November 15 Benny Parsons wins the season finale at Ontario Motor Speedway as Dale Earnhardt captures his first NASCAR Winston Cup Grand National title.

Dale Earnhardt took the points lead after the Daytona 500 and held on to capture the 1980 NASCAR Winston Cup Grand National title. Earnhardt became the first driver to win Rookie of the Year and championship honors back to back.

Richard Petty was within 48 points of Earnhardt in late July, but he broke his neck in a crash at Pocono. Petty concealed the injury from NASCAR so he could continue racing. Relief drivers assisted Petty but he fell from contention.

Cale Yarborough began his rally in September. He trailed by 173 points following the Sept. 7 Richmond event, but then posted a series of top-10 finishes. Going into the season finale at Ontario, Calif., Earnhardt had a narrow 29-point lead.

Earnhardt fell a lap off the pace at Ontario, but muscled his way back onto the lead lap and scrambled to a fifth-place finish. The effort put him 19 points ahead of Yarborough, who took third at Ontario, and gave Earnhardt his first title.

1980 NASCAR Winston Cup GN Points Race

Rank	Driver	Points	Wins	Top 5	Top 10	Winnings
1	Dale Earnhardt	4661	5	19	24	$671,990.40
2	Cale Yarborough	4642	6	19	22	$567,890.20
3	Benny Parsons	4278	3	16	21	$411,518.68
4	Richard Petty	4255	2	15	19	$397,317.16
5	Darrell Waltrip	4239	5	16	17	$405,710.64
6	Bobby Allison	4019	4	12	18	$378,969.12
7	Jody Ridley	3972	0	2	18	$204,882.60
8	Terry Labonte	3766	1	6	16	$222,501.08
9	Dave Marcis	3745	0	4	14	$150,164.04
10	Richard Childress	3742	0	0	10	$157,419.56

◄ Buddy Baker leads a pack of cars off the fourth turn in the Feb. 17 Daytona 500. The Charlotte native drove his Ranier Racing Oldsmobile to an impressive victory after many years of hard luck in "The Great American Race." It was Baker's 18th Daytona 500 start. He won $102,175, the first time a NASCAR winner took home more than $100,000 in a single event.

▶ Dale Earnhardt wheels his #2 Chevrolet under Buddy Baker during the early laps of the April 13 CRC Chemicals Rebel 500 at Darlington Raceway. Baker crashed early and Earnhardt fell out with engine problems. Earnhardt's Osterlund Racing team picked up sponsorship from Mike Curb Productions in 1980. During his rookie campaign of '79, Earnhardt competed all year without the aid of a sponsor.

David Pearson, who lost his ride with the Wood Brothers in 1979, started his first race of the '80 season in the April 13 Darlington event. Driving the #1 Hoss Ellington/Hawaiian Tropic Chevrolet, Pearson started on the front row, bolted to the lead, and was holding down first place when rain curtailed the event five laps after the halfway point. It was the 105th and final career NASCAR Winston Cup Grand National victory for Pearson.

Sophomore Terry Labonte waves to the crowd after scoring an upset victory in the 31st Southern 500. Labonte was running a distant fourth with three laps to go when leaders David Pearson, Dale Earnhardt, and Benny Parsons slid through a patch of oil deposited by Frank Warren, who had blown an engine. All three leaders were taken out of contention as Labonte tiptoed his way through the carnage. The Sept. 1 race marked the young Texan's first career NASCAR Winston Cup Grand National win.

1981

January 17 Due to new guidelines requiring the use of downsized cars (110-inch vs. 115-inch wheelbase), Richard Petty tests a Dodge Mirada at Daytona. The car is unable to run competitive speeds, so Petty gives up any idea of returning to Chrysler.

February 15 Richard Petty wins his record seventh Daytona 500. Petty's longtime crew chief Dale Inman quits two days later to accept a job with the Rod Osterlund/Dale Earnhardt team.

April 26 Rookie Morgan Shepherd drives to an upset win in the Virginia 500 at Martinsville, giving the Pontiac nameplate its first NASCAR Winston Cup Grand National win since 1963.

May 3 Bobby Allison wins the Winston 500 at Talladega in a Harry Ranier-owned Buick. The Ranier-Allison team was forced to switch from the Pontiac LeMans to the Buick when new rules made the LeMans uncompetitive.

June 7 Benny Parsons wins at Texas World Speedway. Only 18,000 spectators turn out to watch the race at the financially troubled two-mile track.

August 16 Richard Petty wins at Michigan. Dale Earnhardt, in his first start with the Richard Childress team, finishes ninth.

November 22 Bobby Allison wins the season finale at Riverside as Darrell Waltrip's sixth-place finish clinches his first NASCAR Winston Cup Grand National championship.

Darrell Waltrip rallied to bag his first NASCAR Winston Cup Grand National championship in 1981. Bobby Allison finished second for the fourth time in his career.

Waltrip was seemingly out of the title hunt in early June, but he began to whittle away at Allison's lead with a series of top-five finishes. With six races to go, Waltrip took the points lead with a runner-up finish at Dover. In the final six races, Waltrip extended his lead and finished 53 points ahead of Allison.

Waltrip won 12 races, while Allison won five times. No one else was close in the points race. Harry Gant finished third, 670 points behind Waltrip, and failed to record a single victory.

1981 NASCAR Winston Cup GN Points Race

Rank	Driver	Points	Wins	Top 5	Top 10	Winnings
1	Darrell Waltrip	4880	12	21	25	$799,134.00
2	Bobby Allison	4827	5	21	26	$680,957.00
3	Harry Gant	4210	0	13	18	$280,047.60
4	Terry Labonte	4052	0	8	17	$348,702.84
5	Jody Ridley	4002	1	3	18	$267,604.80
6	Ricky Rudd	3988	0	14	17	$395,684.00
7	Dale Earnhardt	3975	0	9	17	$353,971.40
8	Richard Petty	3880	3	12	16	$396,071.80
9	Dave Marcis	3507	0	4	9	$162,212.60
10	Benny Parsons	3449	3	10	12	$311,092.60

Darrell Waltrip, in his first start for the Junior Johnson team, won the pole for the Jan. 11 season opener at Riverside in his Mountain Dew Chevrolet. Waltrip skidded off course on the fourth lap, and later had to pit to replace fouled spark plugs. He returned and managed to finish 17th. Bobby Allison won the 500-kilometer event in a 1977 Chevy Monte Carlo. The race marked the final appearance for full-size cars in NASCAR Winston Cup competition.

Richard Petty's #43 Buick chases the fleet #28 Pontiac LeMans of Bobby Allison in the Feb. 15 Daytona 500. The King of stock car racing was seemingly out of the hunt late in the race, running a distant fifth with 25 laps remaining. Petty outsmarted the field, however, by making a splash-and-go stop during his final visit to the pits. Petty got back onto the track ahead of the leaders, all of whom took tires on their final pit stop. Petty was able to protect his advantage in the final laps.

Freshman driver Ron Bouchard (#47) snookered Darrell Waltrip and Terry Labonte on the final lap of the Aug. 2 Talladega 500 to provide one of NASCAR's biggest upsets in spectacular fashion. Waltrip led entering the final lap and faded high off the fourth turn to deflect Labonte's charge on the high side. Bouchard, making only his 11th NASCAR Winston Cup Grand National start, shot into the open lane to the inside and won by a bumper in a three-abreast finish.

The 1981 season was tumultuous for defending NASCAR Winston Cup Grand National champion Dale Earnhardt. Rod Osterlund sold the team to the mysterious and somewhat shady J.D. Stacy in May, a move that stunned the racing community. By August, Earnhardt had quit Stacy's team and joined the Richard Childress operation. Earnhardt took the Wrangler sponsorship to Childress' #3 Pontiac team, while Joe Ruttman replaced Earnhardt in the J.D. Stacy #2 Pontiac.

1982

February 21 Dave Marcis stays on the track as rain begins to fall at Richmond Fairgrounds Raceway and is the surprise winner when NASCAR officials call the race after 250 of 400 laps. Marcis is the only driver on the lead lap not to pit during the rain shower.

April 4 Dale Earnhardt ends an 18-month famine with a victory in the Rebel 500 at Darlington Raceway. It is Earnhardt's first career win in a Ford.

April 25 Harry Gant scores his first win in his 107th career start in the Virginia National Band 500 at Martinsville.

May 2 Darrell Waltrip passes Benny Parsons on the final lap and wins the Winston 500 at Talladega. Parsons starts on the pole with a record 200.176-mph qualifying lap, the first time in history a lap of 200 mph is surpassed in official qualifications.

June 13 Tim Richmond posts his first career NASCAR Winston Cup Grand National victory in the 400-kilometer race at Riverside International Raceway.

August 1 Darrell Waltrip becomes the first driver to win the Talladega 500 twice. Entering the race, 13 different drivers had won the 13 previous runnings of the midsummer classic.

October 17 Darrell Waltrip wins the Old Dominion 500 at Martinsville and takes the championship points lead. Bobby Allison suffers an engine failure for the second straight race and trails Waltrip by 37 points in the title chase.

November 21 Tim Richmond wins the season finale at Riverside. Darrell Waltrip finishes third and captures his second straight NASCAR Winston Cup Grand National championship.

For the second straight season, Darrell Waltrip rallied past Bobby Allison to take the NASCAR Winston Cup Grand National championship. Waltrip lagged behind in the points race as Terry Labonte and Allison held the top spots most of the summer. With four races remaining, Waltrip seized the points lead with an October victory at Martinsville.

For Allison, it was another frustrating end as he finished second in points for the fifth time in his career. Waltrip's win gave team owner Junior Johnson his fifth NASCAR Winston Cup Grand National championship in the last seven years.

Waltrip won 12 races along the way to his 72-point victory. Allison won eight races. Labonte, who led the standings most of the season despite failing to record a victory, faded to third place, 278 points behind Waltrip.

1982 NASCAR Winston Cup GN Points Race

Rank	Driver	Points	Wins	Top 5	Top 10	Winnings
1	Darrell Waltrip	4489	12	17	20	$923,150.60
2	Bobby Allison	4417	8	14	20	$795,077.80
3	Terry Labonte	4211	0	17	21	$398,634.52
4	Harry Gant	3877	2	9	16	$337,581.24
5	Richard Petty	3814	0	9	16	$465,792.96
6	Dave Marcis	3666	1	2	14	$249,026.40
7	Buddy Arrington	3642	0	0	8	$178,158.12
8	Ron Bouchard	3545	0	3	15	$375,758.12
9	Ricky Rudd	3537	0	6	13	$217,139.49
10	Morgan Shepherd	3451	0	6	13	$166,029.84

Joe Millikan loses the grip on his #50 Pontiac in front of #71 Dave Marcis during the Feb. 21 Richmond 400 at the Richmond Fairgrounds Raceway. Both drivers continued in the race with Marcis scoring a popular upset triumph. Marcis was running sixth when Joe Ruttman's spin brought out a caution flag. With rain clouds hovering close to the ½-mile track, Marcis was the only driver on the lead lap to bypass a pit stop. He was in front when a cloudburst halted the race after 250 of the scheduled 400 laps.

◄ Harry Gant drove the #33 Skoal Bandit Buick to his first NASCAR Winston Cup Grand National win in the May 24 Virginia National Bank 500 at Martinsville Speedway. Gant had finished second 10 times before in 106 starts, but never first. After the race, the unassuming Taylorsville, N.C., driver said, "We just got some good luck today. You have to have luck to win a race." Gant was indeed lucky to avoid a major mishap as the race featured nine caution flags. Only 14 of the 31 cars that started were running at the finish.

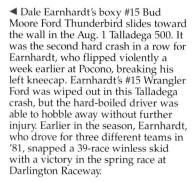

◄ Dale Earnhardt's boxy #15 Bud Moore Ford Thunderbird slides toward the wall in the Aug. 1 Talladega 500. It was the second hard crash in a row for Earnhardt, who flipped violently a week earlier at Pocono, breaking his left kneecap. Earnhardt's #15 Wrangler Ford was wiped out in this Talladega crash, but the hard-boiled driver was able to hobble away without further injury. Earlier in the season, Earnhardt, who drove for three different teams in '81, snapped a 39-race winless skid with a victory in the spring race at Darlington Raceway.

Number 11 Darrell Waltrip prepares to pass a smoking #88 Bobby Allison in the Oct. 3 Holly Farms 400 at North Wilkesboro Speedway. Allison's engine blew after 141 laps, and Waltrip went on to grab the lead in the championship points race with his 10th win of the year.

1983

February 20 Cale Yarborough wins his third Daytona 500 in a backup car. Yarborough topped the 200-mph barrier on his first qualifying lap but flipped and destroyed the car on the second lap.

March 13 Richard Petty ends a 43-race winless streak in the Carolina 500 at Rockingham. The triumph is the 196th of Petty's career.

May 15 Bobby Allison takes the points lead with a narrow victory over Darrell Waltrip in the Mason-Dixon 500 at Dover Downs International Speedway.

July 4 Buddy Baker scoots into the lead and wins the Firecracker 400 at Daytona when Terry Labonte runs out of fuel two laps from the finish. It is Baker's 19th career NASCAR Winston Cup Grand National win and his first with the Wood Brothers team.

July 16 Dale Earnhardt drives his Ford to victory in the Nashville 420 for his first short-track win in three years.

October 9 Richard Petty scores a controversial win in Charlotte's Miller High Life 500. It is Petty's 198th career NASCAR Winston Cup Grand National win, but his team is fined $35,000 and docked 104 points when a postrace inspection reveals illegal tires and an oversized engine. The incident becomes known as "Pettygate."

November 18 Richard Petty announces he will leave Petty Enterprises at the end of the 1983 season after 26 years.

November 20 Bill Elliott scores his first career win in the season finale at Riverside. Bobby Allison finishes ninth and wraps up his first NASCAR Winston Cup Grand National championship.

Bobby Allison held off a rally by Darrell Waltrip to secure his first NASCAR Winston Cup Grand National championship in 1983. Allison held a comfortable 170-point lead in late July, but Waltrip shaved the margin down to 41 points by September. Allison responded with three straight wins, and held off a last-ditch surge by Waltrip to win by 47 points.

The points lead changed hands six times among six drivers during the season. In the early weeks of the campaign, Cale Yarborough, Joe Ruttman, Harry Gant, Bill Elliott, and Neil Bonnett traded the lead. Allison took the lead at Dover in May and held it to the end of the season.

Allison and Waltrip each won six races. Elliott, making his first attempt at the championship, won one race and finished third in the final standings.

1983 NASCAR Winston Cup GN Points Race

Rank	Driver	Points	Wins	Top 5	Top 10	Winnings
1	Bobby Allison	4667	6	18	25	$883,009.40
2	Darrell Waltrip	4620	6	22	25	$865,184.47
3	Bill Elliott	4279	1	12	22	$514,029.22
4	Richard Petty	4042	3	9	21	$508,883.76
5	Terry Labonte	4004	1	11	20	$388,418.62
6	Neil Bonnett	3842	2	10	17	$453,585.09
7	Harry Gant	3790	1	10	16	$414,352.36
8	Dale Earnhardt	3732	2	9	14	$465,202.88
9	Ricky Rudd	3693	2	7	14	$275,399.14
10	Tim Richmond	3612	1	10	15	$262,138.14

▶ Bobby Allison wheels his #22 Buick around the lapped car of #08 Rick McCray in the Budweiser 400 at Riverside International Raceway on June 5. Although he finished 22nd in the Riverside road race, Allison maintained his NASCAR Winston Cup Grand National points lead. The Hueytown, Ala., veteran finally cashed in on NASCAR's most elusive prize in 1983 by winning the championship. Allison took the lead in the standings in May and held on the rest of the way, fending off Darrell Waltrip's late-season charge.

◀ Cale Yarborough's Chevrolet spirals through the air after bouncing off the wall during qualifications for the Feb. 20 Daytona 500. Yarborough was the first driver to officially top the 200-mph barrier at Daytona, piercing the timing lights at 200.550 mph. On his second qualifying lap, he lost control and demolished his car in this spectacular spill. Yarborough turned in the quickest time on pole day, but the car was withdrawn from the 500, and he lost the pole position and the record.

Dale Earnhardt drove Bud Moore's sleek #15 Wrangler Ford to a pair of victories in 1983, including the July 31 Talladega 500. Earnhardt placed eighth in the final NASCAR Winston Cup Grand National points standings as 13 DNFs prevented him from challenging for the championship. Earnhardt drove for Moore for two seasons, then reunited with Richard Childress in '84.

◀ Bill Elliott ran the full schedule for the first time in 1983, and performed well. Driving Harry Melling's #9 Ford Thunderbird, Elliott scored his first NASCAR Winston Cup Grand National win in the season finale at Riverside. The Dawsonville, Ga., driver also finished an impressive third in the final championship points standings on the strength of 22 top-10 finishes in 30 starts.

1984

February 19 Cale Yarborough wins his fourth Daytona 500.

April 29 Geoff Bodine scores his first career NASCAR Winston Cup Grand National win in Martinsville's Sovran Bank 500. The triumph also gives team owner Rick Hendrick his first NASCAR win in the team's eighth career start.

May 6 Cale Yarborough wins Talladega's Winston 500. It is the most competitive race in NASCAR history. Thirteen drivers swap the lead a record 75 times.

May 12 Neil Bonnett finishes first, but Darrell Waltrip is declared the winner of the controversial Nashville 420. Waltrip leads as the caution flag comes out with two laps to go. Although the field is given the yellow flag, Bonnett continues to race and passes Waltrip. NASCAR reverses the decision the following day.

May 20 Richard Petty drives his Mike Curb-owned Pontiac to victory in the Budweiser 500 at Dover for his 199th career NASCAR Winston Cup Grand National triumph.

June 10 Bill Elliott posts his first win on a superspeedway by taking the Miller 400 at Michigan International Speedway.

July 4 With President Ronald Reagan in attendance on the nation's birthday, Richard Petty wheels his Pontiac to victory in the Pepsi Firecracker 400 at Daytona. It is Petty's 200th NASCAR Winston Cup Grand National victory, a milestone that will likely live in NASCAR's record books forever.

August 25 Terry Labonte wins the Busch 500 at Bristol International Raceway and takes the lead in the championship points race.

November 11 Dale Earnhardt wins the Atlanta Journal 500. Terry Schoonover, in his second career NASCAR Winston Cup Grand National start, is fatally injured in a single-car crash.

November 18 Geoff Bodine wins the season finale at Riverside International Raceway. Terry Labonte finishes third and wins the 1984 NASCAR Winston Cup Grand National championship.

Pole-sitter Cale Yarborough jumps out to an early lead at the start of the Feb. 19 Daytona 500. Yarborough was in the hunt all day, playing a game of patience until the final lap. Perched on Darrell Waltrip's rear bumper for 38 laps, Yarborough motored past his rival in the final mile. It was the sixth time Yarborough won with a last-lap pass.

Ricky Rudd pushes his #15 Ford past #3 Dale Earnhardt in the Feb. 26 Miller High Life 400 at Richmond Fairgrounds Raceway. Rudd won the race in his second start with the Bud Moore team. Earnhardt left Bud Moore's team for the Richard Childress operation in 1984, taking the Wrangler sponsorship with him. A fine relationship with Moore prompted Wrangler to sponsor cars for two different teams.

Darrell Waltrip powers his #11 Budweiser Chevrolet under teammate #12 Neil Bonnett en route to an impressive win in the April 1 Valleydale 500 at Bristol International Speedway. Waltrip's victory gave team owner Junior Johnson his eighth straight win on the paved oval. Bonnett struggled most of the way and finished a disappointing 11th. Bonnett failed to win in 1984, but posted seven top-five and 14 top-ten finishes, and placed eighth in championship points.

Terry Labonte overtook Dale Earnhardt with 10 races to go and held off a late charge by Harry Gant to win the 1984 NASCAR Winston Cup Grand National championship. Labonte moved into the lead with a victory at Bristol in August.

Gant, who trailed by 131 points in mid August, pulled to within 42 points of Labonte in the season's closing weeks. Labonte ran third in the season finale on the Riverside, Calif., road course to seal his first title by 65 points over Gant.

Labonte won two races, one short-track event and one on a road course. He became the first driver since 1973 to win the NASCAR Winston Cup Grand National championship without posting a superspeedway victory.

1984 NASCAR Winston Cup GN Points Race

Rank	Driver	Points	Wins	Top 5	Top 10	Winnings
1	Terry Labonte	4508	2	17	24	$767,715.94
2	Harry Gant	4443	3	15	23	$673,059.48
3	Bill Elliott	4377	3	13	24	$680,343.82
4	Dale Earnhardt	4265	2	12	22	$634,670.18
5	Darrell Waltrip	4230	7	13	20	$731,022.54
6	Bobby Allison	4094	2	13	20	$641,048.88
7	Ricky Rudd	3918	1	7	16	$497,778.24
8	Neil Bonnett	3802	0	7	14	$282,532.58
9	Geoff Bodine	3734	3	7	14	$413,747.26
10	Richard Petty	3643	2	5	13	$257,931.94

Number 28 Cale Yarborough runs just ahead of #43 Richard Petty and #12 Neil Bonnett in the May 6 Winston 500 at the Alabama International Motor Speedway. The 188-lap contest around Talladega's massive 2.66-mile tri-oval featured the most official lead changes in the history of NASCAR Winston Cup Grand National racing. Thirteen drivers swapped the lead 75 times in the race, with Yarborough pulling off the last lead change when he passed Harry Gant on the final lap for the win.

◀▼ Richard Petty races mere inches ahead of Cale Yarborough (below) back to the yellow flag in the final three laps of the July 4 Firecracker 400 at Daytona International Speedway. Doug Heveron's spin brought out the caution flag and both Petty and Yarborough were aware that whoever got back to the caution flag first would win the race. Petty prevailed by the width of a bumper to score his much-awaited 200th career NASCAR Winston Cup Grand National win. President Ronald Reagan (left) witnessed the milestone from the broadcast booth. Motor Racing Network's Ned Jarrett (shown next to the President) interviewed Reagan on MRN's radio broadcast of the race. It marked the first time a sitting President attended a NASCAR Winston Cup Grand National event.

Terry Labonte drove Billy Hagan's #44 Piedmont Airlines Chevrolet to the 1984 NASCAR Winston Cup Grand National championship. Labonte won a short-track event at Bristol and prevailed on Riverside's road course along the way to the title. Labonte became the first NASCAR champion to win the title without a superspeedway victory since '73.

Harry Gant guns his #33 Chevrolet across the finish line to win the Sept. 16 Delaware 500 at Dover Downs International Speedway. Trevor Boys, in the #48 Chevrolet, posted a 10th-place finish, nine laps behind Gant's fleet Chevy. Gant put on a late-season charge and challenged Terry Labonte for the championship. Gant placed second in the final tally, 65 points behind.

1985

February 17 Bill Elliott dominates Daytona's Speedweeks. He leads 136 of the 200 laps to win the Daytona 500, takes the pole at more than 205 mph, and nearly laps the field in the Twin 125-mile qualifier.

March 17 Driving with a broken leg, Bill Elliott wins Atlanta's Coca-Cola 500. Elliott wins two of the first four races, but ranks fifth in points.

May 5 Bill Elliott rallies from a five-mile deficit without the aid of a caution flag to win Talladega's Winston 500.

May 25, 26 Darrell Waltrip wins the inaugural The Winston NASCAR all-star race at Charlotte Motor Speedway. Waltrip wins the World 600 the next day, earning $290,733 for the weekend.

September 1 Bill Elliott grabs his 10th win of the season and pockets the inaugural offering of the Winston Million $1 million bonus in Darlington's Southern 500. Elliott leads the championship chase by 206 points.

September 29 Harry Gant wins the Holly Farms 400 at North Wilkesboro Speedway as Darrell Waltrip takes the points lead. Bill Elliott finishes out of the top 10 for the fourth straight race.

November 3 Bill Elliott wins the Atlanta Journal 500 for his 11th superspeedway victory of the season. Elliott tops David Pearson's 1973 record of 10 superspeedway wins in a season.

November 17 Ricky Rudd wins the season finale at Riverside as Darrell Waltrip finishes seventh and wraps up his third championship. Bill Elliott experiences transmission problems early, erasing his title hopes.

The NASCAR Winston Cup Grand National points system came under fire in 1985 as Bill Elliott, who won a record 11 super-speedway races, was blown away in the points race by three-time winner Darrell Waltrip.

Waltrip, who won his third title, also questioned the points system. "There's not enough incentive for winning the race," said Waltrip. "This year I was the beneficiary of the points system. I've been on the other end of it, too. I will be the first to admit that with the year Bill had, he deserved to be the champion."

Elliott led virtually every category, but lost the championship to Waltrip by 101 points—the biggest margin of victory since 1978.

Elliott squandered a 206-point lead in the final two months of the season. Waltrip took a commanding lead by finishing 13th at North Wilkesboro in September. He was never threatened again.

1985 NASCAR Winston Cup GN Points Race

Rank	Driver	Points	Wins	Top 5	Top 10	Winnings
1	Darrell Waltrip	4292	3	18	21	$1,318,374.60
2	Bill Elliott	4191	11	16	18	$2,433,186.30
3	Harry Gant	4033	3	14	19	$804,286.48
4	Neil Bonnett	3902	2	11	18	$530,144.64
5	Geoff Bodine	3862	0	10	14	$565,867.82
6	Ricky Rudd	3857	1	13	19	$512,440.98
7	Terry Labonte	3683	1	8	17	$694,509.16
8	Dale Earnhardt	3561	4	10	16	$546,595.32
9	Kyle Petty	3528	0	7	12	$296,366.40
10	Lake Speed	3507	0	2	14	$300,325.50

Lake Speed spins his #75 Pontiac at Bristol during the April 6 Valleydale 500. Speed recovered to finish seventh. Number 3 Dale Earnhardt avoided the crash and won the race despite a power-steering failure. Speed, who leaped from go-kart racing directly into NASCAR Winston Cup competition in 1980, led the points standings briefly in the '85 campaign. The Jackson, Miss., driver eventually finished 10th in the championship race with 14 top-10 finishes in 28 starts.

Smoke erupts from the #9 Coors Ford of Bill Elliott in the May 5 Winston 500 at Talladega. Elliott was holding a solid lead when a broken oil fitting required him to limp into the pits for repairs. Elliott returned to the track running 26th, 2.03 seconds from going two laps down. At that point, Elliott began one of the most memorable comebacks in NASCAR history. Without the aid of a caution flag, he rallied from the five-mile deficit, grabbed the lead 97 laps later, and scored his fourth win of the season.

Darrell Waltrip beams from Charlotte's victory lane after a big win in the May 26 Coca-Cola 600. Waltrip won back-to-back races on Saturday and Sunday, including the first The Winston all-star race. Waltrip also moved into contention for the NASCAR Winston Cup Grand National championship with his first win of the year.

Ricky Rudd powers his #15 Bud Moore Ford around turn nine on his way to victory in the Winston Western 500 at Riverside International Raceway on Nov. 17. Title contender Darrell Waltrip, leading Bill Elliott by 20 points entering the race, wrapped up the championship with a seventh-place finish. Elliott's title hopes were dashed by transmission problems early in the race.

1986

January Following an announcement in late 1985, NASCAR changes the names of its premier stock car racing series and its second-ranked division. The official titles of NASCAR's two leading stock car racing series become NASCAR Winston Cup and NASCAR Busch Grand National.

February 23 Kyle Petty posts his first career NASCAR Winston Cup victory in the Miller High Life 400 at Richmond Fairgrounds Raceway.

April 6 Rusty Wallace leads the final 101 laps at Bristol to score his first career NASCAR Winston Cup win.

May 4 Bobby Allison fends off Dale Earnhardt in the Winston 500 at Talladega. Allison ends a two-year drought with the victory.

June 15 Bill Elliott outruns Harry Gant to win the Miller American 400 at Michigan. Gant makes a miraculous comeback from serious injuries, including a bruised heart, suffered in a crash a week earlier at Pocono. The race is billed as Richard Petty's 1000th career start, but it is actually his 999th career NASCAR Winston Cup race.

July 27 Bobby Hillin, Jr., a 22-year-old Texan, wins the Talladega 500, becoming the third youngest driver ever to win a NASCAR Winston Cup race.

August 10 The NASCAR Winston Cup Series makes its first visit to Watkins Glen since 1965, and Tim Richmond wins the 219-mile event.

November 16 Tim Richmond wins his seventh race of the season at Riverside, Calif. Dale Earnhardt finishes second and captures his second NASCAR Winston Cup championship.

▶ Number 3 Dale Earnhardt and #25 Tim Richmond battle side-by-side in the Oct. 5 Oakwood Homes 500 at Charlotte Motor Speedway. Earnhardt rallied from a two-lap deficit early in the event. Two cut tires dropped him four miles off the pace, but with the aid of a rash of caution flags, he was able to scramble back onto the lead lap in just 20 laps. Once back in contention, Earnhardt easily disposed of the field, lapping all rivals except runner-up Harry Gant. The win gave Earnhardt a comfortable 159-point lead in the title chase with just three races to go.

Dale Earnhardt grabbed his second NASCAR Winston Cup championship in 1986, finishing a comfortable 288 points ahead of runner-up Darrell Waltrip.

Earnhardt claimed the points lead in early May with a runner-up finish in Talladega's Winston 500. The determined Richard Childress Chevrolet driver never let anybody challenge his lead for the remainder of the season.

Tim Richmond compiled the biggest numbers during the season, winning seven races and eight poles. But Richmond's slow start to the season made it impossible for him to overtake Earnhardt. Waltrip won three races and edged Richmond for second place by only six points.

1986 NASCAR Winston Cup Points Race

Rank	Driver	Points	Wins	Top 5	Top 10	Winnings
1	Dale Earnhardt	4468	5	15	23	$1,768,879.80
2	Darrell Waltrip	4180	3	21	22	$1,099,734.90
3	Tim Richmond	4174	7	13	17	$973,220.92
4	Bill Elliott	3844	2	8	16	$1,049,141.92
5	Ricky Rudd	3823	2	11	17	$671,547.74
6	Rusty Wallace	3762	2	4	16	$557,353.94
7	Bobby Allison	3698	1	6	15	$503,094.96
8	Geoff Bodine	3678	2	10	15	$795,110.96
9	Bobby Hillin, Jr.	3546	1	4	14	$448,451.46
10	Kyle Petty	3537	1	4	14	$403,241.98

Neil Bonnett's #12 Chevrolet dives down to the apron as Joe Ruttman's #26 Buick darts toward the wall in the Feb. 16 Daytona 500. A broken wheel on Bonnett's car triggered the pileup. No drivers were injured. Numerous crashes brought out 120 miles of caution flags, depleting the field. Geoff Bodine won unchallenged after Dale Earnhardt, who was running second, ran out of gas with three laps to go.

Joe Ruttman's #26 Buick is knocked sideways after a tap from #3 Dale Earnhardt during the middle stages of the April 20 First Union 400 at North Wilkesboro Speedway. Ruttman was in contention for the win until the mishap, but he recovered to finish fifth. Earnhardt went on to outrun Ricky Rudd by two car lengths for the win, and from victory lane, made a public apology for spinning Ruttman.

◀ Alan Kulwicki drives his #35 Quincy's Steak House Ford at Richmond en route to a 15th-place finish. Kulwicki's freshman season was quite remarkable. He bought the car from team owner Bill Terry in spring and tackled the NASCAR Winston Cup tour with only one car. Kulwicki managed to log four top-10 finishes. For his determined efforts with a short-handed crew and a single-car operation, Kulwicki was voted 1986 Rookie of the Year.

1987

January 8 Tim Richmond announces he will miss the first part of the 1987 NASCAR Winston Cup season with an illness he says is "double pneumonia." Benny Parsons will replace Richmond until he can return.

February 15 Geoff Bodine runs out of fuel with three laps to go, allowing Bill Elliott to score his second Daytona 500 win. Benny Parsons finishes second as a replacement for Tim Richmond.

April 12 Dale Earnhardt bangs Sterling Marlin out of the lead near the midway point and speeds to victory in the Valleydale 500 at Bristol. Richard Petty finishes a close second.

May 3 Bill Elliott wins the pole for the Winston 500 at Talladega with a record run of 212.809 mph. Rookie Davey Allison wins the race in his 14th career NASCAR Winston Cup start. The event is marred by a scary crash when Bobby Allison sails into the catch fence.

June 14 Still seriously ill, Tim Richmond makes his first start of the season and wins the Miller High Life 500 at Pocono. The nature of Richmond's illness hasn't been revealed, but he is suffering from the AIDS virus.

August 16 Bill Elliott wins the Champion Spark Plug 400 at Michigan International Speedway. Tim Richmond, driving in his final NASCAR Winston Cup event, finishes 29th.

September 27 Darrell Waltrip barges through Dale Earnhardt and Terry Labonte on the final lap to score his first win with Hendrick Motorsports in the wild Goody's 500 at Martinsville Speedway. Labonte and Earnhardt spin in the third turn as Waltrip shoots the gap to score the win.

October 25 Bill Elliott wins the AC Delco 500 at Rockingham as Dale Earnhardt clinches his third NASCAR Winston Cup championship. Earnhardt finishes second and has a 515-point lead with two races left in the season.

November 22 Bill Elliott leads 162 of the 328 laps at Atlanta and wins the season finale. Newly crowned NASCAR champion Dale Earnhardt finishes second.

Bill Elliott won the pole for the Feb. 15 Daytona 500 with a record speed of 210.364 mph. His time trial came in an era before NASCAR mandated carburetor restrictor plates for the ultrafast speedways in Daytona and Talladega. In May, Elliott qualified at an all-time record 212.809 mph at Talladega. That mark will likely live in the record books forever because NASCAR officials take measures to ensure the 200-mph barrier will never be topped again.

Tim Richmond, the flashy NASCAR star afflicted with the AIDS virus, made his return to competitive racing in the May 17 The Winston all-star race. The Ashland, Ohio, driver finished third behind Dale Earnhardt and Terry Labonte. Richmond returned in June and immediately posted back-to-back victories at Pocono and Riverside. He competed in eight races over the next nine weeks before his failing health forced him to sit out for the remainder of the year. Richmond never got back into a race car and eventually passed away on Aug. 13, 1989.

The May 17, 1987, all-star race at Charlotte Motor Speedway still ranks as one of the series' most memorable races. The race has been unofficially christened "The Pass in the Grass," though no such pass was made. After Dale Earnhardt caused Bill Elliott and Geoff Bodine to crash a few laps earlier, Earnhardt led Elliott by a narrow margin late in the race. Elliott faked to the high side and swept down low. Earnhardt blocked both moves, but fenders made contact. Earnhardt angled across the racing surface and into the grass. Miraculously, he came back onto the track still in the lead. Elliott made one final attempt to pass on the high side. Again, Earnhardt blocked the move, nearly forcing Elliott into the wall. Elliott blew a tire and fell off the pace two laps later, placing 14th. Earnhardt sped to victory. After the race, Elliott weaved his Ford through traffic and ran into the rear bumper of Earnhardt's Chevrolet. "Earnhardt turned left into me and tried to push me into the grass," Elliott said. "Then he tried to run me into the wall. It's pretty obvious what he did."

Dale Earnhardt blasted out of the starting blocks by winning six of the first eight races in 1987 and coasted to his third championship. By September, Earnhardt had built up a hefty 608-point lead.

On the strength of 11 victories in his 29 starts, Earnhardt finished 489 points in front of runner-up Bill Elliott, who won six races. Earnhardt finished out of the top five in only eight races. The championship was never in doubt past April.

Elliott led the points standings after the first two races, but Earnhardt charged into the lead with a victory at Richmond on March 8. By the sixth race of the year, Earnhardt held a lead of more than 100 points. He clinched the championship after the 27th race of the season at Rockingham.

1987 NASCAR Winston Cup Points Race

Rank	Driver	Points	Wins	Top 5	Top 10	Winnings
1	Dale Earnhardt	4696	11	21	24	$2,069,243
2	Bill Elliott	4207	6	16	20	$1,599,210
3	Terry Labonte	4007	1	13	20	$805,054
4	Darrell Waltrip	3911	1	6	16	$511,768
5	Rusty Wallace	3818	2	9	16	$690,652
6	Ricky Rudd	3742	2	10	13	$653,508
7	Kyle Petty	3737	1	6	14	$544,437
8	Richard Petty	3708	0	9	13	$445,227
9	Bobby Allison	3530	1	4	13	$515,894
10	Ken Schrader	3405	0	1	10	$375,918

1988

February 14 Bobby and Davey Allison finish first and second in the Daytona 500. Richard Petty survives a wild tumble. NASCAR's "tire wars" begin as ten teams use Hoosier tires at Daytona.

March 6 Neil Bonnett wins the Goodwrench 500 at Rockingham's North Carolina Motor Speedway. The first four finishers are running Hoosier tires.

March 20 Lake Speed speeds to his first NASCAR Winston Cup triumph in Darlington Raceway's TranSouth 500.

April 10 Bill Elliott overcomes a late spinout and rallies past Geoff Bodine to score his first career short-track win in the Valleydale 500 at Bristol.

May 1 Phil Parsons posts his first career NASCAR Winston Cup victory in Talladega's Winston 500. It is Parsons' 111th start.

June 12 Rusty Wallace wins the Budweiser 400 at Riverside International Raceway. It is the final NASCAR Winston Cup race staged at the venerable Southern California road course.

June 19 Geoff Bodine drives to victory after Bobby Allison is critically injured in an opening-lap crash in Pocono's Miller High Life 500. Allison's Buick suffers a flat tire and spins, then is hit in the driver's door by Jocko Maggiacomo.

July 31 Ken Schrader wins Talladega's DieHard 500. The race is Buddy Baker's last, as he is forced to retire when a blood clot is discovered in his brain.

August 27 Dale Earnhardt holds off Bill Elliott to win the Busch 500 at Bristol. Elliott takes a 16-point lead over Rusty Wallace in the championship chase.

November 6 Alan Kulwicki posts his first career NASCAR Winston Cup win at Phoenix International Raceway. It is the first NASCAR Winston Cup event on the one-mile track.

November 20 Bill Elliott's 11th-place finish seals his first NASCAR Winston Cup championship as Rusty Wallace wins the season finale at Atlanta. For Cale Yarborough and Benny Parsons, it is the last race of their careers.

Bobby Allison's #12 Buick crosses the finish line two car lengths ahead of runner-up Davey Allison's #28 Ford at the conclusion of the Daytona 500. The 1-2 finish by father and son was the first in NASCAR history since Lee and Richard Petty ran 1-2 in a race a Heidelberg, Penn., on July 10, 1960. It was the 85th and final victory of the elder Allison's storied career.

Richard Petty's spectacular crash on the 106th lap of the Feb. 14 Daytona 500 spewed parts all over the frontstretch at Daytona International Speedway. Petty brushed bumpers with Phil Barkdoll, then was hit by A.J. Foyt. Petty's Pontiac went airborne and tumbled for a couple hundred yards before being hit by Brett Bodine. The King was shaken up, but not seriously injured in the incident.

Bill Elliott's #9 Ford spins wildly after a tap from Geoff Bodine knocked him out of the lead in the waning laps of the April 10 Valleydale 500 at Bristol International Raceway. The incident occurred with nine laps remaining. Elliott made a quick trip to the pits to replace the flat-spotted tires, and resumed the chase. It took Elliott only three laps to run down Bodine and pass him for the lead. Elliott went on to notch the first short-track victory of his NASCAR Winston Cup career.

Ricky Rudd guns his #26 Buick to the low side of #3 Dale Earnhardt in the Oct. 16 Holly Farms 400 at North Wilkesboro Speedway. Rudd and Earnhardt engaged in a bumping feud during the race. Rudd bumped Earnhardt out of the groove to take the lead on the 459th lap. Earnhardt retaliated and knocked Rudd into a spin one lap later. Both drivers were disciplined by NASCAR after the race. Rusty Wallace won the race after a bumping incident of his own with Geoff Bodine.

Bill Elliott overcame challenges by Rusty Wallace and Dale Earnhardt to win the 1988 NASCAR Winston Cup championship. After leading the standings from June until late August, Wallace stumbled in September and was 124 points behind with five races remaining.

Wallace won four of the final five races, but Elliott performed well enough in those events to wrap up his first title. He finished 24 points ahead of Wallace. Earnhardt led the standings from March through early June, but fell off the pace in the second half of the season and finished third.

For Elliott, it was sweet redemption for his bitter defeat in the 1985 NASCAR Winston Cup title chase.

1988 NASCAR Winston Cup Points Race

Rank	Driver	Points	Wins	Top 5	Top 10	Winnings
1	Bill Elliott	4488	6	15	22	$1,554,639
2	Rusty Wallace	4464	6	19	23	$1,411,567
3	Dale Earnhardt	4256	3	13	19	$1,214,089
4	Terry Labonte	4007	1	11	18	$950,781
5	Ken Schrader	3858	1	4	17	$631,544
6	Geoff Bodine	3799	1	10	16	$570,643
7	Darrell Waltrip	3764	2	10	14	$731,659
8	Davey Allison	3631	2	12	16	$844,532
9	Phil Parsons	3630	1	6	15	$532,043
10	Sterling Marlin	3621	0	6	13	$521,464

1989

February 19 In his 17th Daytona 500 start, Darrell Waltrip prevails in an economy run. Waltrip runs the final 132.5 miles without a pit stop and coasts across the finish line. Most of the field runs on Hoosier tires as Goodyear pulls out of the race due to safety concerns with its new radial tire.

April 2 Harry Gant ends a 90-race winless drought in Darlington's TranSouth 500. It is Gant's 10th career NASCAR Winston Cup victory.

April 16 Dale Earnhardt wins the First Union 400 at North Wilkesboro Speedway as the new Goodyear radial tire makes its NASCAR Winston Cup debut.

May 8 Bob Newton, president of Hoosier Tire Co., announces his company will withdraw from NASCAR competition following the 1989 season. Newton's 18-employee Indiana-based company began making tires for NASCAR Winston Cup cars in '88. Hoosier stood toe-to-toe with Goodyear for two seasons, and registered more than a dozen victories.

July 30 By pocketing $47,965 for his second-place finish in the Talladega 500, Darrell Waltrip becomes NASCAR's first $10-million winner.

October 8 Ken Schrader wins the All Pro Auto Parts 500 at Charlotte as Rusty Wallace takes the points lead with an eighth-place finish. A broken crankshaft on the 13th lap relegates Dale Earnhardt to a last-place finish and causes him to lose the points lead.

October 22 Mark Martin survives a rash of caution flags and notches his first career NASCAR Winston Cup win in the AC Delco 500 at Rockingham. Championship contenders Rusty Wallace and Dale Earnhardt tangle midway through the race, causing major damage to Earnhardt's Chevrolet. Wallace now has a 109-point lead over Earnhardt in the standings.

November 19 Dale Earnhardt wins the season-ending Atlanta Journal 500 as Rusty Wallace wraps up his first NASCAR Winston Cup title with a 15th-place finish. Wallace nips Earnhardt by 12 points in the final tally.

Darrell Waltrip drove his #17 Hendrick Motorsports/Tide Chevrolet into the lead four laps from the finish and went on to win the Feb. 19 Daytona 500. Waltrip, who was making his 17th start in The Great American Race, rode across the finish line with a near-empty fuel tank. Hendrick Motorsports cars finished first and second, with Waltrip beating Ken Schrader by 7.64 seconds.

Harry Gant throttles his #33 Oldsmobile under #5 Geoff Bodine in the late stages of the April 2 TranSouth 500. Gant ended a 90-race drought with a win. His most recent victory had come at North Wilkesboro in 1985. "The Bandit is back," said a cheerful Gant in victory lane. "I was confident before the race that we had the car to beat."

Ken Schrader tags the wall with his #25 Chevrolet in the early laps of the April 9 Valleydale 500 at Bristol International Raceway. Schrader fell on hard times after his fine showing in Daytona's Speedweeks. The Bristol crash was the third in his last five races. He would recover to finish fifth in the finals points standings.

Rusty Wallace overtook Dale Earnhardt with five races to go to win the 1989 NASCAR Winston Cup championship.

Wallace and Earnhardt engaged in a hard-fought battle during the season. While racing side by side at Rockingham in the 27th race of the 29-race campaign, Wallace slid into Earnhardt, forcing him into a spin. Earnhardt left Rockingham trailing by 109 points, but he staged a furious rally in the final two events.

Needing only to finish 18th or better in the season finale at Atlanta, Rusty nursed his Pontiac to a 15th-place finish as Earnhardt dominated the race. Wallace squeaked out a narrow 12-point decision over Earnhardt to take his first title.

Wallace won six times during his championship season, while Earnhardt took five victories. Mark Martin, who scored his first career win at Rockingham, finished third in points.

1989 NASCAR Winston Cup Points Race

Rank	Driver	Points	Wins	Top 5	Top 10	Winnings
1	Rusty Wallace	4176	6	13	20	$2,237,950
2	Dale Earnhardt	4164	5	14	19	$1,432,230
3	Mark Martin	4053	1	14	18	$1,016,850
4	Darrell Waltrip	3971	6	14	18	$1,312,479
5	Ken Schrader	3876	1	10	14	$1,037,941
6	Bill Elliott	3774	3	8	14	$849,370
7	Harry Gant	3610	1	9	14	$639,792
8	Ricky Rudd	3608	1	7	15	$533,624
9	Geoff Bodine	3600	1	9	11	$619,494
10	Terry Labonte	3569	2	9	11	$703,806

Rusty Wallace keeps his #27 Pontiac ahead of #3 Dale Earnhardt in the opening laps of the April 17 First Union 400. Wallace qualified on the pole, but had conventional bias-ply Goodyears on his car. Earnhardt's Richard Childress team mounted the new radial tires on his #3 Chevy, which proved better on long runs. Earnhardt went on to win the race, while Wallace ran a distant ninth.

◄ Davey Allison took the lead in the final six laps and motored his #28 Robert Yates Racing/ Havoline Ford to victory in the July 1 Pepsi 400 at Daytona. Allison held off underdog hopefuls Morgan Shepherd and Phil Parsons to score his second win of the year. A series of crashes eliminated 13 cars from the race.

The Hendrick Motorsports crew pushes Darrell Waltrip's #17 Chevrolet Lumina toward victory lane after the May 28 Coca-Cola 600 at Charlotte Motor Speedway. Waltrip was in the new Lumina that Chevrolet introduced in the spring of '89 as a '90 model. The car took the place of the highly successful Monte Carlo model starting with the May 7 Winston 500 at Talladega.

▲ Ricky Rudd attempted to duck under Dale Earnhardt's #3 Goodwrench Chevy in the first turn of the final lap in the Oct. 15 Holly Farms 400 at North Wilkesboro Speedway. As Rudd pulled his #26 Quaker State Buick down low, Earnhardt swept down to block the move. With Rudd already having established his position, the two cars collided, and both spun into the wall. Geoff Bodine seized on the opportunity and drove the #5 Levi Garrett Chevrolet to victory, leading only the final lap. Rudd and Earnhardt recovered from the spin and finished ninth and 10th, respectively.

Rusty Wallace and Dale Earnhardt staged one of the best championship races in NASCAR Winston Cup history. Wallace took the points lead from Earnhardt on Oct. 8 and led by 78 points entering the final race at Atlanta. Wallace needed to finish within 19 positions of Earnhardt in the Nov. 19 Atlanta Journal 500 to claim the title. Earnhardt won the race, but Wallace overcame several minor problems to place 15th and claim the championship. Wallace and the Blue Max Racing team also overcame internal strife in '89. Wallace filed a lawsuit in July to get out of the remaining year of his contract, but had agreed to stay one more year by the end of the season.

Chapter Six:
NASCAR Goes Big Time

THE 1990s ARRIVED with NASCAR's stock car racing wheels churning progressively forward. Several motivated, energetic, youthful drivers were pressing the seasoned veterans for membership in the elite of NASCAR Winston Cup racing.

The 32nd annual running of the Daytona 500 kicked off the 1990s with its usual flair. Dale Earnhardt was sharply focused on ending the Daytona 500 void that had plagued him throughout his career. Earnhardt motored away from all rivals, leading for 155 of the 200 laps. No driver passed Earnhardt under green flag conditions for the entire race. However, while leading in the final lap, Earnhardt ran over a piece of shrapnel on the backstretch and punctured a tire, leaving unheralded Derrike Cope with an upset victory.

Throughout the 1990 NASCAR Winston Cup campaign, Earnhardt and Mark Martin battled ferociously for the title. Martin gained the upper hand toward the end of the season, and was on the doorstep of NASCAR's championship. But Earnhardt didn't flinch in the heat of battle, taking command with an overwhelming victory at Phoenix in November. The Intimidator cruised to a third-place finish in the season finale at Atlanta and sewed up his fourth title by 26 points over a discouraged Martin.

Earnhardt added another championship to his sparkling portfolio in 1991, taking the points lead in early May and never giving up the top spot. As Earnhardt galloped to an easy championship run, 51-year-old Harry Gant was drawing the most national attention. During the month of September, the mild-mannered Gant went undefeated in NASCAR Winston Cup competition and won a couple of NASCAR Busch Grand National races for good measure.

The 1992 NASCAR Winston Cup season was most memorable, but was tainted by the unfortunate loss of NASCAR founder Bill France. On the morning of June 7, William Henry Getty France died in his sleep in Ormond Beach, Fla. He was 82. France, who founded NASCAR in 1948 and guided the sport into the progressive modern age, had been in declining health for eight years.

The 1992 championship chase was one of the closest in years. It featured an array of challengers. Alan Kulwicki stayed in the hunt during most of the season. Kulwicki was one of the new breed to hit the NASCAR trail in the late 1980s. A self-styled loner who left Greenfield, Wis., in '86 to tackle the NASCAR Winston Cup Series, Kulwicki set up his own skeleton racing operation with little more than passion and a far-

fetched dream to carry him to stock car racing's highest level.

An accomplished short-track racer with a degree in engineering, Kulwicki methodically approached obstacles that loomed in his path. Calm and devoid of flair, Kulwicki possessed a burning desire and a work ethic that were unsurpassed. Against overwhelming and perhaps impossible odds, Kulwicki took on the giants of the sport with his homegrown, lightly regarded team.

Kulwicki was able to win the 1986 Rookie of the Year award while using an arsenal of just two cars. Most teams had more than a dozen finely groomed machines at their disposal. Kulwicki attracted the attention of several top-ranked team owners, including Junior Johnson. On at least two occasions, Johnson offered Kulwicki a ride with his established and well-funded team. Kulwicki politely turned down the offers. His decision jolted nearly everyone in the sport. "Junior's offer was a helluva opportunity," said Kulwicki. "People will think I'm crazy for not accepting the offer."

Kulwicki managed to keep the leaders within sight during the first half of the 1992 title chase. Bill Elliott, who joined the Junior Johnson team, shot out of the starting blocks and won four of the first five races. Elliott had things well in hand going into late September. At that point, the wheels came off the Elliott-Johnson chariot. Uncharacteristic mechanical problems and unforeseen gremlins erased the comfortable cushion and invited five other drivers to battle for top honors in the season finale at Atlanta. The wrap-up at Atlanta had many story lines, ranging from the tight points race, to the final hurrah of King Richard Petty, to the maiden voyage into NASCAR Winston Cup racing by youngster Jeff Gordon.

In late 1991, Petty announced the '92 NASCAR Winston Cup season would be his 35th and final one. Petty would call it his "Fan Appreciation Tour." "It's not a farewell tour or anything like that," said the adored King. "Heck, I ain't going nowhere. This will be our way of telling the fans how much we appreciate their support over the last 34 years."

While NASCAR and Atlanta Motor Speedway promoters were preparing for a snazzy send-off for Petty, the championship contenders were geared up for the epic 500-mile battle. Title contenders Davey Allison, Mark Martin, and Kyle Petty all fell victim to problems and bowed out of the championship chase. In the end, Elliott motored to victory while Kulwicki took second. Kulwicki prevailed by the narrowest margin in championship history, a mere 10 points. Credit the lone wolf

Kulwicki, whose team carefully calculated the number of laps he needed to lead to clinch the lap-leader bonus. Kulwicki led a single lap more than Elliott, which was the difference in winning the championship and finishing second.

The 1993 NASCAR Winston Cup season was more tragic than any in nearly 30 years. Kulwicki perished in a private plane crash on April 1, and Davey Allison died due to injuries suffered in a July 13 helicopter crash at Talladega. Two of NASCAR's brightest young stars were gone, leaving a void for years to come.

Rusty Wallace hit stride in 1993, winning 10 races including five of the last eight. But he was no match for the consistent Earnhardt, who took his sixth NASCAR Winston Cup championship and his fifth in the last eight years. Earnhardt stepped into Richard Petty's shadows, only one title away from the seven Petty won during his career.

By 1994, Jeff Gordon, a 21-year-old starry-eyed youngster, had become a polished and skillful driver. Gordon was flashy and spectacular as a rookie, but he missed earning a trip to victory circle. While Gordon was getting acquainted with NASCAR Winston Cup racing in '94, Dale Earnhardt and Rusty Wallace were engaged in their customary battle for the championship. Wallace won twice as many races as Earnhardt, eight to four, but was no match in the points race. Earnhardt ran away with the championship, finishing 444 points ahead of Mark Martin. For Earnhardt, the joys of his title season were tempered by the death of close friend Neil Bonnett, who lost his life in a practice crash at Daytona.

Trackside attendance for NASCAR races was figuratively going through the roof by the end of 1994. Bolstered by the addition of the Brickyard 400 at Indianapolis Motor Speedway, NASCAR Winston Cup races drew 4,896,000 spectators for the 31 events, an increase of more than one million over '93. Many track owners and promoters were forced to add grandstands to accommodate public demand. Television ratings were also showing a significant increase.

While the sport was experiencing tremendous growth, Earnhardt's prowess remained at its peak in 1995. Earnhardt clearly ruled the NASCAR Winston Cup roost in the early '90s, but he was starting to get company at the top in the form of Jeff Gordon. A blend of bravery, computerized reflexes, and infallible judgment aided Gordon's ascent to NASCAR's elite. Gordon won three of the first six races in '95 and was poised to make a run at his first NASCAR Winston Cup title.

The crafty and wise Earnhardt and the new golden boy Gordon traded the point lead in the early weeks. Gordon assumed command and bolted ahead by 309 points in late September. Only a case of late-season jitters by Gordon and a relentless rally by Earnhardt made the race close. Earnhardt sliced the deficit mightily over the last six races and came within a whisker of recording his eighth title. Gordon prevailed by a mere 34 points in only his third full season.

In 1996, NASCAR expanded to New York City, establishing an office devoted to further developing and servicing corporate marketing and sponsorship relations. As NASCAR was going full speed ahead off the track, Jeff Gordon was grabbing the headlines on the track. He enjoyed a fine year in '96, winning 10 races. Terry Labonte, a revitalized warrior who joined the Hendrick Motorsports operation in '94, won twice and somehow squeezed Gordon off the championship throne. Labonte prevailed by 39 points.

Gordon began the 1997 season with a victory in the Daytona 500, leading a 1-2-3 sweep for Hendrick Motorsports machinery. It represented the first step of a two-year onslaught by Gordon. With his image and skills buffed to a high gloss, Gordon clearly became the most accomplished star on the NASCAR Winston Cup trail. Gordon won 10 races in '97 and bagged his second championship.

The 1998 season was the 50th anniversary for NASCAR, and a promotional bonanza was already in high gear by the time Daytona's Speedweeks rolled around in February. Dale Earnhardt whisked away two decades of frustration by winning the Daytona 500 in his 20th attempt. Earnhardt kept his black Chevy ahead of the pack for most of the race, leading for 107 laps. Several challengers made repeated attempts to get by, but even with drafting help, no one was able to deny Earnhardt. The Daytona 500 was Earnhardt's only win of the season, and he wound up eighth in the final points standings. Gordon took his third NASCAR title on the strength of 13 victories.

The decade of the 1990s closed with Dale Jarrett securing his first NASCAR Winston Cup championship after a season-long battle with Bobby Labonte and Mark Martin. A new fleet of youthful talent had made their way to the NASCAR scene, with Tony Stewart leading the way. Stewart won three races in his freshman campaign, the most wins by a rookie since Dick Hutcherson posted the all-time record of nine victories in his 1965 rookie campaign.

As NASCAR prepared for the new millennium, the television ratings on the major networks and cable channels were at an all-time high. The sport had stepped into mainstream America in convincing fashion. NASCAR stock car racing had become the second most popular professional sport in America, ranking ahead of everything except the National Football League.

1990

February 18 Dale Earnhardt cuts a tire on the final lap, allowing for Derrike Cope to post his first NASCAR Winston Cup win in the Daytona 500.

February 25 Mark Martin finishes first at Richmond's Pontiac Excitement 400. Martin's Roush Racing Ford team is docked 46 points and crew chief Robin Pemberton is fined $40,000 when NASCAR officials find an unapproved carburetor spacer plate. Martin is allowed to keep the win.

March 4 Kyle Petty wins the GM Goodwrench 500 at North Carolina Motor Speedway and pockets $284,550. The total includes $220,400 in Unocal 76 money that goes to a driver who wins the pole and the race.

April 1 Dale Earnhardt drives to victory in the TranSouth 500 at Darlington, an event in which veteran Neil Bonnett is injured in a crash. Bonnett suffers a concussion and amnesia.

June 10 Rusty Wallace posts a win at Sears Point in Sonoma, Calif. It is Wallace's fifth win in his last seven starts on road courses.

July 7 A 24-car crash on the second lap depletes the Pepsi 400 field and Dale Earnhardt breezes to an easy win at Daytona International Speedway.

August 25 Ernie Irvan passes Dale Earnhardt in the final 50 miles and speeds to his first NASCAR Winston Cup victory in Bristol's Busch 500.

September 30 Mark Martin wins the Tyson Holly Farms 400 at North Wilkesboro Speedway. Rookie driver Rob Moroso finishes 21st. A few hours later, Moroso and another motorist are killed in a highway accident.

November 4 Dale Earnhardt dominates the 312-mile Checker 500 at Phoenix. Earnhardt takes the points lead as leading contender Mark Martin struggles to finish 10th.

November 18 Morgan Shepherd wins the season finale at Atlanta as Dale Earnhardt finishes third and captures his fourth NASCAR Winston Cup title by 26 points over Mark Martin.

Greg Sacks takes the #46 Chevrolet to the high side in a battle with #25 Ken Schrader in the 1990 Daytona Twin 125-miler. Sacks was driving one of the cars prepared by Hendrick Motorsports for the upcoming feature-length film *Days of Thunder*. To get authentic racing scenes from in-car cameras, NASCAR permitted a handful of the movie cars to run a few laps in the Twin 125-milers and the early laps of the Daytona 500. Despite the cooperative efforts of the sanctioning body, Hendrick Motorsports, and several expert consultants, *Days of Thunder* turned out to be another dreadful Hollywood film about NASCAR.

Number 3 Dale Earnhardt and #10 Derrike Cope race side by side in the Feb. 18 Daytona 500. Earnhardt clearly had the car to beat, leading for 155 of the 200 laps. He was seemingly on his way to victory when a tire blew in the final turn of the final lap, opening the door for Cope to steal his first NASCAR Winston Cup victory. It was also Cope's first career top-five finish.

Ricky Rudd's #5 Chevrolet lurches sideways as #42 Kyle Petty slaps the wall and #27 Rusty Wallace finds his line blocked in the April 1 TranSouth 500 at Darlington. All three got back into the race after repairs. Petty finished 13th, Wallace 18th, and Rudd 24th. Another crash left Neil Bonnett with a concussion and amnesia, causing him to give up his ride in the Wood Brothers Ford to Dale Jarrett. Dale Earnhardt won the race.

Dale Earnhardt and Mark Martin battled down to the wire for the 1990 NASCAR Winston Cup championship. Earnhardt rallied in the season's final two races to claim his fourth title.

Martin led the standings from June through October, but Earnhardt won the season's second to last event in Phoenix and took third in the finale at Atlanta. He prevailed by 26 points over Martin.

Martin's loss was bitter for his Jack Roush team. Martin won at Richmond in February, but NASCAR officials discovered that his carburetor spacer was ½ inch too thick. The team was fined $40,000 and stripped of 46 points.

In October, Earnhardt left the pits at Charlotte with the left-side wheels unattached, and they flew off in the first turn. His pit crew ran out and secured the tires in place, ignoring a NASCAR official's command to stay away from the car. Rules state that a pit crew can't work on a car when it is on the racing surface. Earnhardt rejoined the race without losing much time. NASCAR didn't impose a penalty and Earnhardt went on to win the title.

1990 NASCAR Winston Cup Points Race

Rank	Driver	Points	Wins	Top 5	Top 10	Winnings
1	Dale Earnhardt	4430	9	18	23	$3,308,056
2	Mark Martin	4404	3	16	23	$1,302,958
3	Geoff Bodine	4017	3	11	19	$1,131,222
4	Bill Elliott	3999	1	12	16	$1,090,730
5	Morgan Shepherd	3689	1	7	16	$666,915
6	Rusty Wallace	3676	2	9	16	$954,129
7	Ricky Rudd	3601	1	8	15	$573,650
8	Alan Kulwicki	3599	1	5	13	$550,936
9	Ernie Irvan	3593	1	6	13	$535,280
10	Ken Schrader	3572	0	7	14	$769,934

Davey Allison keeps his #28 Ford just ahead of #6 Mark Martin in a frantic last-lap duel in the Valleydale Meats 500 at Bristol Motor Speedway. The two cars crossed the finish line in a near dead heat with Allison prevailing by a margin of no more than eight inches. Before promoters at Bristol laid down the concrete surface in 1993, the asphalt track afforded quite a bit of side-by-side action. Allison's victory over Martin was the closest in Bristol history.

Brett Bodine wheels his #26 Buick down pit road after winning the April 22 First Union 400 at North Wilkesboro Speedway. For Bodine, it was his first NASCAR Winston Cup victory. He was credited with leading the final 83 laps and finished less than one second in front of runner-up Darrell Waltrip.

◄ Number 27 Rusty Wallace leads #26 Brett Bodine, #21 Morgan Shepherd, and the rest of a hungry pack off Pocono's flat third turn during the June 17 Miller Genuine Draft 500. Harry Gant, pictured at the rear of this shot, stormed through the field, passed Wallace with 12 laps to go, and scored the win. Gant's victory ended a personal 14-month winless skid and made him the oldest driver to win a NASCAR Winston Cup race at the age of 50 years, 158 days.

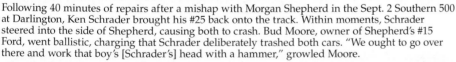

Following 40 minutes of repairs after a mishap with Morgan Shepherd in the Sept. 2 Southern 500 at Darlington, Ken Schrader brought his #25 back onto the track. Within moments, Schrader steered into the side of Shepherd, causing both to crash. Bud Moore, owner of Shepherd's #15 Ford, went ballistic, charging that Schrader deliberately trashed both cars. "We ought to go over there and work that boy's [Schrader's] head with a hammer," growled Moore.

Dale Earnhardt finished third in the 1990 season finale at Atlanta Motor Speedway, enabling him to wrap up the NASCAR Winston Cup championship by a narrow 26-point margin over Mark Martin. Earnhardt won nine races during the season and led 2438 laps, while Martin won three times and led 451 laps. Despite the lopsided numbers, Earnhardt had to rally in the championship chase, taking command in the next-to-last race of the season.

◄ Davey Allison salutes the crowd with a wave as he crosses the finish line to win the Oct. 7 Mello Yello 500 at Charlotte Motor Speedway. Allison muscled his way around Michael Waltrip with 12 laps to go and drove to a 2.59-second victory over runner-up Morgan Shepherd. It was Allison's eighth career NASCAR Winston Cup win.

1991

February 19 Ernie Irvan surges past Dale Earnhardt with six laps to go and scores an upset win in the Daytona 500. Earnhardt spins out with two laps remaining and takes out contenders Davey Allison and Kyle Petty.

April 21 Ending a 19-month victory drought, Darrell Waltrip outruns Dale Earnhardt to win the First Union 400 at North Wilkesboro Speedway.

May 6 Harry Gant finishes the Winston 500 at Talladega on fumes and coasts across the finish line ahead of runner-up Darrell Waltrip. Kyle Petty breaks his leg in a crash, knocking him out of action for three months.

July 6 Bill Elliott posts a resounding triumph in the Pepsi 400 at Daytona. Darrell Waltrip survives a wicked tumble down the backstretch.

August 11 Ernie Irvan wins the 218.52-mile race at Watkins Glen, a tragic affair that takes the life of veteran campaigner J.D. McDuffie.

August 18 Dale Jarrett noses out Davey Allison in a photo finish to win his first NASCAR Winston Cup event in the Champion Spark Plug 400. Jarrett edges Allison by 10 inches for the closest finish ever at Michigan International Speedway.

September 22 Harry Gant, the new "Mr. September," grabs his fourth consecutive win at Martinsville Speedway, overcoming a crash late in the race that knocks him a lap off the pace.

September 29 Harry Gant's late-race brake failure opens the door for Dale Earnhardt to win the Tyson Holly Farms 400 at North Wilkesboro. Gant was attempting to become the first driver to win five straight races since 1971.

November 3 Davey Allison wins the Pyroil 500 at Phoenix. Rusty, Mike, and Kenny Wallace all compete in the race, the first triple brother act in NASCAR's top series since 1961.

November 17 Mark Martin scores his first win of the season in the finale at Atlanta. Dale Earnhardt clinches his fifth NASCAR Winston Cup championship by simply starting the race.

After losing his sponsor Zerex, Alan Kulwicki faced the prospect of competing in 1991 without financial backing. For the Feb. 19 Daytona 500, Kulwicki sported Army sponsorship. In a display of unity during the Gulf War, Winston also lined up Marines, Coast Guard, Air Force, and Navy sponsorships for other drivers.

Ernie Irvan crosses under the checkered flag to win the Daytona 500 while running on the apron of Daytona International Speedway. Irvan snatched the lead from Dale Earnhardt with six laps remaining. Earnhardt crashed a lap later, resulting in the ninth caution period of the day. Irvan, who was low on fuel, tooled around the last couple of laps on the flat part of the track to conserve fuel. Sterling Marlin finished second in the #22 Ford Thunderbird.

Dale Jarrett's #21 Ford goes airborne after ramming the concrete retaining barrier in the April 7 TranSouth 500 at Darlington Raceway. The accident occurred on the 31st lap when rookie Bill Measell pinched #33 Harry Gant into a spin in the third turn. Gant darted into Jarrett, sending both on a harrowing 150-mph slide. Gant continued in the race, but Jarrett was sidelined.

Dale Earnhardt claimed his fifth NASCAR Winston Cup championship in 1991, winning four races and finishing comfortably ahead of runner-up Ricky Rudd.

Earnhardt assumed command of the points race in early May and never trailed again. Rudd managed to cling to second place in the points standings despite only one win and nine top-five finishes in the 29-race season.

Ageless Harry Gant provided the most fireworks during the season, winning four races in a row in September. The 51-year-old Gant won five races for the year and had six more top-five finishes than Rudd, but finished a distant fourth in the title race.

1991 NASCAR Winston Cup Points Race

Rank	Driver	Points	Wins	Top 5	Top 10	Winnings
1	Dale Earnhardt	4287	4	14	21	$2,416,685
2	Ricky Rudd	4092	1	9	17	$1,093,765
3	Davey Allison	4088	5	12	16	$1,712,924
4	Harry Gant	3985	5	15	17	$1,194,033
5	Ernie Irvan	3925	2	11	19	$1,079,017
6	Mark Martin	3914	1	14	17	$1,039,991
7	Sterling Marlin	3839	0	7	16	$633,690
8	Darrell Waltrip	3711	2	5	17	$604,854
9	Ken Schrader	3690	2	10	18	$772,434
10	Rusty Wallace	3582	2	9	14	$502,073

Mark Martin's #6 Ford flies down the backstretch of Talladega Super-speedway during a multicar collision on the 71st lap of the May 6 Winston 500. Prior to the advent of roof flaps, NASCAR Winston Cup machinery often went airborne on NASCAR's speediest tracks. Martin's car came down on all four wheels without flipping over. "I don't like getting upside down, and I was fixin' to," said Martin. "I closed my eyes when I went into the air."

Bill Elliott drove the blue #9 Coors Light Ford during the 1991 NASCAR Winston Cup season. In what was destined to be his final year driving for team owner Harry Melling, Elliott scored one win—at the July 6 Pepsi 400. Following the disappointing 1991 season, in which Elliott finished 11th in the final points standings, he left to join the Junior Johnson operation.

Number 90 Dick Brooks and #14 Coo Coo Marlin head into the first turn of the special Winston Legends event staged at Charlotte Motor Speedway on May 19. Winston invited 22 of NASCAR's legendary heroes to compete in a race on the flat ¼-mile speedway located between the frontstretch and pit road. The 30-lap event was the biggest hit of Charlotte's May Speedweek, and the retired racers put on one whale of a show. Elmo Langley came from the 16th starting position to win, passing Cale Yarborough on the final lap.

Ernie Irvan wheels his #4 Chevrolet through a series of turns at Watkins Glen en route to a big win in the Aug. 11 Budweiser at the Glen event in picturesque upstate New York. Irvan withstood a challenge from Mark Martin on the final lap to record his first road-course win. Irvan won twice for the Morgan-McClure team in 1991 and finished fifth in the final points standings.

▲ Richard Petty's #43 Pontiac lifts into the air after a collision with Chad Little in the early stages of the Sept. 29 Tyson Holly Farms 400 at North Wilkesboro Speedway. Both drivers recovered and continued in the event. Petty finished 19th, while Little brought his Ford home 21st.

◄ Dale Earnhardt nips at the heels of Harry Gant's fleet Oldsmobile in the closing stages of the Tyson Holly Farms 400. Gant was on his way to his fifth consecutive NASCAR Winston Cup victory when a malfunctioning O-ring caused a brake failure. The 10-cent part cost Gant $170,000 when Earnhardt passed him with nine laps to go and drove to victory.

1992

Davey Allison noses out Morgan Shepherd to win the Feb. 16 Daytona 500. After a 92nd-lap crash eliminated or crippled nine of the 16 cars that were on the lead lap, Allison and Shepherd emerged as prime contenders for the most sought after prize in NASCAR. Allison kept the #28 Robert Yates Racing/ Havoline Ford on the point for the final 30 laps and prevailed by a car length.

February 16 Davey Allison wins the Daytona 500. A 14-car crash eliminates nine of the 16 cars on the lead lap.

March 29 Bill Elliott breezes to his fourth consecutive NASCAR Winston Cup triumph at Darlington's TranSouth 500. Elliott has now won four of the first five NASCAR Winston Cup races, but doesn't lead the points standings.

May 3 Davey Allison wins Talladega's Winston 500, giving Ford a victory in all nine races thus far in the season.

May 24 Dale Earnhardt exceeds the 55-mph speed limit down pit road on his final stop, then outruns Ernie Irvan to win the Coca-Cola 600 at Charlotte. Other contenders howl in protest.

June 7 NASCAR founder William Henry Getty France passes away in an Ormond Beach, Fla., hospital at the age of 82. Ernie Irvan wins the race at Sears Point as flags fly at half-staff.

September 20 Ricky Rudd wins the Peak AntiFreeze 500 at Dover Downs International Speedway. Alan Kulwicki is eliminated in an early crash, leaving him 278 points behind in the title chase.

October 11 Mark Martin edges Alan Kulwicki to win Charlotte's Mello Yello 500 for his second win of the season. Points leader Bill Elliott departs with mechanical problems, leaving six drivers within 114 points of the leader.

November 1 Davey Allison snatches the lead in the NASCAR Winston Cup title chase with a win in the Pyroil 500 at Phoenix. Allison leads Alan Kulwicki by 30 points and Elliott by 40 points heading into the finale at Atlanta.

November 15 Bill Elliott scores a narrow victory in the season-ending Hooters 500 at Atlanta. Points leader Davey Allison is knocked out of the title hunt by an early crash. Elliott wins the race, but fails to pick up points on Alan Kulwicki, who clings to a narrow 10-point margin in the final standings. It is the closest title race in NASCAR history. Jeff Gordon makes his first NASCAR Winston Cup start as Richard Petty competes in his final event.

Rusty Wallace's #2 Pontiac gets sideways after a tap from #26 Brett Bodine midway through the March 29 TranSouth 500 at Darlington Raceway. Wallace avoided the retaining wall and recovered to finish 12th. Bodine was involved in two skirmishes in the race, but managed to bring his car home sixth. Geoff Bodine, in the #15 Ford, placed eighth.

Alan Kulwicki made a miraculous comeback to win the 1992 NASCAR Winston Cup championship by the closest margin in the history of the sport.

Kulwicki trailed Bill Elliott by 278 points with six races to go, but a flurry of late-season mechanical problems allowed several contenders back into the hunt. Elliott led the standings from August through October, but a mechanical failure at Phoenix gave the points lead to Davey Allison going into the season finale.

Allison, who took a 30-point lead into the season-ending Hooters 500 at Atlanta, was eliminated in an early crash, leaving Elliott and Kulwicki to battle it out for the title.

Elliott took the lead with 13 laps to go and won the race. But Kulwicki led the most laps and earned the five-point bonus that goes to the lap leader of each race. Kulwicki edged Elliott by 10 points. In the final analysis, maintaining the lead for a single caution-flag lap was all the difference.

1992 NASCAR Winston Cup Points Race

Rank	Driver	Points	Wins	Top 5	Top 10	Winnings
1	Alan Kulwicki	4078	2	11	17	$2,322,561
2	Bill Elliott	4068	5	14	17	$1,692,381
3	Davey Allison	4015	5	15	17	$1,955,628
4	Harry Gant	3955	2	10	15	$1,122,776
5	Kyle Petty	3945	2	8	17	$1,107,063
6	Mark Martin	3887	2	10	17	$1,000,571
7	Ricky Rudd	3735	1	9	18	$793,903
8	Terry Labonte	3674	0	4	16	$600,381
9	Darrell Waltrip	3659	3	10	13	$876,492
10	Sterling Marlin	3603	0	6	13	$649,048

Mark Martin guides his #6 Roush Racing/Valvoline Ford down the frontstretch on his way to victory in the April 26 Hanes 500 at Martinsville Speedway. Martin outran Sterling Marlin and outlasted a host of rivals to capture the 500-lap event on the flat, paper clip-shaped ½-mile oval. Broken axles foiled many contenders, including Dale Earnhardt, Alan Kulwicki, and Ernie Irvan. Most NASCAR teams were experimenting with cambered rear ends—slightly bending the rear axle inward to give the tires a wider "footprint." While cornering speeds were enhanced, the stress on the axles proved to be a noteworthy risk.

Davey Allison crashes into the concrete retaining barrier after tangling with Kyle Petty at the finish of the May 16 The Winston race at Charlotte Motor Speedway. The annual NASCAR all-star event was presented under the lights for the first time in 1992, attracting a sell-out crowd. Allison and Petty slapped quarter-panels in the dash to the checkered flag, causing Allison's Ford to dart out of control. Allison crossed the finish line first, albeit backward. The young Alabama driver was transported to the hospital with minor injuries. Victory lane ceremonies went on as scheduled, without the winning driver.

Darrell Waltrip's #17 Chevrolet hooks up in a tight battle with Ricky Rudd's #5 Tide Chevrolet in the Aug. 29 Bud 500 on Bristol International Raceway's new concrete surface. Raceway officials put down the low-maintenance concrete slats after the asphalt surface had peeled apart several times under the heavy NASCAR artillery. Waltrip made the decisive pass on Rudd with 33 laps to go. It was one Waltrip's three wins in 1992 behind the wheel of his self-owned Western Auto Chevy.

Alan Kulwicki scampers past Darrell Waltrip during the Nov. 1 Pyroil 500 at Phoenix International Raceway along the way to a fourth-place finish. Kulwicki made a miraculous comeback in the season's final weeks, rallying from a 278-point deficit in mid September to challenge for the NASCAR Winston Cup title. Following the Phoenix event, Kulwicki trailed points leader Davey Allison by 30 points heading into the season finale at Atlanta.

NASCAR icon Dale Earnhardt passes newcomer Jeff Gordon in the early laps of the Nov. 15 Hooters 500 at Atlanta Motor Speedway. Driving the #24 Hendrick Motorsports/DuPont Chevrolet, Gordon qualified 21st and placed 31st, falling victim to a crash after 164 laps. Earnhardt closed out a disappointing year by finishing 26th at Atlanta and 12th in the final points standings. It was the first time Earnhardt had finished out of the top ten in points since 1982. The Atlanta 500 also marked the end for a legend. Richard Petty crashed on the 95th lap and finished 35th in his 1184th and final race.

The 1992 season finale at Atlanta Motor Speedway became an instant classic. Davey Allison needed only to finish fifth to wrap up the NASCAR Winston Cup championship, but he crashed on lap 254 and finished 27th. That left Bill Elliott and Alan Kulwicki to duel for top honors in both the race and the title chase. Elliott drove his #11 Budweiser Ford to victory as Kulwicki finished second in the #7 Ford "Underbird." Kulwicki and crew chief Paul Andrews calculated the number of laps he needed to lead to take the five-point lap-leader bonus, and he nabbed it when he led the 310th lap. Kulwicki edged Elliott by 10 points for the title.

1993

February 14 Dale Jarrett passes Dale Earnhardt on the final lap to win the Daytona 500. Jarrett's last-lap heroics thwart Earnhardt's 15th bid for a win in NASCAR's most prestigious event.

March 28 Dale Earnhardt wins the TranSouth 500 at Darlington Raceway, ending a personal 10-month losing skid. Alan Kulwicki finishes sixth in what will be his final race.

April 1 Reigning NASCAR Winston Cup champion Alan Kulwicki perishes in a private plane crash en route to Bristol for the Food City 500. Rusty Wallace wins the race three days later and honors Kulwicki with a ceremonial opposite-direction "Polish victory lap."

May 2 Ernie Irvan wins Talladega's Winston 500. Rusty Wallace flips across the finish line after a tap from Dale Earnhardt. Wallace finishes sixth, but suffers multiple injuries.

May 30 Dale Earnhardt overcomes three penalties, one for rough driving, to win the Coca-Cola 600 at Charlotte Motor Speedway. Earnhardt takes a 129-point lead in the championship chase over Rusty Wallace, who races despite injuries suffered at Talladega.

July 11 Rusty Wallace wins the first NASCAR Winston Cup race staged at New Hampshire International Speedway. The next day, Davey Allison is gravely injured in a helicopter crash on the grounds of Talladega Superspeedway. Allison passes away the following morning.

July 25 Dale Earnhardt beats Ernie Irvan by an eyelash to win the DieHard 500 at Talladega. In one of the closest finishes on record, Earnhardt's margin of victory is a scant .005 second.

September 5 Mark Martin racks up his fourth straight victory with a win in the rain-delayed Mountain Dew Southern 500 at Darlington Raceway.

November 14 Rusty Wallace wins the season finale at Atlanta Motor Speedway. Despite winning 10 races, Wallace falls 80 points shy of winning the championship. Dale Earnhardt takes his sixth NASCAR Winston Cup title.

Pole-sitter #42 Kyle Petty and #18 Dale Jarrett lead the pack at the start of the Feb. 14 "Daytona 500 by STP" at Daytona International Speedway. Petty earned his seventh career pole and was in contention until a late crash put him out of the race. Jarrett went on to win the race, giving team owner Joe Gibbs his first career NASCAR Winston Cup victory.

Rusty Wallace's #2 Pontiac goes airborne in a horrific tumble down the backstretch on the 169th lap of the Daytona 500. Wallace was running in the lead pack when #30 Michael Waltrip and #98 Derrike Cope rubbed together. Cope spun and clipped the rear of Wallace's car, sending him into a series of rollovers. The veteran campaigner suffered only a cut chin in the spectacular mishap. Wallace credited his full-face helmet with preventing major head injuries.

Dale Earnhardt built a big points lead early in the season and cruised to his sixth NASCAR Winston Cup championship in 1993. Earnhardt took the points lead in mid May and held it for the rest of the 30-race campaign.

Rusty Wallace trailed by more than 300 points at one point during the season, but he strung together a flurry of wins and top-five finishes, and gradually worked his way back into contention. Wallace won five of the last eight races and finished 80 points behind Earnhardt.

Earnhardt won six races as Wallace took the checkered flag 10 times. Wallace had more top-five finishes than Earnhardt and an equal number of top-10 finishes, but couldn't overtake his rival in the points chase.

1993 NASCAR Winston Cup Points Race

Rank	Driver	Points	Wins	Top 5	Top 10	Winnings
1	Dale Earnhardt	4526	6	17	21	$3,353,789
2	Rusty Wallace	4446	10	19	21	$1,702,154
3	Mark Martin	4150	5	12	19	$1,657,662
4	Dale Jarrett	4000	1	13	18	$1,242,394
5	Kyle Petty	3860	1	9	15	$914,662
6	Ernie Irvan	3834	3	12	14	$1,400,468
7	Morgan Shepherd	3807	1	3	15	$782,523
8	Bill Elliott	3774	0	6	15	$955,859
9	Ken Schrader	3715	0	9	15	$952,748
10	Ricky Rudd	3644	1	9	14	$752,562

Dale Earnhardt zips his #3 Goodwrench Chevrolet past Mark Martin's #6 Valvoline Ford during the stretch duel in the March 28 TranSouth 500 at Darlington. Earnhardt led all but one of the final 149 laps and posted his 54th career NASCAR Winston Cup victory, which tied him with Lee Petty on the all-time win list. The victory ended a personal 10-month winless skid for the popular NASCAR hero.

Number 3 Dale Earnhardt and #2 Rusty Wallace hooked up in a crowd-pleasing duel in the April 25 Hanes 500 at Martinsville Speedway. Wallace clearly had the upper hand most of the day, leading 409 of the 500 laps. Earnhardt eventually fell victim to engine problems and failed to finish. Wallace rode home with an easy win, his fourth in the season's first eight races.

Rusty Wallace's Pontiac crosses the finish line airborne on the last lap of the May 2 Winston 500 at Talladega. Wallace and Dale Earnhardt were battling for fourth place when Earnhardt flicked Wallace's rear bumper. Air got under Wallace's car and he soared across the finish line in sixth place. Earnhardt finished third. Wallace suffered a broken wrist, a concussion, facial cuts, and a chipped tooth in the incident.

Neil Bonnett's #31 Richard Childress Racing Chevrolet lifts into the air during a frightening crash on the 132nd lap of the July 25 DieHard 500 at Talladega. Bonnett, making his first NASCAR Winston Cup start in 2½ years, slipped sideways while battling Ted Musgrave and Dick Trickle. Bonnett's car crashed into the protective catch fence along the main grandstands, but Bonnett escaped injury.

Bobby Labonte got off to a sluggish start in the #22 Bill Davis/Maxwell House Ford, but he was running well by midsummer. In Talladega's DieHard 500, Labonte was poised to make a run for his first victory, but he ran out of fuel on the final lap and coasted to a 15th-place finish.

Ernie Irvan assumed the driving chores for the Robert Yates #28 Ford in September. Irvan replaced the late Davey Allison, who had died due to injuries suffered in a private helicopter crash at Talladega in July. Irvan dominated the Oct. 10 Mello Yello 500 at Charlotte Motor Speedway, leading all but six of the 334 laps. After taking the checkered flag, Irvan gave a fitting tribute to his fallen comrade by touring the track in a reverse-lap salute.

Rusty Wallace racked up his 10th victory of the season in the Nov. 10 Hooters 500 at Atlanta Motor Speedway, and Dale Earnhardt clinched his sixth NASCAR Winston Cup Championship with a 10th-place finish. After the race, Wallace and Earnhardt carried flags bearing the numbers 28 and 7 to honor fallen heroes Davey Allison and Alan Kulwicki. The moving "Polish victory lap" tribute put an end to an exciting but tragic 1993 campaign.

1994

February 11 Veteran Neil Bonnett loses his life in a practice crash at Daytona International Speedway in preparation for the upcoming Daytona 500.

February 20 Sterling Marlin earns his first career NASCAR Winston Cup victory in the Daytona 500. Marlin's first triumph comes in his 279th start, the longest it has ever taken a driver to post his first win.

March 27 Dale Earnhardt wins the TranSouth 400 at Darlington. The victory is Earnhardt's ninth on the venerable Darlington track, one shy of David Pearson's all-time mark of 10 wins on the 1.366-mile oval.

May 29 Youthful Jeff Gordon hustles past Ricky Rudd with nine laps to go and goes on to win the Coca-Cola 600. It is the first career NASCAR Winston Cup win for the 22-year-old.

July 10 Ricky Rudd, in his first season as owner/driver, wins the Slick 50 300 at New Hampshire International Speedway. It is Rudd's 15th career victory, marking the 12th consecutive season he has won at least one race.

August 6 Sophomore Jeff Gordon holds off Brett Bodine to win the inaugural Brickyard 400 at Indianapolis Motor Speedway. More than 340,000 trackside spectators watch Gordon claim his second career victory.

August 21 Geoff Bodine dominates the Champion Spark Plug 400 at Michigan International Speedway. Ernie Irvan is critically injured in a practice crash the day before the race.

September 4 Bill Elliott ends a 52-race winless skid with a victory in Darlington's Mountain Dew Southern 500.

September 25 Rusty Wallace scores a one-car-length victory over Dale Earnhardt at Martinsville. Despite eight wins to Earnhardt's three, Wallace trails by 222 points and is effectively out of the championship hunt.

October 23 With a win in the AC Delco 500 at Rockingham, Dale Earnhardt locks up a record-tying seventh NASCAR Winston Cup championship.

Sterling Marlin outruns Ernie Irvan by two car lengths to win the Feb. 20 Daytona 500. Irvan won the 1991 Daytona 500 in the #4 Morgan-McClure/ Kodak Chevrolet and enjoyed a successful three-year run with the Virginia-based team. In late '93, Irvan left Larry McClure's team to join forces with Robert Yates' Ford team. Marlin drove the Kodak Chevrolet to his first career victory in The Great American Race. It was Marlin's 279th career start in 18 years of NASCAR Winston Cup competition.

As Dale Earnhardt and Mark Martin raced into the third turn on the 190th lap of the May 29 Coca-Cola 600 at Charlotte Motor Speedway, Martin's #6 Valvoline Ford spun into the high groove. With a pack of cars breathing down his neck, Martin found himself in the middle of a 14-car crash. Number 31 Ward Burton and #32 Dick Trickle were eliminated in the accident, but most of the other damaged cars continued in the event.

Entering the Aug. 21 race at Michigan, Ernie Irvan and Dale Earnhardt were locked in a tight battle for supremacy in the 1994 NASCAR Winston Cup championship race. However, Irvan suffered near-fatal injuries in a practice crash before the GM Goodwrench Dealers 400, leaving Earnhardt uncontested for the title.

Earnhardt finished 444 points ahead of runner-up Mark Martin to record his record-tying seventh championship. Irvan led the standings after 12 of the first 18 races but his unfortunate crash took him out of the chase.

Earnhardt won four races, while Martin won twice. Rusty Wallace was again the season's top winner with eight wins, but he finished a distant third in points.

1994 NASCAR Winston Cup Points Race

Rank	Driver	Points	Wins	Top 5	Top 10	Winnings
1	Dale Earnhardt	4694	4	20	25	$3,300,733
2	Mark Martin	4250	2	15	20	$1,628,906
3	Rusty Wallace	4207	8	17	20	$1,914,072
4	Ken Schrader	4060	0	9	18	$1,171,062
5	Ricky Rudd	4050	1	6	15	$1,044,441
6	Morgan Shepherd	4029	0	9	16	$1,089,038
7	Terry Labonte	3876	3	6	14	$1,125,921
8	Jeff Gordon	3776	2	7	14	$1,779,523
9	Darrell Waltrip	3688	0	4	13	$835,680
10	Bill Elliott	3617	1	6	12	$936,779

Jeff Gordon took the lead from Ricky Rudd 19 laps from the finish and sped to his first NASCAR Winston Cup victory in the 1994 Coca-Cola 600. On the final round of green-flag pit stops, virtually all of Gordon's challengers took on four tires and fuel. When Gordon pitted on lap 381, crew chief Ray Evernham ordered only a two-tire stop. The quick pit stop gave Gordon a lead that he never relinquished.

Geoff Bodine drove his self-owned #7 Ford to an overwhelming victory in the July 17 Miller Genuine Draft 500 at the triangular Pocono International Raceway. Shod with Hoosier tires, Bodine led 156 of the 200 laps. Hoosier Tire Co. made a brief return to NASCAR Winston Cup racing in 1994, but had difficulty signing top drivers. Bodine was the horse of the Hoosier-contracted teams, winning three races and five poles.

▼ Bobby Labonte's #22 Pontiac broke loose on the fifth lap of the Oct. 9 Mello Yello 500 at Charlotte Motor Speedway. Incredibly, the trailing pack of cars managed to miss Labonte's spinning, fire-engulfed car. Labonte bailed out unhurt, but his car was wiped out. Dale Jarrett won the race after failing to qualify for the previous race at North Wilkesboro.

Jimmy Spencer noses his McDonald's Ford ahead of Ernie Irvan a few feet before the finish line in the July 2 Pepsi 400 at Daytona International Speedway. For Spencer, it was his first career NASCAR Winston Cup victory. Spencer dogged Irvan's heels in the final 50 miles and nudged his way in front on the final lap. Irvan led for more than half the race, but Spencer refused to be denied as he gave team owner Junior Johnson his first win of the season.

Geoff Bodine's #7 Ford leads #4 Sterling Marlin and Jeff Gordon as they put a lap on #50 Mike Chase and #44 Bobby Hillin, Jr., in the Aug. 6 Brickyard 400 at Indianapolis Motor Speedway. Bodine led twice and was leading when he and younger brother Brett tangled on lap 100. Geoff spun out, opening the door for Gordon, who had lived in Indiana, to win the historic event.

Dale Earnhardt won his record-tying seventh NASCAR Winston Cup championship in 1994, a feat matched only by Richard Petty. Earnhardt wrapped up the title by winning the third-to-last race of the season at Rockingham. Six of Earnhardt's seven titles came with the Richard Childress-owned RCR Enterprises team; the other was with Rod Osterlund in 1980. Here, Petty joins Earnhardt at the postseason awards banquet in New York.

1995

February 5 NASCAR launches the Super Truck Series with an 80-lap race at Phoenix International Speedway. Mike Skinner becomes the series' first winner after qualifying 16th.

April 2 Jeff Gordon posts his third win in the first six races at Bristol's Food City 500. Gordon ranks only fourth in the points standings.

May 7 Dale Earnhardt records his first career win on a road course with a victory at Sears Point International Raceway. It is Earnhardt's 36th career start on a road course.

May 28 Bobby Labonte motors to his first career win in Charlotte's Coca-Cola 600. Terry Labonte finishes second, marking the first time brothers have finished 1-2 in a NASCAR Winston Cup race since 1971 when Bobby and Donnie Allison did it at Charlotte.

August 5 Dale Earnhardt wins the second annual Brickyard 400 at Indianapolis Motor Speedway.

August 26 Terry Labonte slides across the finish line just ahead of Dale Earnhardt to win the Goody's 500 at Bristol. Earnhardt slaps Labonte sideways in a bid to win. Labonte crashes into the concrete barrier just after taking the checkered flag.

September 17 Jeff Gordon takes a 309-point lead in the championship race with a win in Dover's MBNA 500.

October 1 Mark Martin wins the Tyson Holly Farms 400 at North Wilkesboro. Ernie Irvan, making his first start since his accident at Michigan in August 1994, finishes seventh.

October 22 Ward Burton scores his first NASCAR Winston Cup victory in the AC Delco 400 at Rockingham. Points leader Jeff Gordon finishes 20th, but still clings to a 162-point lead over Dale Earnhardt.

November 12 Dale Earnhardt wins the season-ending NAPA 500 at Atlanta as Jeff Gordon captures his first NASCAR Winston Cup title with a 32nd-place effort. Gordon holds off Earnhardt's furious rally to win the title by 34 points.

After running four exhibition races starting in July 1994, the NASCAR Super Truck Series made its official debut on Feb. 5, 1995, at Phoenix International Raceway. Mike Skinner won the series' inaugural race, and went on to claim the championship with eight wins and 17 top-five finishes in 20 starts. Skinner won $428,096 for his sterling season. Four pioneering off-road team owners—Dick Landfield, Jimmy Smith, Jim Venable, and Frank Vessels—convinced Bill France, Jr., in 1993 that trucks would be a popular racing attraction. "In only 18 months, this series has risen to a level that took the NASCAR Winston Cup Series 20 years to reach," noted France after the first season. The Super Truck series became the NASCAR Craftsman Truck tour in 1996.

Sterling Marlin guides his #4 Chevy out of the pits just ahead of #3 Dale Earnhardt in the Feb. 19 Daytona 500, while #25 Ken Schrader completes his pit stop. Marlin won to become only the third driver to take back-to-back Daytona 500s. The race marked the return to NASCAR for the Chevy Monte Carlo, which replaced the Lumina that ran from 1989 to '94.

Young Jeff Gordon took the points lead after the 16th race of the season at Loudon, N.H., in July and held off a gallant rally by Dale Earnhardt to win the 1995 NASCAR Winston Cup championship. The 24-year-old Gordon became the second-youngest winner of NASCAR's crown.

With six races remaining, Gordon led Earnhardt by 309 points. With a late-season charge, The Intimidator sliced the deficit each week. In the end, Earnhardt lost by only 34 points.

Gordon won seven races, while Earnhardt won five, including two of the final six. Daytona 500 winner Sterling Marlin finished third with three victories.

1995 NASCAR Winston Cup Points Race

Rank	Driver	Points	Wins	Top 5	Top 10	Winnings
1	Jeff Gordon	4614	7	17	23	$4,347,343
2	Dale Earnhardt	4580	5	19	23	$3,154,241
3	Sterling Marlin	4361	3	9	22	$2,253,502
4	Mark Martin	4320	4	13	22	$1,893,519
5	Rusty Wallace	4240	2	15	19	$1,642,837
6	Terry Labonte	4146	3	14	17	$1,558,659
7	Ted Musgrave	3949	0	7	13	$1,147,445
8	Bill Elliott	3746	0	4	11	$996,816
9	Ricky Rudd	3734	1	10	16	$1,337,703
10	Bobby Labonte	3718	3	7	14	$1,413,682

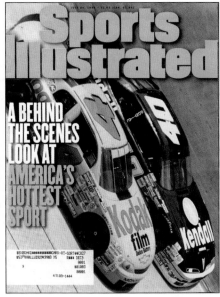

Terry Labonte's #5 Kellogg's Chevrolet leaps over the #21 Citgo Ford of Morgan Shepherd as #3 Dale Earnhardt gets crowded into the wall in a bone-jarring crash on the fifth lap of the April 23 Hanes 500 at Martinsville Speedway. Labonte was unable to get back into the race on the .526-mile oval, while Earnhardt and Shepherd eventually returned, finishing 29th and 31st, respectively. Rusty Wallace led 172 of the 356 laps to win the scheduled 500-lapper, which was delayed by rain and shortened by darkness.

The cover story of the July 24, 1995, *Sports Illustrated* put NASCAR Winston Cup racing on the map with America's other major sports—NFL football, Major League Baseball, NBA basketball, and NHL hockey. *SI* credited NASCAR for its down-home attitude.

▲ Jeff Gordon tapped teammate Ken Schrader's #25 Chevrolet into a wild flip in the July 23 DieHard 500 at Talladega Superspeedway. The incident occurred on the 139th lap and gobbled up nine other cars. Schrader was able to free himself from the mangled mess under his own power. Gordon, who led the most laps until the crash, went on to finish eighth. Sterling Marlin won the race after starting on the pole.

Number 3 Dale Earnhardt and #88 Ernie Irvan battle it out in the Oct. 29 Dura Lube 500 at Phoenix International Raceway. Irvan was the class of the field in his second start since his 1994 injuries, leading for 111 laps before engine failure put him out of the race. Earnhardt went on to finish third. Ricky Rudd won the race, making him the first driver in NASCAR history to win after starting 29th. The win kept Rudd's streak intact for winning at least one race every year since 1983.

Jeff Gordon drove the #24 Hendrick Motorsports Chevrolet to the NASCAR Winston Cup championship in 1995. The 24-year-old Gordon became the youngest winner of the NASCAR crown since 23-year-old Bill Rexford took the title in 1950. Gordon led virtually every category in '95, winning the most races (seven), the most poles (eight), leading the most races (29 of 31), and leading the most laps (2600). He edged Dale Earnhardt by 34 points.

1996

February 18 Dale Jarrett passes Dale Earnhardt with 24 laps remaining and scores his second win in the Daytona 500. Jarrett blocks Earnhardt's final-lap moves to post a .12-second victory.

April 14 Terry Labonte ties Richard Petty's streak of 513 consecutive NASCAR Winston Cup starts, capping a perfect weekend by winning the First Union 400 from the pole.

June 16 Jeff Gordon rolls to his fifth win of the season at Pocono. Dale Earnhardt finishes 32nd, but still leads the championship race by 52 points over Terry Labonte.

July 14 Ernie Irvan caps his amazing comeback from life-threatening injuries by winning the Jiffy Lube 300 at New Hampshire International Speedway.

July 28 Jeff Gordon surges past a thinned-out field to win the shortened DieHard 500 at Talladega for his sixth win of the season. Dale Earnhardt escapes with a broken sternum and a fractured collarbone after a 20-car crash.

September 29 Jeff Gordon racks up his 10th win of the year in the Tyson Holly Farms 400 at North Wilkesboro Speedway. It is the final event in the history of the ⅝-mile oval. New owners Bruton Smith and Bob Bahre will move the track's future race dates to Texas and New Hampshire, respectively.

October 6 Terry Labonte moves to within one point of NASCAR Winston Cup standings leader Jeff Gordon with a win at Charlotte. Gordon has won 10 races to Labonte's two, but the points race is the closest in NASCAR history.

October 27 Bobby Hamilton drives the Petty Enterprises Pontiac to victory in the Dura Lube 500 at Phoenix International Raceway. It is the first NASCAR Winston Cup victory for Petty Enterprises since 1983.

November 10 Bobby Labonte holds off Dale Jarrett to win the season finale at Atlanta, as his brother Terry finishes fifth and wraps up his second NASCAR Winston Cup championship. The elder Labonte finishes 37 points ahead of Jeff Gordon to nail down the title.

Dale Jarrett's #88 Quality Care Ford crosses the finish line two car lengths ahead of runner-up Dale Earnhardt to capture the 39th annual running of the celebrated Daytona 500 on Feb. 18. Jarrett pushed his mount to the front with 24 laps to go and deflected repeated efforts from runner-up Earnhardt to post his second win in NASCAR's most prestigious event. For Earnhardt, it was his third runner-up effort in the last three years.

In the late stages of the Feb. 25 Goodwrench 400 at Rockingham, Bobby Hamilton appeared to be a shoo-in for his first NASCAR Winston Cup victory, and the first for the Petty Enterprises team since 1983. Hamilton was pulling away from the field when a caution flag interrupted his bid for a convincing win. On the restart, Hamilton quickly dashed to the front, passing #3 Dale Earnhardt. But as Hamilton assumed command, Earnhardt flicked the quarter panel of Hamilton's Pontiac, sending it out of control and into the wall. Hamilton blew a tire and crashed two laps later as Earnhardt drove to a controversial victory.

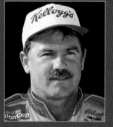

Hendrick Motorsports teammates Terry Labonte and Jeff Gordon battled for the 1996 NASCAR Winston Cup title, but consistency earned Labonte his second championship.

Labonte took the points lead with a third-place finish at Rockingham in late October. Top-five finishes in the final two events were enough to beat Gordon by 37 points.

Gordon won 10 races, while Labonte won twice. Both Chevrolet drivers had 21 top-five finishes and 24 top-10 efforts. Gordon led 2314 laps as Labonte led 973 laps. Gordon seemed to have a better year, but Labonte was able to come out on top of the points race thanks to fewer DNFs.

1996 NASCAR Winston Cup Points Race

Rank	Driver	Points	Wins	Top 5	Top 10	Winnings
1	Terry Labonte	4657	2	21	24	$4,030,648
2	Jeff Gordon	4620	10	21	24	$3,428,485
3	Dale Jarrett	4568	4	17	21	$2,985,418
4	Dale Earnhardt	4327	2	13	17	$2,285,926
5	Mark Martin	4278	0	14	23	$1,887,396
6	Ricky Rudd	3845	1	5	16	$1,503,025
7	Rusty Wallace	3717	5	8	18	$1,665,315
8	Sterling Marlin	3682	2	5	10	$1,588,425
9	Bobby Hamilton	3639	1	3	11	$1,151,235
10	Ernie Irvan	3632	2	12	16	$1,683,313

Bill Elliott's #94 Ford slides off the second turn in the 78th lap of the April 28 Winston Select 500 at Talladega Superspeedway. Elliott's Thunderbird lifted high into the air, soared down the backstretch, and crashed back down to the ground without turning over. Elliott suffered a broken leg in the incident, which sidelined him until July. Sterling Marlin led the final 22 laps to post his fifth career NASCAR Winston Cup victory

The speedy three-abreast formation often seen at Talladega can go awry in an instant. On the 130th lap of the Winston Select 500, one little twitch sent cars flying in all directions. Ricky Craven's #41 Chevrolet climbed over another car and sailed into the catch fence. Craven's car was ripped apart in the multicar accident, but the driver from Newburgh, Maine, climbed out with only bruises—proof that NASCAR machinery can protect a pilot in the most dire situations.

Ernie Irvan's #28 Ford hustles down the front chute at Michigan International Speedway, flanked by #24 Jeff Gordon and #88 Dale Jarrett, in the Aug. 18 GM Goodwrench Dealers 400. Jarrett racked up his fourth win of the NASCAR Winston Cup season. Irvan and Gordon recorded sterling efforts too, finishing fourth and fifth, respectively.

Rusty Wallace steers his #2 Roger Penske/Miller Ford under #9 Lake Speed in the Aug. 24 Goody's Headache Powder 500 at Bristol Motor Speedway. Wallace trounced the field and scored his fifth win of the '96 campaign. The race was the first since Bruton Smith took over management of the popular ½-mile concrete oval. Smith changed the name of the track from Bristol International Raceway to Bristol Motor Speedway.

Terry Labonte cuts a quick lap down Charlotte Motor Speedway's front chute in the Oct. 6 UAW-GM Quality Parts 500. Labonte entered the race trailing NASCAR Winston Cup standings leader Jeff Gordon by 111 points, but shaved that deficit down to a single point with a resounding triumph in the 500-miler. Gordon stumbled, finishing 31st, which put Labonte and Gordon in a virtual dead heat for the championship with three events remaining.

Ricky Rudd keeps his #10 Tide Ford just ahead of #88 Dale Jarrett in the Oct. 20 AC Delco 400 at Rockingham's North Carolina Motor Speedway. Rudd drove away from Jarrett in the final laps to record his first win of the season. The triumph marked the 14th consecutive year Rudd had won a NASCAR Winston Cup race, four years short of the all-time record of 18 set by Richard Petty from 1960 to '77. Terry Labonte took over the points lead with a third-place finish. Labonte finished third and fifth in the final two races to edge out Hendrick Motorsports teammate Jeff Gordon for the NASCAR Winston Cup championship.

1997

February 16 Jeff Gordon drives past Bill Elliott with six laps remaining and leads a 1-2-3 sweep for the Hendrick Motorsports team in the Daytona 500. Gordon, Terry Labonte, and Ricky Craven gang up on Elliott in the stretch drive and take the top three spots.

April 6 Jeff Burton racks up his first career NASCAR Winston Cup win as Texas Motor Speedway stages its inaugural race, the Interstate Batteries 500.

May 10 Mark Martin prevails in the nonstop Winston 500 at Talladega Superspeedway and holds off Dale Earnhardt to win in record time. Martin averages a staggering 188.354 mph. It is Martin's first win since 1995.

June 8 Jeff Gordon sprints to a narrow victory over Jeff Burton, registering his sixth triumph of the season in the Pocono 500 in Pennsylvania. With the win, Gordon ties winless Terry Labonte for the lead in the NASCAR Winston Cup points standings.

June 15 In a crowd-pleasing late-race spurt, Ernie Irvan drives to victory in the Miller 400 at Michigan International Speedway, claiming a win at the track that nearly took his life in August 1994.

June 22 Jeff Gordon wins the inaugural California 500 at California Speedway. Terry Labonte takes second, giving Hendrick Motorsports another 1-2 finish.

August 4 Owner/driver Ricky Rudd gambles on fuel mileage and it pays off with a $571,000 triumph in the Brickyard 400 at Indianapolis.

August 31 Jeff Gordon drives to victory in Darlington's Mountain Dew Southern 500, also claiming the Winston Million bonus. Gordon is the first driver to pocket the $1 million bonus since Bill Elliott won it in 1985.

November 16 Bobby Labonte wins the NAPA 500 at Atlanta Motor Speedway. Dale Jarrett finishes second but falls 14 points short of Jeff Gordon's point total in the NASCAR Winston Cup standings. Gordon finishes 17th, and becomes the youngest driver to capture two championships.

Dale Earnhardt's #3 Chevrolet begins a wild upside-down ride down the backstretch on the 189th lap of the Feb. 16 Daytona 500. Earnhardt had just been passed by Jeff Gordon for second place when his Goodwrench Chevy glanced off the wall. Dale Jarrett, Ernie Irvan, and Terry Labonte got stacked up behind Earnhardt in a chain reaction. Earnhardt's car tumbled over and landed on its wheels. While sitting in the ambulance awaiting the mandatory trip to the infield care center, Earnhardt noticed the wheels were still on the car. "I got out of the ambulance and asked the guy in my car to crank it. When it fired, I told him to give me my car back," Earnhardt said. The hardboiled pilot drove the remaining laps to salvage a 31st-place finish. "My chances of winning the Daytona 500 were over," said Earnhardt, "but I can still win an eighth Winston Cup championship."

A happy Jeff Gordon pumps his fists in celebration in Daytona's victory lane following his win in the 39th annual running of the Daytona 500 as CBS Sports reporter Mike Joy waits to interview the winner. At 25 years of age, Gordon became the youngest winner of the Daytona 500. Richard Petty, who was 26 when he won his first Daytona 500 in 1964, held the distinction for 33 years.

Mark Martin drove his #6 Valvoline/Roush Racing Ford to victory in the May 10 Winston 500 at Talladega Superspeedway. Martin started midpack, led the final 31 laps, and edged Dale Earnhardt at the finish. The race was rained out twice in April and held on a Saturday in May. Martin averaged 188.354 mph, a record for a 500-mile NASCAR Winston Cup event.

Jeff Gordon prevailed in a three-way showdown with Dale Jarrett and Mark Martin to win the 1997 NASCAR Winston Cup championship.

Gordon took the points lead with a September victory in Darlington's Mountain Dew Southern 500 and maintained the narrow advantage for the rest of the year. Gordon posted his second NASCAR Winston Cup championship by only 14 points over runner-up Jarrett. Martin was only 29 points behind in the closest three-way title chase in the history of NASCAR competition.

The points lead changed hands seven times among four drivers. Gordon led most of the season, but Jarrett, Martin, and Terry Labonte each led briefly.

Gordon racked up 10 wins during the season, while Jarrett won seven events and Martin grabbed four victories.

1997 NASCAR Winston Cup Points Race

Rank	Driver	Points	Wins	Top 5	Top 10	Winnings
1	Jeff Gordon	4710	10	22	23	$6,375,658
2	Dale Jarrett	4696	7	20	23	$3,240,542
3	Mark Martin	4681	4	16	24	$2,532,484
4	Jeff Burton	4285	3	13	18	$2,296,614
5	Dale Earnhardt	4216	0	7	16	$2,151,909
6	Terry Labonte	4177	1	8	20	$2,270,144
7	Bobby Labonte	4101	1	9	18	$2,217,999
8	Bill Elliott	3836	0	5	14	$1,607,827
9	Rusty Wallace	3598	1	8	12	$1,705,625
10	Ken Schrader	3576	0	2	8	$1,355,292

John Andretti's 100th career NASCAR Winston Cup start was a memorable one. Driving Cale Yarborough's #98 RCA Ford in the Pepsi 400 at Daytona, Andretti was in contention the entire race. By the 137th lap, Andretti had motored his way into the lead. He held off Terry Labonte, Sterling Marlin, and Dale Earnhardt to post his first career win. It was the first and only win for Yarborough as a team owner.

Dale Earnhardt drifts into the upper groove in the opening laps of the Aug. 31 Mountain Dew Southern 500 at Darlington as #1 Lance Hooper, #17 Darrell Waltrip, and #43 Bobby Hamilton steer clear. Earnhardt suffered a lapse of consciousness on the opening lap and grazed the wall. Two laps later, Earnhardt drove into the pits, where he was replaced by Mike Dillon, who took the car to a 30th-place finish. Earnhardt was examined by a team of doctors, but the cause of the blackout went unresolved. "We were told [by doctors] they found no medical reason he couldn't race," said a NASCAR spokesperson. "That was good enough for us." Earnhardt competed at Richmond six days later.

▼ Rusty Wallace holds the low line in his #2 Ford in a three-abreast battle with #28 Ernie Irvan and #24 Jeff Gordon in the Oct. 5 UAW-GM Quality 500 at Charlotte Motor Speedway. Gordon, who went on to finish fifth behind race winner Dale Jarrett, maintained a healthy 125-point lead over Mark Martin in the NASCAR Winston Cup championship chase. Wallace managed to finish 12th, while Irvan struggled and placed 18th.

▲ Terry Labonte crosses the finish line a ahead of #18 Bobby Labonte at the conclusion of the Oct. 12 DieHard 500 at Talladega Superspeedway. The Labonte brothers teamed up and whisked around leader Ken Schrader with two laps to go. "You have to have help to pass somebody in these restrictor plate races," said the winner. "I was glad to see Bobby behind me." Terry recorded the 11th win for Chevrolet in '97, but it was the first for anyone other than Jeff Gordon.

Jeff Gordon drove his #24 DuPont Chevrolet to the 1997 NASCAR Winston Cup championship. Gordon racked up his second consecutive 10-win season, edging Dale Jarrett by 14 points to secure his second NASCAR title. At the age of 26, Gordon became NASCAR's youngest two-time champion.

1998

February 15 With the Thunderbird no longer available, Ford introduces the Taurus for competition in NASCAR's 50th Anniversary season. Dale Earnhardt ends two decades of frustration at the Daytona 500. It is the 71st win of Earnhardt's career and it snaps a victory drought that dates to 1996.

March 1 Mark Martin wins the inaugural NASCAR Winston Cup event at Las Vegas Motor Speedway.

May 24 Jeff Gordon runs down Rusty Wallace with 10 laps to go and hustles to victory in the Coca-Cola 600 at Charlotte Motor Speedway. With the pass, Gordon denies Wallace a shot at the Winston No Bull 5 $1-million bonus. Gordon also takes the points lead.

June 21 Jeremy Mayfield holds off Jeff Gordon and Dale Jarrett in a stirring finish to bag his first career NASCAR Winston Cup win in the Pocono 500.

July 4 Forest fires in Florida force Daytona International Speedway officials to postpone the Pepsi 400. It is the first time the holiday classic has been postponed in the track's history.

September 6 Jeff Gordon bags his sixth victory in the last seven races and wins another Winston No Bull 5 $1-million bonus with a victory in the Pepsi Southern 500 at Darlington. Gordon pads his lead in the NASCAR Winston Cup standings to 199 points over Mark Martin.

September 27 Ricky Rudd wins the NAPA Autocare 500 at Martinsville, giving him a victory in 16 consecutive NASCAR Winston Cup seasons. Rudd's feat leaves him two years shy of the all-time mark of 18 set by Richard Petty.

October 17 For the first time, a race is staged under the lights at Daytona as Jeff Gordon wins the rescheduled Pepsi 400. Gordon wins for the 11th time in the season and is virtually assured of taking his third title.

November 8 Jeff Gordon bags the finale at Atlanta for his 13th win of the season. Gordon finishes 364 points ahead of runner-up Mark Martin in the final NASCAR Winston Cup standings.

Dale Earnhardt leads a pack of cars down the front chute as they approach the white flag of the Feb. 15 Daytona 500. Using the lapped car of #75 Rick Mast to prevent Jeremy Mayfield and Bobby Labonte from passing him, Earnhardt won the race back to the caution flag. The final lap was run under caution due to an accident involving John Andretti and Lake Speed. Earnhardt finally prevailed in NASCAR's crown-jewel event after 20 years of trying. He also halted a career-long 59-race winless streak that stretched back to the 1996 season.

After the conclusion of the 40th annual Daytona 500, which kicked off NASCAR's 50th Anniversary celebration, winner Dale Earnhardt was congratulated by a reception line that included crews of virtually every other team. "To see all those guys come out [on pit road] was pretty impressive," said Earnhardt, who led the final 61 laps in a dominating performance. Earnhardt earned $1,059,805 for the win.

Jeff Gordon moved past Jeremy Mayfield in late June to take the NASCAR Winston Cup points lead, and left all rivals to battle over the leftovers. Gordon motored to a 364-point win to capture his third championship during the NASCAR's 50th anniversary celebration.

Gordon won 13 races, tying a modern-era mark established by Richard Petty in 1975. Mark Martin finished a distant second to Gordon; it was his third runner-up finish.

The points lead changed hands five times among four drivers before Gordon set sail. Rusty Wallace, Dale Earnhardt, and Mayfield traded the lead before Gordon assumed command.

1998 NASCAR Winston Cup Points Race

Rank	Driver	Points	Wins	Top 5	Top 10	Winnings
1	Jeff Gordon	5328	13	26	28	$9,306,584
2	Mark Martin	4964	7	22	26	$4,309,006
3	Dale Jarrett	4619	3	19	22	$4,019,657
4	Rusty Wallace	4501	1	15	21	$2,667,889
5	Jeff Burton	4415	2	18	23	$2,626,987
6	Bobby Labonte	4180	2	11	18	$2,980,052
7	Jeremy Mayfield	4157	1	12	16	$2,332,034
8	Dale Earnhardt	3928	1	5	13	$2,990,749
9	Terry Labonte	3901	1	5	15	$2,054,163
10	Bobby Hamilton	3786	1	3	8	$2,089,566

Veteran Mark Martin drove his Roush Racing Ford to victory in the inaugural NASCAR Winston Cup event at Las Vegas Motor Speedway on March 1. Martin drove past Geoff Bodine with 23 laps remaining and banked $313,900 for winning the first annual Las Vegas 400. Along with the cash prize, Martin also had the privilege to share the victory lane celebration with a couple of Las Vegas lovelies.

Number 4 Bobby Hamilton battles with #43 John Andretti late in the April 20 Goody's 500 at Martinsville Speedway. Hamilton led 378 of the 500 laps and racked up his third career win in his first season driving for team owner Larry McClure. Andretti's bid was foiled when he ran out of fuel with six laps to go. The heartbreaking experience dropped Andretti from second to 18th place.

Jeff Gordon sails down the frontstretch at Indianapolis Motor Speedway en route to victory in the Aug. 1 Brickyard 400. Gordon started third, grabbed the lead on the 19th lap, and kept his #24 DuPont Chevrolet on the point for most of the race. He outran runner-up Mark Martin to become the first driver to win the Brickyard 400 twice and to claim the Winston No Bull 5 $1-million bonus.

Jeff Gordon swept both road-course events in 1998, prevailing at Sears Point in June and Watkins Glen in August. In the Aug. 9 The Bud At The Glen, Gordon overcame a slow pit stop, rallied from an 11-second deficit, and raced past leader Mike Skinner with four laps remaining. The victory gave Gordon an 82-point lead in the championship chase and put him in position to capture his third title in four years.

Dale Earnhardt runs three abreast with #4 Bobby Hamilton and #12 Jeremy Mayfield during the Oct. 11 Winston 500 at Talladega Superspeedway. Earnhardt suffered mechanical problems that relegated him to 32nd place. Hamilton finished 15th, while Mayfield placed fifth. Mayfield led the points standings in late spring, but a rash of problems dropped him to seventh in the final tally.

Daytona International Speedway's Pepsi 400, traditionally a mid-summer classic, was run in October. The event was postponed to Oct. 17 when wildfires swept through central Florida. The 400-miler was also the first race run under Daytona's new lights. Jeff Gordon won to take a 358-point lead, virtually assuring him of his third championship.

Sterling Marlin slides his #40 Chevrolet in front of #26 Johnny Benson, Jr., during the Nov. 1 AC Delco 400 at North Carolina Speedway. Marlin recovered and finished a credible 13th. Jeff Gordon continued his winning spree at Rockingham, scoring his 12th win of the season and clinching the 1998 NASCAR Winston Cup championship.

1999

February 14 Jeff Gordon staves off a charge by Dale Earnhardt to win his second Daytona 500.

March 21 Jeff Burton's crumpled Ford lies in a smoking heap on the front-stretch at Darlington Raceway as rain begins to fall, securing his victory in one of the zaniest finishes in NASCAR history. Burton is involved in a crash on lap 163, but manages to keep his car rolling until heavy rains halt the race.

May 30 Jeff Burton wins the Coca-Cola 600 at Lowe's Motor Speedway. Tony Stewart makes history, finishing ninth in the Indianapolis 500 and fourth in the NASCAR 600-miler on the same day.

June 13 Dale Jarrett wins the Kmart 400 at Michigan Speedway. The race is uninterrupted by a single caution flag. It is the first caution-free NASCAR Winston Cup event since 1997.

August 7 Dale Jarrett wins the Brickyard 400 at Indianapolis Motor Speedway and pockets $712,240 for his fourth win of the season. Jarrett's victory puts him 274 points ahead of Mark Martin in the championship chase.

September 11 Rookie Tony Stewart leads 333 of the 400 laps and dominates the Exide Batteries 400 at Richmond International Raceway. It is the first NASCAR Winston Cup win for the talented freshman driver.

October 17 Dale Earnhardt wins the Winston 500 at Talladega Superspeedway. It is Earnhardt's 74th career NASCAR Winston Cup triumph.

November 14 Tony Stewart breezes to an easy 5.2-second victory over Bobby Labonte in the first NASCAR Winston Cup event at Homestead-Miami Speedway. It is Stewart's third win of the season, the most victories for a rookie driver since 1965 when Dick Hutcherson won nine times.

November 21 Bobby Labonte comes from a provisional starting spot to win the season-ending NAPA 500 at Atlanta Motor Speedway. Dale Jarrett finishes second and wraps up his first NASCAR Winston Cup championship by a 201-point margin over Labonte.

After scrubbing fenders with teammate Kenny Irwin, Jr., Dale Jarrett's #88 Ford lurched out of control on the 135th lap of the Feb. 14 Daytona 500. The ensuing collision involved more than a dozen cars, sidelining six, including Jarrett. Irwin, Jr., driving Robert Yates' #28 Ford, went on to finish third—his best career effort in the NASCAR Winston Cup Series.

Number 24 Jeff Gordon battles #3 Dale Earnhardt and #99 Jeff Burton in the 41st Daytona 500. In the closing laps, the top 12 cars were separated by less than a half second. Gordon took a risky dive to the apron to swing past Rusty Wallace, nearly clipping Ricky Rudd, who was accelerating slowly after a pit stop. The daring move propelled Gordon into the lead, which he never gave up. Earnhardt took second.

John Andretti and The King, Richard Petty, enjoy the victory lane ceremonies following Andretti's come-from-behind win in the Goody's Body Pain 500 at Martinsville. Andretti spun his Petty Pontiac in the early laps, but battled back from a one-lap deficit. Andretti raced past Jeff Burton with four laps remaining to record the win. It was Andretti's second career NASCAR Winston Cup victory.

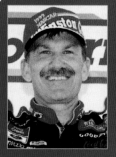

Dale Jarrett moved into the NASCAR Winston Cup points lead in May with a victory at Richmond and never looked back along the way to his first championship. Jarrett won four races during the 34-race campaign and finished a comfortable 201 points ahead of runner-up Bobby Labonte.

Jarrett became the second second-generation driver to reach the pinnacle of NASCAR Winston Cup stock car racing. He and his father Ned joined Lee and Richard Petty as the only father-son combinations to wear the championship crown.

Labonte won five races en route to the runner-up spot in the title chase. Two-time winner Mark Martin came in third.

Jarrett gave team owner Robert Yates his first career NASCAR Winston Cup championship.

1999 NASCAR Winston Cup Points Race

Rank	Driver	Points	Wins	Top 5	Top 10	Winnings
1	Dale Jarrett	5262	4	24	29	$6,649,596
2	Bobby Labonte	5061	5	23	26	$4,763,615
3	Mark Martin	4943	2	19	26	$3,509,744
4	Tony Stewart	4774	3	12	21	$3,190,149
5	Jeff Burton	4733	6	18	23	$5,725,399
6	Jeff Gordon	4620	7	18	21	$5,858,633
7	Dale Earnhardt	4492	3	7	21	$3,048,236
8	Rusty Wallace	4155	1	7	16	$2,454,050
9	Ward Burton	4062	0	6	16	$2,405,913
10	Mike Skinner	4003	0	5	14	$2,499,877

Dale Earnhardt leads his son Dale Earnhardt, Jr., in the May 30 Coca-Cola 600 at Lowe's Motor Speedway. The younger Earnhardt, a third-generation NASCAR driver, was making his first start in stock car racing's elite series. He performed well, qualifying eighth and finishing 16th. The elder Earnhardt started 15th and finished sixth. Jeff Burton won the race, nosing out runner-up Bobby Labonte. Bruton Smith, chairman of Charlotte Motor Speedway, changed the name of his 1½-mile track to Lowe's Motor Speedway prior to the 1999 season, making it the first NASCAR facility to take on a corporate sponsor's name.

▶ Dale Jarrett hugs the low line at Indianapolis Motor Speedway during the sixth annual running of the Brickyard 400. The Aug. 7 event was another notch in Jarrett's holster. He dominated the 400-miler, leading 116 of the final 121 laps on the rectangular 2½-mile track. It was Jarrett's second win in the midsummer classic, and it padded his NASCAR Winston Cup lead to 274 points. Bobby Labonte ran second, followed by Jeff Gordon and Mark Martin.

▼▶ Mark Martin drives onto the slick racing surface during a practice session at Watkins Glen International prior to the Aug. 15 Frontier At The Glen. Goodyear had developed a treaded rain tire (inset) for use on a road course in inclement weather. Racing in the rain is impossible on high-speed ovals but makes for an interesting possibility on a road course. The competitors used the rain tires in practice, but NASCAR chose to cancel qualifying and start the field in order of points earned. Rain tires have never been used in an official NASCAR Winston Cup race.

▼ Bobby Labonte leads Jeff Gordon to the finish line before a packed house in Michigan Speedway's Aug. 22 Pepsi 400 Presented by Meijer. Labonte snatched the lead from Dale Earnhardt with 17 laps to go and outran Gordon by less than a second to post his fourth win of the season. Labonte's pass was daring, as he scampered around Earnhardt and Gordon on the high side in one fell swoop to grab the lead for keeps.

Number 3 Dale Earnhardt zeroes in on #5 Terry Labonte late in the Aug. 28 Goody's Headache Powder 500 at Bristol Motor Speedway. Labonte passed Earnhardt just before the white flag and took a high line through the first and second turns, staying clear of Earnhardt. Earnhardt darted into Labonte's rear bumper anyway, spinning him out. Earnhardt went on to win his second race of the season.

Tony Stewart and Kenny Irwin, Jr., tangled three times during the Oct. 3 NAPA Autocare 500 at Martinsville Speedway. Stewart finally spun when Irwin, Jr., rapped his rear bumper. After exiting his car, Stewart tossed his heel pads at Irwin and tried to climb inside the rolling #28 Ford to further "discuss" matters. Stewart settled for 41st place. Jeff Gordon won in his first start with new crew chief Brian Whitesell.

Chapter Seven:
The New Millennium

WITH RECORD ATTENDANCE and increased television ratings, NASCAR Winston Cup racing experienced tremendous growth throughout the 1990s. The new millennium promised continued interest. Strong and steady administration was guiding NASCAR's development. By the end of '99, negotiations were under way to revamp the entire television package. In the negotiations, NASCAR required that, starting with the 2001 season, it would have a unified television package with the sanctioning body as the nucleus and more events aired on the major networks.

On Nov. 11, 1999, NASCAR announced that FOX and NBC had landed the multibillion-dollar television package, with a number of races to be televised on the TNT cable system and FOX cable affiliates. Under the new pact, which went into effect in 2001, the parties agreed on a 500-percent revenue increase that would fill the coffers for competitors, track promoters, and NASCAR itself. "The important thing is that this process elevates NASCAR as a true professional sport against other professional sports," said NASCAR president Mike Helton. Left out were incumbents CBS, ABC, and ESPN, along with CBS' cable outlet TNN, but each would continue to honor their agreements through the 2000 season.

The first half of the 2000 season underscored a disturbing trend. Side-by-side competition and the thrill-a-minute exploits on the track were no longer what they used to be. The enhanced aerodynamic packages that NASCAR Winston Cup teams used had made passing difficult. Lead changes at Daytona were a fraction of what they once were. For example, there were 19 lead changes in the 900 miles of racing at Daytona in 2000 compared to 108 in 1974.

To increase on-track competition, NASCAR issued a new set of rules for the Oct. 15, 2000, Talladega race. A small blade was attached to the roofs of all NASCAR Winston Cup cars, creating "dirty air" that flowed over the top of each vehicle. The blade made the cars less stable, thus reacquainting the drivers with the nervy and tedious aspects of superspeedway racing that had been so commonplace years earlier.

The 500-miler at Talladega Superspeedway turned out to be the most exciting event of the 2000 campaign. Dale Earnhardt, who was running in 20th with four laps to go, blasted his way past all rivals and won the high-speed, 500-mile thriller. Earnhardt's high-speed, flawless drive became a magical moment in NASCAR history. The race had 49 official lead changes, the most in a NASCAR Winston Cup race in 11 years.

Aerodynamic rules identical to Talladega remained in place for the 2001 Daytona 500, and swarms of cars battled through-

out the race. In one of the most spectacular 500s in memory, the lead swapped hands 49 times, the most in 20 years. In the closing stages, Michael Waltrip, never a winner in his 462-race career, was dueling with Dale Earnhardt and Dale Earnhardt, Jr., for the lead. Entering the final lap, Waltrip led Earnhardt, Jr., off the fourth turn. Then, pandemonium broke loose behind them. As the field battled three-abreast, Dale Earnhardt squeezed a tad low and clipped the front of Sterling Marlin's Dodge. Earnhardt's car darted out of control and delivered a solid shot to the concrete barrier. Waltrip bolted under the checkered flag as Earnhardt's skidding car came to a halt inside the fourth turn.

Waltrip, whose career had been revitalized when Earnhardt signed him to drive for Dale Earnhardt, Inc. in late 2000, finally earned a trip to victory lane. It was supposed to be a joyous occasion, but something had gone terribly wrong in that final-lap crash. Schrader, the first driver to check on Earnhardt, frantically motioned for an emergency crew.

Emergency crews cut the top off Earnhardt's car and administered to the stricken driver. He was transported to the hospital and pronounced dead at 5:16 P.M. The life of NASCAR's most dynamic hero had passed. The official announcement came nearly two hours later when NASCAR president Mike Helton, who had taken over the position at the start of the 2000 season, uttered the words nobody wanted to hear: "Today … we lost Dale Earnhardt."

Earnhardt's death was the fourth in a nine-month period in NASCAR's top three racing divisions. Head injuries were blamed in all four fatalities. Within several weeks, all drivers were required to wear the HANS device, a safety collar designed to prevent the head from snapping forward in a head-on accident. Other increased safety-awareness programs followed as the sanctioning body reacted to the death of its most cherished star.

Following Earnhardt's tragic demise, team owner Richard Childress hired NASCAR Busch Series driver Kevin Harvick to take the wheel of the Goodwrench Chevrolet. Driving the #29 Chevy, Harvick nosed out Jeff Gordon in a thriller in Atlanta in just his third career NASCAR Winston Cup start. The ghost of Dale Earnhardt remained prominent. "There was somebody in the car making it go a lot better than I was," declared Harvick.

Waltrip and Harvick provided two fresh faces in victory lane in the season's first four races. Elliott Sadler scored his first career win at Bristol, giving the Wood Brothers their first NASCAR Winston Cup win since 1993. Ricky Craven completed

a successful comeback from injuries with his first win at Martinsville. And Robby Gordon nabbed his initial win in the season finale at New Hampshire. Overall, the 2001 season featured five first-time winners, the most since 1966.

Sterling Marlin ushered in Dodge's first Winston Cup win since 1977 when he took the checkered flag at Michigan in August. Dodge was back in NASCAR with a full-fledged factory effort for the first time in more than a quarter century.

During the first half of the 2001 season, FOX telecasts recorded the highest ratings in the history of NASCAR coverage. The races televised in the first half of the season combined to average a 5.3 rating for FOX and its cable affiliate FX. That represented a hefty 29 percent increase over the same races a year earlier. NBC picked up the television coverage in July and the ratings bonanza continued. Despite rain delays and rainouts, NBC's average ratings for the second half of the season mounted to 3.9, 34 percent higher than the 2001 telecasts.

Jeff Gordon won his fourth NASCAR Winston Cup title in 2001. At age 31, he became the youngest four-time champion. A record 44 drivers topped the million-dollar earnings mark during the year, with Gordon pocketing $10,879,757. Nineteen drivers won races, matching the all-time record.

The 2002 season dawned with promise. The television agreement signed in late 1999 stipulated that FOX and NBC would alternate covering the Daytona 500. So, NBC televised "The Great American Race" for the first time. The aero package used in 2001 was no longer in place, having been scrapped due to safety concerns in the wake of the Earnhardt crash.

Despite the new rules, the 2002 Daytona 500 was a thrilling event, though it was punctuated by crashes that sidelined eight cars and crippled at least 25 others. Ward Burton, who missed a pair of wrecks by paper-thin margins, took the lead late in the race and went on to win. NBC's ratings for the annual Speedweeks finale were an all-time record 10.9.

NASCAR's "young guns" dominated the headlines in early 2002. Jimmie Johnson racked up his first win at California in April. Ryan Newman, a former Sprint Car driver, prevailed in NASCAR's all-star race at Charlotte and at New Hampshire in September. Sophomore Kurt Busch won four races, including three of the final five. Rookie Jamie McMurray, temporarily stepping in for an injured Sterling Marlin, won at Charlotte in only his second career start, becoming the quickest winner at NASCAR's top level since Johnny Rutherford won his first start at Daytona in 1963. Youthful exuberance had the upper hand on crafty veterans as the season closed.

Young-gun Tony Stewart, in his fourth full season, prevailed in the chase for the championship, taking the points leads for keeps in October. Stewart edged Mark Martin by 38 points.

The 2003 NASCAR campaign was marked by change. R.J. Reynolds, title sponsor of the Winston Cup Series since

1971, announced it would bow out after 33 years if NASCAR could find a proper suitor. In June, Nextel Communications signed a pact with NASCAR to become the title sponsor beginning with the 2004 season. Winston had helped guide the sport to the lofty status it enjoys today, but increasing pressure on tobacco companies to halt racing sponsorships led R.J. Reynolds to sever ties with NASCAR. Nextel, a young, aggressive company, may have the marketing expertise to take NASCAR deeper into the nation's mainstream.

In September, NASCAR chairman Bill France, Jr., turned over the reigns of the sport to his 41-year-old son Brian. There was even talk of changing the points system for the first time in nearly 30 years. Finally, in October, Pontiac announced it wouldn't return in 2004, leaving Chevrolet as the lone GM marque on the tour.

Meanwhile, on the track, Matt Kenseth was building a healthy points lead. In 2002, Kenseth won more races than any other driver, but finished a distant eighth in the final points standings. Kenseth adjusted his plan of attack in '03. While winning only once, Kenseth was remarkably consistent, clicking off top-10 finishes in bundles. By July, Kenseth's led by more than 200 points. Kenseth's effort was enough to comfortably beat sophomore Ryan Newman, who won a season-high eight races but lost out in the points race due to several wrecks.

The 2004 NASCAR campaign was punctuated by an additional flurry of changes. Under the direction of new chairman Brian Z. France, NASCAR's movement from the Southeast to the West hit full stride. Rockingham's North Carolina Speedway hosted its final race, and the venerable Darlington Raceway staged the final Southern 500. Meanwhile, Phoenix and Texas each acquired a second race date for the '05 season.

NASCAR's most high-profile change was the "Chase for the NASCAR NEXTEL Cup," which called for the top 10 drivers after the season's first 26 races to compete in a final 10-race "chase." The chase worked according to NASCAR's plan, with the championship coming down to the final lap of the season. Kurt Busch's eight-point margin of victory over a game Jimmie Johnson was the closest in NASCAR's 56-year history. Near the end of the chase, television ratings surged upward nearly 30 percent from 2003.

More changes loom for the 2005 NASCAR NEXTEL Cup season. The top 35 teams in the points standings will be guaranteed a spot in the starting lineup for each '05 race, no matter how they qualify.

The aggressive changes, France claims, allow NASCAR to keep abreast with other major league sporting organizations, particularly the NFL. In 2004, the plan worked. The new championship system helped solidify NASCAR's position as the number-two sport in the country. The future has never looked brighter for America's most exciting motorsport.

2000

February 20 Dale Jarrett wins his third Daytona 500. After following Johnny Benson, Jr., for 50 miles, Jarrett makes the decisive pass with four laps to go.

March 12 Dale Earnhardt wins the Cracker Barrel 500 at Atlanta Motor Speedway. It is Earnhardt's 75th career NASCAR Winston Cup victory.

March 19 Ward Burton ends a five-year victory famine with a win in the mall.com 400 at Darlington Raceway.

April 2 Third-generation driver Dale Earnhardt, Jr., wins the DirecTV 500 at Texas Motor Speedway for his first NASCAR Winston Cup victory.

April 16 Jeff Gordon posts his 50th career win in Talladega's DieHard 500.

July 9 Tony Stewart is declared the winner of the thatlook.com 300 at New Hampshire when a thunderstorm shortens the scheduled 300-lapper to 273 laps. Kenny Irwin, Jr., a promising young star, is killed in a practice crash.

August 13 Steve Park wins in an upset at Watkins Glen for his first victory on the NASCAR Winston Cup Series.

September 3 Bobby Labonte, who fails to lead a single green-flag lap, wins the rain-shortened Pepsi Southern 500 at Darlington Raceway. Labonte grabs the lead with a quick caution-flag pit stop and is out front when a thunderstorm brings the race to a halt.

September 17 Jeff Burton wins the Dura-Lube/Kmart 300 at New Hampshire International Speedway. Burton becomes the first driver to lead every lap in a superspeedway event since Fireball Roberts did it at Hanford, Calif., in 1961.

November 20 Jerry Nadeau posts his first career victory in the season finale at Atlanta Motor Speedway. Bobby Labonte finishes fifth and takes the NASCAR Winston Cup championship. Darrell Waltrip uses a champion's provisional to enter the race and finishes 34th in his final career start.

November 28 Mike Helton succeeds Bill France, Jr., as NASCAR president.

Dale Earnhardt, sporting an orange paint scheme on his #3 Chevrolet, races with his son Dale, Jr., in the early laps of the Feb. 20 Daytona 500. The elder Earnhardt, regarded as the master of the Daytona International Speedway, uncharacteristically sloshed through the 500 in the middle of the pack. He never led the race and finished a disappointing 21st. "Little E," competing in his first Daytona 500, finished 13th.

◀ Number 88 Dale Jarrett crosses the finish line with #99 Jeff Burton riding his bumper as the 2000 Daytona 500 concludes under a caution flag. Jarrett powered his way past Johnny Benson, Jr., with four laps remaining and was in front when a Jimmy Spencer crash brought out the yellow flag for the final two laps. The win earned Jarrett a king's ransom, as he banked $2,277,975, which included the $1-million Winston No Bull 5 bonus.

▲ Flashy rookies Dale Earnhardt, Jr., and Matt Kenseth battle in the April 2 DirecTV 500 at Texas Motor Speedway. Earnhardt, Jr., in only his 12th NASCAR Winston Cup start, drove the #8 Chevrolet to his first career victory. He led the most laps and drove away from all challengers down the stretch. Kenseth was in contention until a cut tire forced him into the wall on the 290th lap.

Bobby Labonte gave team owner Joe Gibbs his first NASCAR Winston Cup championship to go with the former Washington Redskins coach's three Super Bowl rings in 2000. Labonte took the points lead with a runner-up finish at California Speedway in April and held on to record his first career championship.

Labonte posted four victories and held off a mild late-season rally by Dale Earnhardt to win the title by 265 points. Earnhardt won twice.

Four-time race winner Jeff Burton finished third, 29 points behind Earnhardt. Super sophomore Tony Stewart racked up the most wins with six, including the first of his career, and finished sixth in the championship points race.

2000 NASCAR Winston Cup Points Race

Rank	Driver	Points	Wins	Top 5	Top 10	Winnings
1	Bobby Labonte	5130	4	19	24	$7,361,386
2	Dale Earnhardt	4865	2	13	24	$4,918,886
3	Jeff Burton	4836	4	15	22	$5,959,439
4	Dale Jarrett	4684	2	15	24	$5,984,475
5	Ricky Rudd	4575	0	12	19	$2,974,970
6	Tony Stewart	4570	6	12	23	$3,642,348
7	Rusty Wallace	4544	4	12	20	$3,621,468
8	Mark Martin	4410	1	13	20	$3,098,874
9	Jeff Gordon	4361	3	11	22	$3,001,144
10	Ward Burton	4152	1	4	17	$2,699,604

Rookie Matt Kenseth rides down pit road in his #17 Ford after winning the May 28 Coca-Cola 600 at Charlotte's Lowe's Motor Speedway. The 28-year-old rookie held off Bobby Labonte in a final-lap shootout to record his first NASCAR Winston Cup victory. Kenseth was the 11th different winner in the first 12 races of the 2000 season. Kenseth and fellow freshman Dale Earnhardt, Jr., became the first pair of rookies to win since 1981 when Morgan Shepherd and Ron Bouchard accomplished the feat.

Tony Stewart blazes down the front chute at Dover Downs International Speedway during the June 4 MBNA Platinum 400. Stewart authored a decisive romp in the 400-miler on Dover's "Monster Mile," leading 242 of the 400 laps. The sophomore sensation drove aggressively as most of his rivals took a conservative approach due to heavy tire wear. Stewart wore the competition down and scampered to an easy victory over rookie Matt Kenseth.

Jeff Gordon runs through one of the tight corners at Sears Point Raceway during the June 25 Save Mart/Kragen 300. Gordon pulled off one of racing's most astonishing feats by winning his sixth consecutive NASCAR Winston Cup event on a road course. Gordon led the final 27 laps on the 1.949-mile California track and drove to a comfortable win over runner-up Sterling Marlin. Marlin, not known for his finesse on road courses, remarked, "Road racing is like having a friend with a mean dog. If you're going to spend time with the friend, you've gotta learn to love the dog."

Steve Park, who cut his teeth on the short tracks of NASCAR's New England Modified Tour, pulled off a shocker on Watkins Glen's twisty road course in the Aug. 13 Global Crossing @ The Glen. Park guided his #1 Pennzoil/DEI Chevrolet around Ricky Rudd with 27 laps remaining and staved off Mark Martin to rack up his first career NASCAR Winston Cup victory.

A three-car collision knocked #88 Dale Jarrett, #01 Ted Musgrave, and #24 Jeff Gordon out of contention in the Oct. 8 UAW-GM Quality 500 at Lowe's Motor Speedway. The crash relegated Jarrett to a 40th-place finish and effectively ended his bid for a second NASCAR Winston Cup championship. Bobby Labonte won the race, building his lead to 252 points with five races remaining.

In a show of respect, Dale Earnhardt points to #25 Jerry Nadeau moments after Nadeau beat him to the finish line in the Nov. 20 season finale at Atlanta Motor Speedway. Nadeau led the final seven laps of the NAPA 500 and nipped Earnhardt at the checkered flag for his first career NASCAR Winston Cup victory. Nadeau became the 14th different winner of the season, and was one of four drivers to score his first career win in 2000.

2001

February 18 Michael Waltrip nips Dale Earnhardt, Jr., at the finish line to win the Daytona 500, a tragic affair in which Dale Earnhardt is fatally injured in a last-lap crash. It is Waltrip's first NASCAR Winston Cup victory.

March 11 Kevin Harvick, replacing the late Dale Earnhardt, wins the Cracker Barrel Old Country Store 500 at Atlanta Motor Speedway in only his third career NASCAR Winston Cup start.

March 25 Elliott Sadler becomes the third first-time winner in the first six races of the season with a triumph in Bristol's Food City 500.

May 27 Jeff Burton ends a personal slump with a big victory in the Coca-Cola 600 at Lowe's Motor Speedway. Tony Stewart finishes third after his sixth-place effort in the Indianapolis 500 on the same day.

July 15 Rookie Kevin Harvick holds off Robert Pressley to win the inaugural race at Chicagoland Speedway. Jeff Gordon and Dale Jarrett are locked in a tie for the lead in the points race.

August 19 Sterling Marlin drives a Dodge to victory in the Pepsi 400 at Michigan Speedway for his first win of the season. It is the first win for Dodge since Neil Bonnett won in 1977.

September 30 Jeff Gordon wins the Protection One 400 at the new Kansas Speedway, giving him a 222-point lead over Ricky Rudd in the title chase.

October 15 Underdog Ricky Craven posts his first career NASCAR Winston Cup win in the Old Dominion 500 at Martinsville Speedway.

November 11 Bill Elliott ends a personal seven-year drought with a victory at Homestead-Miami Speedway. Elliott gives Ray Evernham his first win as a NASCAR Winston Cup team owner.

November 23 Robby Gordon posts his first NASCAR Winston Cup win in the season finale at New Hampshire International Speedway. The race was postponed from Sept. 16 after the Sept. 11 terrorist attacks. Jeff Gordon nabs his fourth NASCAR Winston Cup title.

The Feb. 18 Daytona 500 was the most competitive since 1974 with 49 official lead changes among 14 different drivers. NASCAR-mandated rules requiring a strip of aluminum on each car's roof enhanced the on-track action, but concerns about a big crash still remained. On the 174th lap, Robby Gordon's #4 Chevrolet tapped #22 Ward Burton into a spin, triggering a 19-car collision on the backstretch. In the mishap, Tony Stewart's #20 Pontiac soared high into the air. Stewart was shaken but uninjured in the spectacular accident.

◄ Michael Waltrip's #15 NAPA Chevrolet leads teammate #8 Dale Earnhardt, Jr., across the finish line at the conclusion of the 2001 Daytona 500. Waltrip, taking his first ride with the DEI team, scored his first victory in his 463rd NASCAR Winston Cup Series start. While the DEI cars ran 1-2, it was a tragic day for the entire NASCAR community. NASCAR legend Dale Earnhardt lost his life in an accident on the final turn of the final lap. It was the first death to occur in the history of the Daytona 500.

Steve Park drives his #1 Chevrolet off the final corner just ahead of #18 Bobby Labonte in the Feb. 26 Dura Lube 400 at North Carolina Speedway. Park nipped Labonte at the finish line by an eyelash to pocket his second career NASCAR Winston Cup victory. After the race, Park drove around the track in a reverse victory lap holding a Dale Earnhardt hat out the window.

Jeff Gordon took the NASCAR Winston Cup points lead with an eighth-place finish at Pocono in July, then romped to his fourth championship. After being locked in a tight battle during the first half of the season, Gordon left all challengers in the dust as he won by a 349-point cushion over runner-up Tony Stewart.

The points lead changed hands seven times among five drivers as several contenders jockeyed for points early in the year. By late summer, it was a one-horse race with Gordon leading by more than 300 points in August.

Gordon won six races along the way to his fourth title. Stewart overcame a sluggish start to finish second with three wins.

2001 NASCAR Winston Cup Points Race

Rank	Driver	Points	Wins	Top 5	Top 10	Winnings
1	Jeff Gordon	5112	6	18	24	$10,879,757
2	Tony Stewart	4763	3	15	22	$4,941,463
3	Sterling Marlin	4741	2	12	20	$4,517,634
4	Ricky Rudd	4706	2	14	22	$4,878,027
5	Dale Jarrett	4612	4	12	19	$5,377,742
6	Bobby Labonte	4561	2	9	20	$4,786,779
7	Rusty Wallace	4481	1	8	14	$4,788,652
8	Dale Earnhardt, Jr.	4460	3	9	15	$5,827,542
9	Kevin Harvick	4406	2	6	16	$4,302,202
10	Jeff Burton	4394	2	8	16	$4,230,737

Rookie Kevin Harvick, replacement for the late Dale Earnhardt, made his third career NASCAR Winston Cup start in the March 11 Cracker Barrel Old Country Store 500 at Atlanta Motor Speedway. On the final lap, Harvick's #29 Goodwrench Chevy washed out to the high side, leaving the door open for #24 Jeff Gordon to challenge for first place. Harvick got back on the throttle and nipped Gordon at the finish line by .006 second in one of the closest finishes in NASCAR history. After the race, Harvick drove around the track in reverse direction showing three fingers in honor of the fallen Dale Earnhardt.

Elliott Sadler pulled a major upset in the March 25 Food City 500 at Bristol Motor Speedway. Coming from his 38th starting position, Sadler stayed on the lead lap throughout the first half of the race as cautions kept the field bunched up. He took the lead with 70 laps to go when #29 Kevin Harvick encountered tire problems, and led the rest of the way. The win was the first for the Wood Brothers team since 1993 and the first of Sadler's NASCAR Winston Cup career.

Rusty Wallace keeps his #2 Ford just ahead of #24 Jeff Gordon in the decisive last lap of the April 29 NAPA Auto Parts 500 at California Speedway. Wallace snagged his 54th career NASCAR Winston Cup victory by holding off Gordon's late surge. The triumph gave Wallace a win in 16 consecutive seasons, two years short of Richard Petty's all-time record.

Bobby Hamilton seemed to have the Oct. 15 Old Dominion 500 at Martinsville well in hand until the closing laps. Number 29 Kevin Harvick drilled Hamilton's rear bumper, sending the #55 Chevy spinning and dropping Hamilton to 13th in the final order. Harvick was penalized a lap for rough driving and finished 22nd. Kevin Lepage, who placed 21st, talked about the short tempers usually found at Martinsville. "Martinsville is not an anger management seminar," said Lepage. "In fact, it might do you some good to attend one of those before the race."

Ricky Craven flashes his #32 Ford across the finish line, beating #88 Dale Jarrett by less than a second to post his first career NASCAR Winston Cup win in Martinsville's Oct. 14 Old Dominion 500. Having been injured at Texas in 1997, Craven lost his ride and his recuperation was lengthy. With his Martinsville triumph, he filled a void in the victory column—and also became the first driver to ever win in a car bearing the number 32.

Bobby Labonte's #18 Pontiac runs side by side with Dale Earnhardt, Jr.'s #8 Chevy in the Nov. 18 NAPA 500 at Atlanta Motor Speedway. Labonte came from his 39th starting position to win, taking advantage of Jerry Nadeau's fuel-starved car on the final lap. Labonte's second win of the year enabled the 2000 NASCAR Winston Cup champion to finish sixth in the '01 final points standings. Jeff Gordon's sixth-place finish assured him of his fourth championship.

2002

February 17 Ward Burton leads only the final five laps and scores an upset win in the Daytona 500. Sterling Marlin is penalized by NASCAR when he pulls a bent fender off his right front tire during a late red flag.

March 24 Sophomore Kurt Busch sprints to his first career NASCAR Winston Cup victory at Bristol.

April 28 Rookie Jimmie Johnson surges into the lead with 13 laps remaining and outruns Kurt Busch to win the California 500. Johnson's first NASCAR Winston Cup victory comes in his 13th career start.

May 26 Mark Martin wins the Coca-Cola 600 at Lowe's Motor Speedway. Martin's victory ends a 25-month drought.

August 4 Bill Elliott scores a popular win in the Brickyard 400 at Indianapolis Motor Speedway. It is the 43rd victory of Elliott's career.

August 24 Jeff Gordon wins the Sharpie 500 at Bristol Motor Speedway, ending a 31-race losing streak.

September 15 Freshman driver Ryan Newman is only a car length ahead of Kurt Busch when rain curtails the New Hampshire 300 after 207 of the scheduled 300 laps. Newman's first career win comes in his 34th start.

October 13 Jamie McMurray, making his second start since replacing the injured Sterling Marlin, wins the UAW-GM Quality 500 at Lowe's Motor Speedway. McMurray becomes the quickest winner in NASCAR Winston Cup history since Johnny Rutherford won in his first start at Daytona in 1963.

November 3 Johnny Benson, Jr., posts his first NASCAR Winston Cup victory in his 227th start in Rockingham's Pop Secret 400. It is also the first win for team owner Read Morton.

November 17 Kurt Busch wins his fourth race of the year at Homestead-Miami Speedway, and Tony Stewart coasts to an 18th-place finish to put the lid on his championship campaign. Stewart beats runner-up Mark Martin by 38 points to capture the title.

During a red flag five laps from the finish of the Feb. 17 Daytona 500, Sterling Marlin climbed from his #40 Dodge on the backstretch and pulled a bent fender away from his right front tire. Marlin, who was leading, had crumpled the fender in a skirmish with Jeff Gordon. NASCAR rules prohibit any work from being done to a car during a red flag, and Marlin was flagged to the pits when the race continued. Marlin resumed the chase in 14th place, and battled back to finish eighth.

Jimmy Spencer, in the #41 Dodge, and #97 Kurt Busch battled ferociously in the final laps of the March 24 Food City 500 at Bristol Motor Speedway. Spencer and Busch swapped the lead before a packed house that exceeded 150,000. Busch scrubbed his way past Spencer for the final time on lap 445 and sped to his first NASCAR Winston Cup victory.

Dale Earnhardt, Jr., plants a bumper on the rear of Tony Stewart's car during the April 14 Virginia 500 at Martinsville. Rattling the rear bumper of a rival is a driving technique that has been in stock car racing since the beginning. A craftsman like Earnhardt, Jr., can swat a competitor just enough to make him wobble out of the groove and leave room for a critical pass. Bobby Labonte won the 2002 Virginia 500.

Bad-boy Tony Stewart rallied from a last-place finish in the season-opening Daytona 500, scrambled back into contention, and delivered a late-season kick to capture the 2002 NASCAR Winston Cup championship.

Stewart took the points lead with a runner-up finish at Talladega in the 30th of 36 races. Rookie Jimmie Johnson led going into the Talladega event, becoming the first rookie to lead the standings since Dick Hutcherson in 1965.

Sterling Marlin led in points from February through late September, but his season ended when he injured his neck at Kansas Speedway. Mark Martin, Johnson, and Stewart all led the standings in the final stretch.

Stewart cruised to an 18th-place finish in the season finale at Homestead-Miami Speedway to seal his first title. He finished 38 points ahead of runner-up Martin, who finished second for the fourth time in his career.

2002 NASCAR Winston Cup Points Race

Rank	Driver	Points	Wins	Top 5	Top 10	Winnings
1	Tony Stewart	4800	3	15	21	$9,163,761
2	Mark Martin	4762	1	12	22	$7,004,893
3	Kurt Busch	4641	4	12	20	$5,105,394
4	Jeff Gordon	4607	3	13	20	$6,154,475
5	Jimmie Johnson	4600	3	6	21	$3,788,268
6	Ryan Newman	4593	1	14	22	$5,346,651
7	Rusty Wallace	4574	0	7	17	$4,785,134
8	Matt Kenseth	4432	5	11	19	$4,514,203
9	Dale Jarrett	4415	2	10	18	$4,421,951
10	Ricky Rudd	4323	1	8	12	$4,444,614

Two of NASCAR's top-ranked young guns, #48 Jimmie Johnson and #97 Kurt Busch, battle side by side in the April 28 NAPA Auto Parts 500 at California Speedway. Busch dominated the race on the two-mile oval until the late stages when Johnson galloped into the lead 14 laps from the finish. Johnson scored his first NASCAR Winston Cup victory as Busch ran second.

Roush Racing teammates #17 Matt Kenseth and #6 Mark Martin battled down to the wire in the May 26 Coca-Cola 600 at Lowe's Motor Speedway. Martin, riding a 73-race losing streak into the Charlotte race, took the lead with 40 laps to go and held off Kenseth's dynamic efforts in the final laps. Martin collected his 33rd career NASCAR Winston Cup victory and the $1-million Winston No Bull 5 bonus.

Ward Burton provided the night's most notable display of anger during the Aug. 24 Sharpie 500 at Bristol Motor Speedway. Dale Earnhardt, Jr., bumped Burton into a spin and crash in the final 50 miles. As Junior drove past under the caution flag, Burton threw the heat shields of his driving shoes at the #8 car. Burton was saddled with a 37th-place finish, while Earnhardt placed third.

Rookie Ryan Newman, who had posted four runner-up finishes, broke through with his first NASCAR Winston Cup victory in the Sept. 15 New Hampshire 300 at New Hampshire International Speedway. Newman kept his #12 Dodge in front of Kurt Busch over the final 41 laps. Rain curtailed the event after 207 of the scheduled 300 laps. Newman went on to beat out Jimmie Johnson for Rookie of the Year honors.

Jamie McMurray, a rookie who replaced the injured Sterling Marlin in the #40 Dodge, stunned the NASCAR community by winning the Oct. 13 UAW-GM Quality 500 at Lowe's Motor Speedway in only his second career start. Joining him in victory lane is team owner Chip Ganassi. McMurray stormed into the lead with 31 laps to go and kept Bobby Labonte at bay in the final shootout.

Tony Stewart gave team owner Joe Gibbs his second NASCAR Winston Cup title in the last three years with a come-from-behind victory in the championship chase. The season started slowly for Stewart, who finished last in the Daytona 500. He clawed his way into contention by late summer, and moved to the top of the heap in early October. Stewart won three races and beat runner-up Mark Martin by 38 points.

2003

February R.J. Reynolds confirms it has offered to step away from its Winston Cup sponsorship of NASCAR's premier stock car racing series.

February 16 Michael Waltrip wins the rain-shortened Daytona 500. Waltrip's Chevrolet is out front when the race is called after 272.5 miles and 109 laps.

March 16 Ricky Craven edges out Kurt Busch to win the Carolina Dodge Dealers 400 at Darlington Raceway. The official margin of victory is 0.002 seconds, the closest finish since NASCAR began using electronic timing systems in 1993.

April 6 Dale Earnhardt, Jr., makes a decisive pass with a rule-violating trip across the out-of-bounds line and wins the Aaron's 499 at Talladega. NASCAR officials rule that Earnhardt, Jr., completed the pass on Matt Kenseth and Jimmie Johnson before he crossed the line.

June 19 NASCAR announces that Nextel Communications will become the title sponsor of its top racing series in 2004. Nextel will replace Winston, which has provided sponsorship since 1971.

August 17 Ryan Newman wins the Michigan 400 at Michigan International Speedway. Jimmy Spencer and Kurt Busch fight in the garage after the race. NASCAR suspends Spencer for one week for punching Busch.

August 31 Terry Labonte wins the Southern 500 at Darlington Raceway. It is the last Labor Day weekend Southern 500 at NASCAR's original superspeedway. NASCAR has announced that beginning in 2004, the race date will be moved to California Speedway.

September 13 Bill France, Jr., steps down as chairman and chief executive officer of NASCAR and names his 41-year-old son Brian as his successor.

October 28 Pontiac announces it is withdrawing from NASCAR competition, leaving Chevrolet as the lone General Motors make for 2004.

November 9 With a fourth-place finish in the Pop Secret 400 at Rockingham's North Carolina Speedway, Matt Kenseth wraps up his first NASCAR Winston Cup Championship.

On the 56th lap of the Feb. 16 Daytona 500, Ward Burton clipped Ken Schrader's #49 Dodge, triggering a pileup. Schrader's car veered into the path of Ryan Newman. The two hit and Newman's #12 Dodge went airborne, flipping violently onto the infield grass along the front chute. Newman's car disintegrated, but the talented sophomore escaped unharmed. Michael Waltrip won the race, which was shortened to 109 of the scheduled 200 laps due to rain.

Matt Kenseth's Robbie Reiser-led crew services the #17 DeWalt Ford during the March 2 UAW-DaimlerChrysler 400 at Las Vegas Motor Speedway. Kenseth led the final 32 laps and sped to victory. The win propelled Kenseth to within three points of the NASCAR Winston Cup points lead. A week later, Kenseth took command in the points race with a fourth-place finish at Atlanta. He never trailed again even though he failed to post another win. Benny Parsons was the last driver to win the championship with only one win; he did it in 1973.

With smoke spitting off their cars, #32 Ricky Craven and #97 Kurt Busch grind toward the finish line in the thrilling conclusion of the March 16 Carolina Dodge Dealers 400 at Darlington Raceway. Craven nipped Busch by 0.002 seconds, the closest finish in NASCAR Winston Cup history. Craven's was the only triumph for the Pontiac nameplate in '03, and perhaps its last victory in NASCAR's top series. In October, Pontiac announced it was withdrawing from NASCAR effective in 2004.

Matt Kenseth dominated the 2003 season with amazing consistency. The Wisconsin native only won one race but held the points lead for most of the year. With a fourth-place finish in the March 9 Bass Pro Shops MBNA 500 at Atlanta, Kenseth moved atop the points standings and never trailed again. He had only two DNFs the entire year.

Kenseth coasted home 90 points in front of runner-up Jimmie Johnson. Kenseth became only the fourth driver to capture the title with only one win.

Kenseth led the points after 33 of the 36 races, the most dominating performance since Dale Earnhardt led all but two races in 1987. He also led the standings more than any driver since Richard Petty led after 41 of 48 races in '71.

Kenseth, who gave owner Jack Roush his first title, was also the final champion crowned by series sponsor Winston. Effective in 2004, Nextel Communications became the title sponsor for NASCAR's top stock car racing series.

2003 NASCAR Winston Cup Points Race

Rank	Driver	Points	Wins	Top 5	Top 10	Winnings
1	Matt Kenseth	5022	1	11	25	$9,422,764
2	Jimmie Johnson	4932	3	14	20	$7,745,530
3	Dale Earnhardt, Jr.	4815	2	13	21	$6,880,807
4	Jeff Gordon	4785	3	15	20	$6,622,002
5	Kevin Harvick	4770	1	11	18	$6,237,119
6	Ryan Newman	4711	8	17	22	$6,100,877
7	Tony Stewart	4549	2	12	18	$6,131,633
8	Bobby Labonte	4377	2	12	17	$5,505,018
9	Bill Elliott	4303	1	9	12	$5,008,530
10	Terry Labonte	4162	1	4	9	$4,283,625

Matt Kenseth's #17 Ford runs three-abreast with #29 Kevin Harvick and #8 Dale Earnhardt, Jr., late in the April 6 Aaron's 499 at Talladega Superspeedway. Kenseth and Earnhardt, Jr., were involved in a controversial late-race pass. As Kenseth battled Jimmie Johnson for the lead, Earnhardt, Jr., swept low to overtake both rivals, making the decisive pass with his left tires below the yellow "out of bounds" line. NASCAR ruled that Earnhardt, Jr., had completed the pass before going below the line, a decision that outraged many competitors. Earnhardt went on to win the race, Harvick took second, and Kenseth drifted to ninth.

Number 97 Kurt Busch and #7 Jimmy Spencer ran in close quarters quite often during the 2003 campaign. During the Aug. 17 Michigan 400 at Michigan International Speedway, Busch and Spencer got into a bumping match near the end of the race. Busch admittedly moved into Spencer, who registered his complaints immediately after the race with a couple of short jabs to Busch's nose. Spencer was reprimanded by NASCAR for his actions and had to sit out the following week's race at Bristol. Ryan Newman won the Michigan event when Busch ran out of fuel in the final four miles.

Terry Labonte authored a heartwarming triumph in the Aug. 31 Southern 500 at Darlington Raceway. In a season dominated by the young guns, the Texas veteran's late-race gallop was perhaps *the* "feel good" story of 2003. Labonte claimed the lead for keeps with a quick pit stop on lap 335, and went on to post his 22nd career win. The 54th annual running of the Labor Day weekend event at Darlington was a bittersweet affair for many NASCAR traditionalists. Earlier in the year, NASCAR announced that California Speedway would assume Darlington's holiday race date beginning in 2004.

Elliott Sadler's #38 Ford gyrates through the air during a wild tumble in the Oct. 28 EA Sports 500 at Talladega Superspeedway. Sadler, who started on the pole, was among the front-runners when the accident occurred with six laps remaining. Dale Earnhardt, Jr., made a move to the inside of a pack of cars and Sadler flinched. Sadler made contact with Kurt Busch, spinning backward and high into the air. Sadler escaped the season's most spectacular wreck unharmed.

Michael Waltrip pops through the roof of his #15 Chevrolet after a dramatic win in Talladega's EA Sports 500. Waltrip staved off a last-lap challenge from Dale Earnhardt, Jr., to score his second win of the season. Waltrip's DEI team was among the first to experiment with the roof hatch as an emergency escape device late in the 2003 season.

Team owner Jack Roush, affectionately nicknamed the "Cat in the Hat," realized a lifelong dream by winning the 2003 NASCAR Winston Cup title. Since joining the NASCAR tour in 1988, Roush's cars had finished second four times, but had never won. In '90, his championship quest was foiled by a 46-point penalty that cost Mark Martin the title. Matt Kenseth's incredibly consistent season in '03 finally gave the crusty mechanical genius from Lavonia, Mich., a much-deserved championship ring.

2004

January 20 NASCAR announces details of the new "Chase for the NASCAR NEXTEL Cup" format. The system calls for the top 10 points winners after the first 26 races to compete for the title over the final 10 races.

April 25 Jeff Gordon wins the Aaron's 499 at Talladega when a caution flag freezes the field as Dale Earnhardt, Jr., attempts a pass for the lead. Rules implemented in 2003 prohibit "racing back to the flag" during a caution flag.

May 14 NASCAR announces that North Carolina Speedway in Rockingham will not host a NASCAR NEXTEL Cup event in 2005, and Darlington Raceway will have only one race in '05. NASCAR also announces that Phoenix and Texas will each host a second race in '05.

September 5 Elliott Sadler wins the Pop Secret 500 at California Speedway. It is the first year for the event, which had been the Labor Day Southern 500 at Darlington Raceway since 1950.

September 11 Jeremy Mayfield wins the final "regular season" race at at Richmond to grab a coveted spot in the "Chase for the NASCAR NEXTEL Cup."

October 3 Dale Earnhardt, Jr., wins at Talladega. In victory lane, he uses the "S" word in response to a TV interviewer's question. A day later, NASCAR docks Earnhardt $10,000 and 25 points.

October 24 The Hendrick Motorsports plane crashes minutes before the Subway 500 at Martinsville Speedway, killing all 10 people on board. Hendrick driver Jimmie Johnson wins and is informed of the tragedy after the race.

November 14 Jimmie Johnson racks up his fourth win in the last five races in the Mountain Dew Southern 500 at Darlington. Johnson has rallied from a 247-point deficit and ninth place in the standings to 18 points behind leader Kurt Busch with one race remaining.

November 21 Kurt Busch finishes fifth in the season finale to claim the 2004 "Chase for the NASCAR NEXTEL Cup" championship. Busch's eight-point win over Jimmie Johnson is the closest margin of victory in the 56 years of NASCAR Cup Series racing.

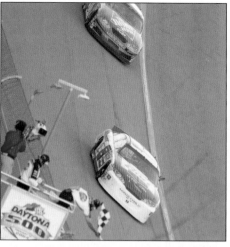

Dale Earnhardt, Jr., drives his #8 Chevrolet across the finish line to win the 46th running of the Daytona 500 on Feb. 15. With the victory, Earnhardt, Jr., became the third son of a former Daytona 500 winner to win "The Great American Race." The previous father-son winners were Lee and Richard Petty and Bobby and Davey Allison.

North Carolina Speedway has been one of NASCAR's most competitive tracks since it opened in 1965. The finish of the Feb. 22 Subway 400 enhanced that reputation as #17 Matt Kenseth held off a late-race charge by rookie #9 Kasey Kahne to score a photo-finish victory. Kahne, a graduate of the rugged Midwestern Sprint Car circuit, was making only his second start in the NASCAR NEXTEL Cup Series. The 400-miler was the final NASCAR Cup Series race at Rockingham. Its race date was moved to Phoenix for 2005.

Jeff Gordon cruises along Talladega Superspeedway's littered frontstretch during the final laps of the April 25 Aaron's 499. Dale Earnhardt, Jr., was passing Gordon for the lead with five laps to go, but Brian Vickers spun out, bringing out the caution flag. NASCAR officials let the race end under yellow, inciting the wrath of the crowd. A rule enacted in 2003 that prevents racing back to the flag when a yellow comes out froze the field and gave Gordon a controversial win. Disappointed fans tossed beverage cans and other debris onto the track.

The first "Chase for the NASCAR NEXTEL Cup" produced a thrilling conclusion to the 2004 season. Five drivers had a shot to win the title entering the season finale. Kurt Busch claimed top honors by a scant eight points over runner-up Jimmie Johnson. Jeff Gordon placed third, only 16 points behind.

Busch overcame numerous problems on his road to the title. Twice during the final 10-race "playoffs," Busch spun in heavy traffic but escaped unscathed. Constantly battling back from deep in the pack, Busch logged nine top-10 finishes in the final 10 races to win the closest points race in NASCAR history.

Busch was the most consistent driver during the important 10-race "chase," with an average finish position of 8.9. Johnson averaged a 10.2 position.

Under the previous points system, Jeff Gordon would have edged teammate Johnson by 47 points. Busch would have placed a distant fourth, 247 points out of first place.

2004 NASCAR NEXTEL Cup Points Race

Rank	Driver	Points	Wins	Top 5	Top 10	Winnings
1	Kurt Busch	6506	3	10	21	$9,677,543
2	Jimmie Johnson	6498	8	20	23	$8,275,721
3	Jeff Gordon	6490	5	16	25	$8,439,382
4	Mark Martin	6399	1	10	15	$5,479,004
5	Dale Earnhardt, Jr.	6368	6	16	21	$8,913,510
6	Tony Stewart	6326	2	10	19	$7,830,807
7	Ryan Newman	6180	2	11	14	$6,354,256
8	Matt Kenseth	6069	2	8	16	$7,405,309
9	Elliott Sadler	6024	2	8	14	$6,244,954
10	Jeremy Mayfield	6000	1	5	13	$4,919,342

The 10 qualifiers for the 2004 "Chase for the NASCAR NEXTEL Cup" pose after the Sept. 11 Chevy Rock & Roll 400 at Richmond International Raceway. From left to right, they are Dale Earnhardt, Jr., Jeff Gordon, Matt Kenseth, Tony Stewart, Jimmie Johnson, Elliott Sadler, Jeremy Mayfield, Kurt Busch, Ryan Newman, and Mark Martin. Mayfield's win at Richmond earned him a spot the 10-race chase and knocked out teammate Kasey Kahne, who finished 24th.

The first ever "Chase for the NASCAR NEXTEL Cup" race was the Sept. 19 Sylvania 300 at New Hampshire International Speedway. Controversy flared when #31 Robby Gordon spun Greg Biffle, also collecting #19 Jeremy Mayfield and Tony Stewart. Gordon admittedly took out Biffle, but he was unaware that the crash would scoop up two title contenders. Kurt Busch won the race and leaped from seventh to a first-place tie in the points chase.

Elliott Sadler's #38 Ford breaks loose in the tri-oval area of Talladega Superspeedway on the final lap of the Oct. 3 EA Sports 500. Dale Earnhardt, Jr., took the checkered flag as Sadler's car sailed through the air and landed on all four wheels near the finish line. Sadler got credit for a 23rd-place finish, losing 10 positions during his 190-mph pirouette.

Jeff Gordon's ill-handling #24 Chevrolet cuts across the front of Rusty Wallace's #2 Dodge on lap 76 of the Oct. 16 UAW-GM Quality 500 at Lowe's Motor Speedway. Gordon fell a lap off the pace, but was able to get it back after the halfway mark. A tremendous rally in the late stages netted Gordon a second-place finish behind teammate Jimmie Johnson.

The Hendrick Motorsports pit crew services Jimmie Johnson's Chevrolet during the Oct. 31 Bass Pro Shops/MBNA 500 at Atlanta Motor Speedway. A message reading "Always In Our Hearts" was placed on the hood of Johnson's car in tribute to the 10 members of the Hendrick Motorsports family that perished in a private plane crash near Martinsville on Oct. 24. Johnson won the Atlanta race to rack up his third straight victory.

▶ Greg Biffle leads Kurt Busch and Jeff Gordon at Homestead-Miami Speedway in the Nov. 21 Ford 400. Biffle drove to victory in the season finale as Busch wrapped up the NASCAR NEXTEL Cup championship with a hard-fought fifth-place finish. Busch won the title by eight points over Jimmie Johnson, who finished second at Miami. Gordon finished third, and also wound up third in the final points standings. Had NASCAR not opted to change its championship system in '04, Gordon would have won his fifth NASCAR Cup Series title by 47 points over Hendrick Motorsports teammate Johnson.

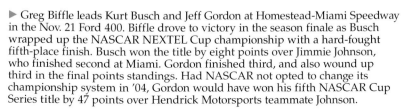

Index

A
Allen, Johnny, 27, 29
Allison, Bobby, 32, 34, 38, 39, 40, 41, 42, 43, 46,
  47, 51, 52, 53, 59, 94
Allison, Davey, 59, 61, 65, 68, 69, 71, 94
Allison, Donnie, 42, 43, 45, 47
American Automobile Association, 8
Andretti, John, 79, 80, 81, 82
Andretti, Mario, 33
Andrews, Paul, 69
Apperson, Bob, 11

B
Baker, Buck, 16, 18, 19, 20, 21, 22
Baker, Buddy, 38, 41, 43, 44, 46, 50
Baker, Erwin "Cannonball," 10
Barkdoll, Phil, 59
Beauchamp, Johnny, 27
Beauchamp, Tom, 23
Benson, Jr., Johnny, 81, 86
Biffle, Greg, 95
Blackburn, Bunkie, 28
Blair, Bill, 17
Blizzard, Ed, 9
Bodine, Brett, 59, 65, 68, 73
Bodine, Geoff, 57, 58, 59, 60, 61, 68, 73, 81
Bonnett, Neil, 53, 54, 55, 57, 64, 71
Bouchard, Ron, 51, 87
Boys, Trevor, 55
Brickhouse, Richard, 35
Brooks, Dick, 39, 43, 67
Brown, Jr., Lamar H., 34
Bruner, Jr., Johnny, 22
Bruner, Sr., Johnny, 23
Burton, Jeff, 82, 83, 86
Burton, Ward, 72, 88, 91, 93
Busch, Kurt, 90, 91, 92, 93, 94, 95
Byron, Red, 10, 11, 14

C
Campbell, Malcolm, 8
Chase, Mike, 73
Chester, Ted, 18
Childress, Richard, 51, 53, 54, 57, 61, 71, 73
Christian, Sara, 10
Clark, Cyrus, 8
Cope, Derrike, 64, 70
Craven, Ricky, 77, 89, 92
Cronkrite, Will, 46

D
Davis, W.R. "Slick," 10
Days of Thunder, 64
DeWitt, L.G., 41
Dillon, Mike, 79
Dolan, Dick, 23

E
Eargle, Pop, 27
Earnhardt, Dale, 43, 46, 47, 50, 52, 53, 54, 56, 57,
  58, 59, 60, 61, 64, 65, 66, 67, 69, 70, 71, 72,
  73, 74, 75, 76, 78, 79, 80, 81, 82, 83, 86, 87,
  88, 89, 92
Earnhardt, Jr., Dale, 83, 86, 87, 88, 89, 90, 91, 93,
  94, 95
Economaki, Chris, 26
Elliott, Bill, 45, 53, 56, 58, 59, 67, 68, 69, 77
Elliott, George, 45
Etheridge, Jack, 10
Evernham, Ray, 73

F
Ferreri, Lynda, 44
Flock, Bob, 10, 16, 19
Flock, Fonty, 9, 10, 11, 15, 16, 17, 19, 21
Flock, Tim, 11, 15, 16, 18, 19, 20, 21, 27
Florian, Jimmy, 14
Foyt, A.J., 30, 31, 39, 40, 59
France, Jr., Bill, 74
France, Sr., William "Big Bill," 8, 9, 23, 27, 35
Frank, Larry, 30

G
Ganassi, Chip, 91
Gant, Harry, 42, 51, 52, 53, 55, 57, 60, 65, 66, 67
Garrett, Levi, 61
Gibbs, Joe, 70, 86, 91
Glotzbach, Charlie, 34, 35, 39
Goldsmith, Paul, 21, 22, 29, 30
Gordon, Jeff, 69, 73, 74, 75, 76, 77, 78, 79, 80, 81,
  82, 83, 87, 88, 89, 90, 94, 95
Gordon, Robby, 88, 95
Gurney, Dan, 32
Guthrie, Janet, 44

H
Hagan, Billy, 55
Hamilton, Bobby, 76, 79, 81, 89
Hamilton, Pete, 38
Harvick, Kevin, 89, 93
Hassler, Friday, 39

Hawkes, Howard, 30
Heveron, Doug, 55
Hillin, Jr., Bobby, 73
Holland, Bill, 18
Holley, Armond, 33
Holloway, Bee Gee, 27
Hooper, Lance, 79
Howard, Richard, 39, 40
Hutcherson, Dick, 31, 90
Hyde, Harry, 38
Hylton, James, 32, 33, 38, 39, 40

I
Irvan, Ernie, 66, 67, 69, 71, 72, 73, 75, 77, 78
Irwin, Jr., Kenny, 82, 83
Isaac, Bobby, 30, 34, 35, 38, 39, 42

J
Jarrett, Dale, 64, 70, 73, 76, 77, 78, 79, 82, 83, 86,
  87, 89
Jarrett, Ned, 27, 28, 30, 31, 55, 82
Johns, Bobby, 26
Johnson, Jimmie, 90, 91, 92, 93, 94, 95
Johnson, Junior, 19, 20, 26, 27, 29, 31, 32, 35, 40,
  44, 45, 46, 51, 52, 54, 67, 73
Joseph, Melvin, 39
Joy, Mike, 78

K
Kahne, Kasey, 94
Keene, Tex, 16
Keller, Al, 18
Kenseth, Matt, 86, 87, 91, 92, 93, 94, 95
Kiekhaefer, Carl, 19, 20, 21
Krauskopf, Nord, 38, 42
Kulwicki, Alan, 57, 66, 68, 69, 71

L
Labonte, Bobby, 71, 73, 79, 80, 83, 86, 87, 88, 89,
  90, 91
Labonte, Terry, 50, 51, 52, 55, 58, 75, 76, 77, 78,
  79, 83, 93
Landfield, Dick, 74
Langley, Elmo, 67
Lepage, Kevin, 89
Little, Chad, 67
Lorenzen, Fred, 28, 29, 30, 31, 32, 33
Lowe, Bosco, 34
Lund, Tiny, 29, 43

M
Manning, Skip, 45
Mansfield, Jayne, 29
Marcis, Dave, 42, 43, 52
Marlin, Coo Coo, 67
Marlin, Sterling, 66, 69, 72, 73, 74, 75, 77, 79, 81,
  87, 90, 91
Martin, Mark, 60, 64, 65, 67, 69, 71, 72, 78, 79, 80,
  81, 82, 83, 87, 90, 91, 93, 95
Mast, Rick, 80
Matthews, Banjo, 28
Mayfield, Jeremy, 80, 81, 95
McClure, Larry, 72, 81
McCray, Rick, 53
McMurray, Jamie, 91
McQuagg, Sam, 31
Measell, Bill, 66
Melling, Harry, 53, 67
Miller, Bill, 16
Millikan, Joe, 52
Moody, Ralph, 28, 44
Moore, Bud, 27, 28, 29, 33, 43, 46, 52, 53, 54, 56,
  65
Mundy, Frank, 10, 11, 15, 20
Musgrave, Ted, 71, 87
Myers, Bobby, 21

N
Nadeau, Jerry, 87, 89
National Championship Stock Car Circuit, 9
Negre, Ed, 43
Newman, Ryan, 91, 92, 93, 95
Nyquist, Ted, 8

O
O'Dell, Don, 26
Osterlund, Rod, 51, 73
Otto, Ed, 23
Owens, Cotton, 21, 23, 32

P
Pagan, Eddie, 22
Page, Lenny, 26
Panch, Marvin, 21, 29, 30, 32
Park, Steve, 87, 88
Parks, Raymond, 11
Parsons, Benny, 39, 41, 43, 44, 45, 46, 50, 92
Parsons, Phil, 61
Paschal, Jim, 17
Pearson, David, 30, 32, 34, 35, 38, 40, 41, 42, 44,
  46, 50

Penske, Roger, 42, 45
Petty, Kyle, 64, 69, 70
Petty, Lee, 9, 11, 14, 17, 18, 19, 22, 23, 26, 27, 28,
  33, 59, 71, 82, 94
Petty, Maurice, 40
Petty, Richard, 17, 19, 23, 26, 28, 29, 30, 31, 33,
  34, 35, 38, 39, 40, 41, 42, 43, 44, 45, 46, 47,
  50, 51, 55, 59, 67, 69, 73, 77, 80, 82, 89, 92,
  94
Pistone, "Tiger" Tom, 27
Pond, Lennie, 43, 46

R
Rainier, Harry, 46
Rathmann, Jim, 28
Reagan, Ronald, 55
Red Line 7000, 30
Rexford, Bill, 14, 15, 75
Ribbs, Willy T., 46
Richmond, Tim, 57, 58
Roberts, Glen "Fireball," 14, 17, 21, 22, 28, 30
Rollins, Shorty, 23
Rose, Mauri, 18
Rossi, Mario, 39
Roush, Jack, 64, 92, 93
Rudd, Ricky, 54, 56, 57, 59, 61, 64, 66, 69, 73, 75,
  77, 82, 87
Rush, Ken, 19
Rutherford, Jack, 8
Ruttman, Joe, 51, 52, 53, 57

S
Sacks, Greg, 64
Sadler, Elliott, 89, 93, 95
Saverance, Ed, 17
Schindler, Bill, 8
Schrader, Ken, 60, 64, 65, 74, 75, 79, 92
Scott, Wendell, 32
Seay, Lloyd, 8
Shepherd, Morgan, 61, 65, 68, 75, 87
Shuman, Buddy, 16
Skinner, Mike, 74, 81
Smith, Bruton, 27, 77, 80
Smith, Jack, 26, 28
Smith, Jimmy, 74
Smith, Louise, 11
Smith, Slick, 17
Snowden, Bill, 9, 11
Sosebee, Gober, 14
Speed, Lake, 56, 77, 80
Spencer, Jimmy, 73, 86, 90, 93
Sports Illustrated, 75
Stacy, J.D., 51
Stewart, Tony, 83, 86, 87, 88, 90, 91, 95

T
Teague, Marshall, 10, 15
Terry, Bill, 57
Thomas, Herb, 14, 15, 16, 17, 18, 19, 20, 21
Thompson, Jimmy, 14
Thompson, Speedy, 20, 21
Thompson, Tommy, 15
Trickle, Dick, 71, 72
Truelove, Russ, 20
Turner, Curtis, 14, 15, 16, 21, 22, 27, 31, 33

V
Venable, Jim, 74
Vessels, Frank, 74
Vickers, Brian, 94
Vogt, Red, 11

W
Wallace, Rusty, 59, 60, 61, 64, 65, 68, 70, 71, 72,
  75, 77, 79, 80, 82, 89, 95
Wallard, Lee, 15
Waltrip, Darrell, 42, 43, 45, 46, 47, 51, 52, 53, 54,
  56, 57, 60, 61, 65, 69, 79
Waltrip, Michael, 65, 70, 88, 92, 93
Warren, Frank, 50
Weatherly, Joe, 23, 26, 28, 29, 30
Welborn, Bob, 21, 23
Wheeler, Humpy, 44
White, Rex, 22, 26, 27
Whitesell, Brian, 83
Wolf, Joe, 11
Wood, Glen, 22, 29
Woods, Ernest, 18

Y
Yarborough, Betty Jo, 45
Yarborough, Cale, 31, 41, 42, 44, 45, 46, 47, 50, 53,
  54, 55, 67, 79
Yarbrough, LeeRoy, 35
Yates, Robert, 61, 71, 72, 82
Yunick, Smokey, 22, 28, 33

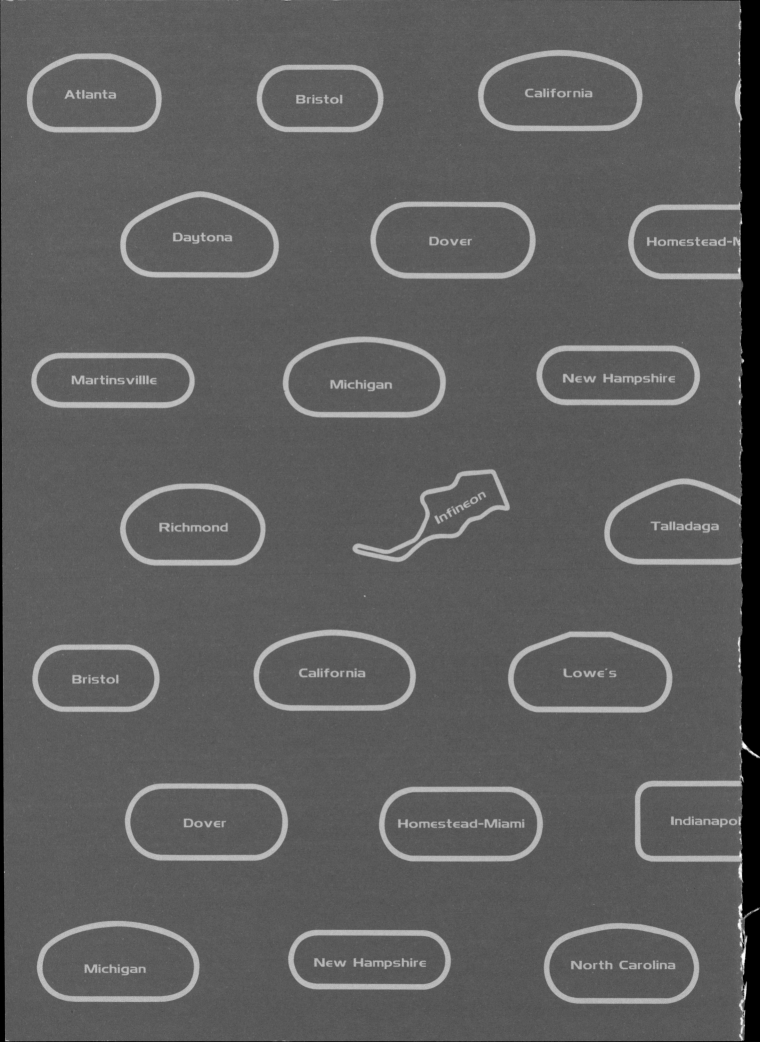